Race and Socia

"Amidst the cacophony of too often shrill and contentious, self-righteous and duplicitous, too infrequently honest and insightful voices of those speaking out on issues that, both in how they have come about as well as in how they are dealt with, structure substantial portions of individual and shared life as it unfolds in America; off-stage, beyond the flashy hype of the new subworld of high-profile, institution-hopping, celebrity scholar-intellectuals are those persons of firmly-held, well-considered convictions who comprise that great bulk of journeyman and journeywoman teacher-scholars and teacher-artists who sustain institutions of higher education and fulfill the crucial roles of cultural critique, creation, and mediation in America's very complex, conflict-ridden unfinished experimental civilization project. These persons are known best by their students and local colleagues, and by a not insignificant few others in various places in America, and are known and respected for their civil and passionate engaging of some of the most challenging of the issues of contemporary social, political, and moral life in America. Howard McGary is one of these persons. Read his essays in this book and you will experience insightful discussion of issues of justice that will likely challenge you by their compelling importance as well as by the model of clarity, patience, thoughtfulness, and principled moderation of passion that he invests in his discussions. Here is a model of informed and informing civil discourse at its best that invites us to join in in like fashion."

Lucius Outlaw, Haverford College

# Race and Social Justice

*Howard McGary*

First published 1999

2 4 6 8 10 9 7 5 3 1

Blackwell Publishers Inc.
350 Main Street
Malden, Massachusetts 02148
USA

Blackwell Publishers Ltd
108 Cowley Road
Oxford OX4 1JF
UK

*Library of Congress Cataloging-in-Publication Data*

McGary, Howard, 1947–
    Race and social justice/Howard McGary.
        p.   cm.
    Includes bibliographical references (p.   ).
    ISBN 0–631–20720–1 (alk. paper).—ISBN 0–631–20721–X (pbk. :
alk. paper)
    1. Afro-Americans—Civil rights—History—20th century.   2. Racism—
United States—History—20th century.   3. Social justice—United States—
History—20th century.   4. United States—Race relations.   5. Race
discrimination—United States—History—20th   century.   I. Title.
E185.615.M352   1998
305.896'073—dc21                                                                98–23968
                                                                                        CIP

*British Library Cataloguing in Publication Data*

A CIP catalogue record for this book is available from the British Library

Typeset in 11½ on 13½ Bembo by York House Typographic Ltd
Printed in Great Britain by M. P. G. Books, Bodmin, Cornwall
This book is printed on acid-free paper

# Contents

# Preface

These essays explore the problems that race and racism have presented for American institutions and practices. If they have to be characterized, I would label them as essays in social philosophy. However, they draw heavily upon other disciplines. In particular, they depend on work in African-American history and literature as well as recent work by legal scholars, political scientists, and sociologists who have wrestled with race and racism.

Racism is clearly a problem that has grabbed the attention of scholars from a host of disciplines. Historians, legal scholars, literary critics, political scientists, social psychologists, and sociologists have each, in their own ways, generated a growing body of literature on this topic. However, professional philosophers have only recently begun to welcome examinations of race and racism by using the methods and techniques that characterize their area of endeavor. A part of the reluctance can be attributed to a widespread view that philosophy is above culture and history, but some of the hesitation is associated with a tendency by some professional philosophers to avoid what they consider to be applied questions. Yet in the last decade work by American pragmatists, applied philosophers, feminist philosophers, and African-American philosophers have called into question traditional ways of doing philosophy, especially the work on abortion and affirmative action by highly visible philosophers like Bernard Boxill, Ronald Dworkin, Thomas Nagel, Judith Jarvis Thomson, and Richard Wasserstrom.

African-American philosophers have also challenged, in direct ways, the view that the African-American experience cannot serve as a source of philosophical inquiry. Some of these philosophers, like Bernard Boxill, Bill Lawson, Tommy Lott, and Laurence Thomas, have employed traditional analytical methods in their examinations. While others, like Leonard Harris, Lewis Gordon, Frank Kirkland, Lucius Outlaw, and Cornel West, have embraced methodologies that are more characteristic of the Continental and Postmodern methodologies. These works, each in their own ways, have started a dialogue that has now worked its way into the pages of academic journals and on to the programs of philosophy conferences and meetings.

Over the last twenty years, I have written a number of articles that address questions of racism, justice, and public policy. Ten articles included in this volume have been published in a variety of places. Some were included in anthologies on alienation, collective responsibility, exploitation, and freedom and others were published in philosophy journals. I have received a number of requests from college teachers who would like to have these papers collected into a single volume. They impressed upon me the need for such a volume as a textbook for courses that address racism and questions of social justice. I have also prepared two new papers for inclusion in the volume.

Recent events like the Rodney King beating, the O .J. Simpson trial, and the Million Man March, make it clear that race does matter and that racial conflict and racial justice are issues that must be high on the political agendas of academics, citizens, and thoughtful politicians. Racial tensions and divisions in the United States are not new, but current events have caused renewed interests in whether a pluralistic society like the United States, with a long history of racial injustice and racial indifference, can achieve justice and fairness for all of its citizens.

The philosopher and social critic Cornel West has argued that race does matter, but that we still have reasons for being optimistic about overcoming racial injustice and intolerance. While, on the other hand, the distinguished legal scholar Derrick Bell is less optimistic about eliminating racism. In fact, Bell argues that we would all be better off, in a strategic sense, if we accepted the inevitability of racism and worked to mitigate its damaging effects. The essays in this volume all address, from a philosophical perspective, how race does, and should, impact some key issues of public and social policy.

# Acknowledgments

Two of the essays included in this volume appear for the first time, and ten are reprinted, with minor editing, from other publications. The author and publishers gratefully acknowledge the following for permission to reproduce copyright material.

1 "Alienation and the African-American Experience," in John P. Pittman and Marx Wartofsky, eds, *African-American Perspectives and Philosophical Traditions* (New York: Routledge, 1996), pp. 282–96. Reprinted here by permission of Routledge, Inc. Copyright ©1996.

2 "Race and Class Exploitation" was originally published in *Exploitation and Exclusion: Race and Class in Contemporary US Society*. Edited by Abebe Zegeye, Leonard Harris, and Julia Maxted (Hans Zell Publishers, 1991), pp. 14–27. Reprinted by permission of the editors and publisher.

3 "Racial Integration and Racial Separatism: Conceptual Clarifications" was originally published in *Philosophy Born of Struggle*. Edited by Leonard Harris (Kendall/Hunt Publishers, 1983), pp. 199–211. Reprinted by permission of the publisher.

4 "The African-American Underclass and the Question of Values" was originally published in *The Underclass Question*. Edited by Bill E. Lawson (Temple University Press, 1992), pp. 57–70. Reprinted by permission of the publisher.

5 "Morality and Collective Liability" was originally published by Kluwer Academic Publishers in *The Journal of Value Inquiry*, 20: 157–65, 1986. Reprinted with kind permission from Kluwer Academic Publishers.

6 "Justice and Reparations" was originally published by *The Philosophical Forum*, 1977–78, vol. 9, nos 2–3, pp. 250–63. Reprinted here by permission of the publisher.

7 "Reparations, Self-Respect, and Public Policy" was originally published in *The Journal* (MBPI, vol. 1, 1984, pp. 15–26). Reprinted here by permission of the publisher.

9 "The Race and IQ Controversy" was originally published as "Power, Scientific Research and Self-Censorship," in *Rethinking Power*. Edited by Thomas E. Wartenberg (State University of New York Press, 1992), pp. 225–39. Reprinted here by permission of the publisher.

10 "Police Discretion and Discrimination" was originally published in *Handled with Discretion*. Edited by John Kleinig (Rowman and Littlefield Publishers, 1996), pp. 131–44. Reprinted here by permission of the publisher.

12 "Racism, Social Justice, and Interracial Coalitions" was originally published in *The Journal of Ethics*, 1: 3, pp. 249–64, 1997. Reprinted here with kind permission from Kluwer Academic Publishers.

The publishers apologize for any errors or omissions in the above list and would be grateful to be notified of any corrections that should be incorporated in the next edition or reprint of this book.

I am extremely grateful to my late father, mother, and grandmother for teaching me that even in times of adversity good things are possible.

I owe a special debt to John Dolan and my other teachers at the University of Minnesota and the late Irving Thalberg, Jr. for his advice and encouragement. More recently, I received a great deal of support from my colleagues at Rutgers University, especially Richard Foley, Douglas Husak, Jorge Garcia, Mary Gibson, Peter Klein, Ernie LePore, Brian McLaughlin, and Bruce Wilshire.

A special debt is owed to my colleagues and friends Bernard Boxill, Melvin Gaines, Frank Kirkland, Bill Lawson, Leonard Harris, Tommy Lott, Charles Mills, Shelby Neherille, Lucius Outlaw, Laurence Thomas, Cornel West, and Wayne Williams. Discussions with the members of the Society for the Study of Africana Philosophy and colleagues at other colleges and universities have been especially helpful and stimulating.

Thanks to my editors at Blackwell Publishers, Stephen Smith and Mary Riso, for their support, and I am grateful to Laurence Thomas for being first to encourage me to publish these essays as a collection.

Last, but certainly not least, thanks to Gaston, La Vern, Heather, Ollie, Roscoe, Valoria, Mya Cherry, Claude, Claudette, Gladys, and the rest of my family for their love and constant support.

# Introduction

These essays concern moral and political questions about race and racism. Most of the issues discussed are not specific to any given profession, but are ones that citizens ponder in their daily lives. Although these issues are dramatic and common place, they can stand to benefit from philosophical scrutiny. Perhaps my personal history and academic training puts me in a good position to clarify some of the concerns raised by the intense debate in the United States and other countries over race and racism. W. E. B. DuBois, a famous African-American sociologist, wrote: "The problem of the twentieth century is the color-line." Unfortunately, this statement is as true now as when it was first made by DuBois.

As a child growing up in South Central Los Angeles in the late fifties and sixties, I was aware of the extent to which members of my community were excluded from full participation in American life. Because of economic and social practices, we were confined to certain areas and directed into substandard schools and jobs. Although Los Angeles in the 1950s and 1960s was not legally segregated, race was a very significant factor in determining where people lived, socialized, studied, and worked.

In 1968, on the heels of widespread social disturbances, the Kerner Commission Report spoke of two Americas: Black and White, separate and not equal. Thirty years after the publication of this report, prominent scholars argue that these conditions have not changed. In fact, some would contend that if we focus on things like illegitimate births, incarceration, substance abuse, and teenage violence things have gotten worse.

In the present political climate in the United States, the plight of urban racialized communities is not high on the political agendas of either of the major political parties. When politicians do discuss these issues, their discussions most often focus on which ideological perspective (conservative or liberal) is superior rather than framing a legislative plan to address the problems of urban America.

The topics in this book address the varied concerns in urban America, but they all share a common theme. All of them, in one way or another, address issues of equity and inclusion. These essays have been written over a twenty-year period, and they not only show the development of my thinking, but they also show how the discourse about race has changed during this period.

Present discussions of race and racism by academics are dominated by anti-essentialist accounts of race. According to these accounts, race as a biological concept is a myth that has no scientific basis. Thus, armed with this conception of race, these theorists argue that we are intellectually obligated to reject the significance of race. While other theorists argue that race has a significance even if the concept is meaningless from a biological perspective.

I tend to side with the latter group. In these essays, I strive to shed light on some crucial issues in the African-American experience. The chapter on alienation explains the nature of the alienation experienced by present-day African-Americans and the difficulties liberalism faces in its attempt to address this alienation. The chapter on race and class exploitation describes the nature of racial exploitation, and then explains why race and class exploitation are not synonymous. One common objection to programs designed to compensate African-Americans by giving them preferences assumes that racial exploitation, if it exists, is not different from other forms of exploitation. The idea is that there is nothing special about racial exploitation. I reject an important premise of this objection by arguing that racial exploitation is different from class exploitation.

Another common objection to the claim that African-Americans as a group are alienated or exploited is the growth of a large visible African-American middle-class. Critics of affirmative action, and other policies designed to uplift African-Americans, often point to the African-American middle-class as evidence of the opportunities available to African-Americans if they are ambitious enough to take advantage of them. They argue that the present dire situation of the underclass is due to personal shortcomings and not racial exploitation or injustice.

In the chapter on the African-American underclass and the question of values, I argue against the view that members of the underclass are down and out because they have inappropriate values. More specifically, I reject the claim that their underclass status can be attributed to laziness or a lack of motivation.

The chapter on racial integration and racial separatism examines a classic debate in African-American political thought. Must African-Americans emigrate to other lands to escape the alienation and exploitation they experience in the United States or can they assimilate or integrate into the mainstream of American life? If emigration is unrealistic, would a better response to racial injustice require African-Americans to form their own separate institutions or communities in the United States? The chapter serves as a prolegomenon to future discussions of these questions.

The four chapters on affirmative action, black reparations, and collective responsibility (chapters 5–8) examine the arguments, pro and con, involved in the controversial and provocative debates surrounding these topics? Some of the questions include: What is affirmative action? Are affirmative action policies necessary and just? Do past legal practices like American slavery, Jim Crow laws, and racial discrimination, justify a duty of reparations to African-Americans as a group? If so, what form should this reparation take? Is affirmative action, as a policy of racial preference, a just reparation? Should affirmative action be justified on grounds other than reparation? Can racial groups be held collectively liable for wrong-doing?

Chapter 9 addresses the reoccurring issue of race and IQ. Instead of examining the empirical question about the connection between race and IQ, I examine a related moral question. My concern is as follows: Should a morally decent scientist cease to examine issues of race and IQ if she knows that her findings will be used by others to cause harm to innocent human beings?

In the next chapter, I examine a topic that is especially important to racial minorities. It has been well documented that a tense relationship exists between African-Americans and the police. The Rodney King beating, and similar incidents around the country, further highlight this relationship. In this chapter, I examine a police practice of using race to single-out African-American motorists from a group of motorists who are all violating traffic laws. I question whether it is just for police officers to use their discretionary powers in this way?

Given the serious and far-ranging problems confronting African-Americans, now more than ever, there is a need for dedicated courageous leaders. Present African-American leadership has been roundly criticized by liberals and neo-conservatives for failing to provide the caliber of leadership once provided by leaders like Frederick Douglass, Martin Luther King Jr., and Malcolm X. In chapter 11, I examine this criticism.

In the final chapter, I offer my latest thinking on race and social justice, and I examine a recent proposal by the scholar activist, Cornel West, for overcoming racial injustice through interracial coalitions.

# PART I
## The Problem of Racism

# 1

# Alienation and the African-American Experience

The term "alienation" evokes a variety of responses. For liberals, to be alienated signals a denial of certain basic rights, e.g., the right to equality of opportunity or the right to autonomy.[1] On the other hand, progressive thinkers believe that alienation involves estrangement from one's work, self, or others because of capitalism.[2] However, recent discussions of alienation have cast doubt on whether either of these theories totally capture the phenomenon. Drawing on the experiences of nonwhite people, some theorists maintain that to be alienated is to be estranged in ways that cannot be accounted for by liberal and Marxist theories of alienation.[3] The concept of alienation is often associated with Marx's conception of human beings in capitalist societies.

However, non-Marxists have also used the term alienation to explain the experiences of human beings in relationship to their society, each other, their work, and themselves. But liberal theories of alienation have been criticized by Marxists for two reasons. First they see liberal theories of alienation as describing a psychological condition that is said to result from a denial of basic individual rights rather than being the result of a systematic failure. Second, liberals have an account of human nature that is ahistorical, one that fails to consider the changes in human nature that result from changes in social conditions.

For the Marxist, alienation is not simply a theory of how people feel or think about themselves when their rights are violated, but a historical theory of how human beings act and how they are treated by others in capitalist society. The Marxist theory of alienation is an explanatory social theory that places human beings at the center of the critique of socioeconomic relations. Marx's human being is not a stagnant given, but a product of an explanatory social theory. For Marx, alienation is something that all human beings experience in capitalist societies; it is not something that certain individuals undergo because they are neurotic or the victims of some unjust law or social practice.

It is clear that African-Americans have not always been recognized and treated as American citizens or as human beings by the dominant white society. Both of these forms of denial have had serious negative consequences and numerous scholars have discussed what these denials have meant to African-Americans and to the rest of society. However, it does not directly follow from the fact of these denials that African-Americans are alienated because of these things. In this chapter, I shall attempt to understand this new challenge to the liberal and Marxist theories of "alienation" and its impact, if any, on the masses of African-Americans.

## The New Account of Alienation

According to the new account of alienation that is drawn from the experiences of nonwhite people, alienation exists when the self is deeply divided because the hostility of the dominant groups in the society forces the self to see itself as loathsome, defective, or insignificant, and lacking the possibility of ever seeing itself in more positive terms. This type of alienation is not just estrangement from one's work or a possible plan of life, but an estrangement from ever becoming a self that is not defined in the hostile terms of the dominant group.

The root idea here is not just that certain groups are forced to survive in an atmosphere in which they are not respected because of their group membership, but rather that they are required to do so in a society that is openly hostile to their very being. The hostility, according to this new account of alienation, causes the victims to become hostile toward themselves. Those who are said to be alienated in this way are thought to be incapable of shaping our common conception of reality and thus they play little, if any, role in their self-construction. The self is imposed upon them by social forces, and what is even more disturbing, no individual self can change the social forces that impose upon members of certain groups their negative and hostile self-conceptions.

Is this new account of alienation just another way of saying that nonwhite people have had their humanity called into question? We might begin to explore this question by examining the claim that having one's humanity recognized and respected means having a say about things that matter in one's life, and having such a say means that one is unalienated. To be more specific, having opinions about things and the ability and freedom to express one's opinions is the mark of the unalienated person. This response is helpful, but it does not fully capture what recent writers have meant by alienation. It assumes that the alienated self is secure, but constrained by external forces that prevent the person from becoming fully actualized: from having one's voice recognized and respected in the moral or political process.

The above account of what it means to recognize and respect a person's humanity fails to fully appreciate that human selves result, at least in part, from social construction. How we define who we are, our interests, and our relationship with others, involves a dynamic process of social interaction. The assumption that alienation is the failure by some to be able to express and have their opinions heard misses the mark. This view of things assumes that (1) people are clear about their interests, but have not been allowed to express them and (2) those who have power and privilege will be able to understand and fairly assess claims made by those who lack power and privilege if they were only allowed to express their opinions. Even if (1) and (2) are true, we still have not captured what recent writers have meant by alienation. This account focuses incorrectly on what the self is prevented from doing by forces external to it. However, the new account of alienation primarily concentrates on the fragility and insecurity of the self caused by the way people who are victims view and define themselves. According to this view, even if the external constraints were removed, the self would still be estranged because it has been constructed out of images that are hostile to it.

One might think that this new account of alienation is not novel because Americans (including African-Americans) have always believed that people should be free to decide what kind of people they want to be provided that in doing so they don't violate the rights of others. At least, in principle, Americans have endorsed this idea. If this is so, what is new in these recent accounts of alienation? Perhaps we can gain some insight into this question by taking a closer look at the African-American experience.

African-Americans have had a paradoxical existence in the United States. On the one hand, they have rightfully responded negatively to the second-class status that they are forced to endure. On the other hand, they believe that America should have, and has, the potential to live up to the ideas so eloquently expressed in the Bill of Rights and in Martin Luther King, Jr.'s "I Have a Dream" speech.[4] It is clear that there was a time when African-Americans were prevented from participating in the electoral process and from having a say in the shaping of basic institutions. Many would argue that there are still barriers that prevent African-Americans from participating in meaningful ways in these areas. If this is so, does this mean that most (many) African-Americans are alienated from themselves and the dominant society?

African-American leaders from the moderate to the militant have emphasized the importance of African-Americans making their own decisions about what is in their interests.[5] The right to self-determination has been seen as a crucial weapon in the battle against the evils of racial discrimination. These thinkers have also recognized that one must have an adequate understanding of one's predicament if one is to devise an effective strategy for overcoming the material and psychological consequences of racial injustice.

Insight into the African-American experience has come from a variety of sources. Some of these insights have been offered by social and political theorists, others have been advanced in literature and the arts. Ralph Ellison, in his brilliant novel *The Invisible Man*, describes what he takes to be a consuming evil of racial discrimination.[6] According to Ellison, African-Americans are not visible to the white world. They are caricatures and stereotypes, but not real human beings with complex and varied lives.

In very graphic terms, Ellison reveals what it is like to be black in a world where black skin signifies what is base and superficial. Ellison skillfully describes how blacks are perceived by white society, but he also tells us a great deal about how blacks perceive themselves. It is clear that African-Americans have struggled to construct an image of themselves different from the ones perpetrated by a racist society, but this is not an easy thing to do. W. E. B. DuBois spoke to the struggle and the dilemma that confronts African-Americans when he identified what he called "the problem of double-consciousness" in *The Souls of Black Folk*:

> It is a peculiar sensation, this double-consciousness, this sense of always looking at one's self through the eyes of others, of measuring one's soul by the tape of a world that looks on in amused contempt and pity. One ever feels his twoness – an American, a Negro; two warring ideals in one dark body, whose dogged strength alone keeps it from being torn asunder.[7]

DuBois is pointing to what he takes to be the mistaken belief held by many blacks and whites, namely that a person cannot be both black and an American. According to DuBois, for far too many people this was a contradiction in terms.

DuBois strongly disagreed and spent a great deal of his energy arguing against this conclusion. But why this false view was held by so many people can be traced to an inadequate conception of what it means to be "black" and what it meant to be "American." According to DuBois, race and class exploitation contributed greatly to these false conceptions. For DuBois, it was no surprise that African-Americans had such a difficult time identifying their true interests.

## The Liberal Response

Liberal political theorists rarely discuss alienation. This is in a large part because alienation is seen as something that comes from within. For them alienation often is the result of injustice, but even so, it is something that can be overcome if only the individual would stand up for her rights. Liberals may realize that this might come at some serious personal cost to the individual, but they believe that the individuals can and should bear these costs if they are to remain autonomous unalienated beings. For example, liberals often sympathize with white, highly educated, wealthy women who live alienated lives, but they believe that it is within the power of these women to end their estrangement or alienation even though it may be extremely difficult for them to do so. The critics of the liberal account of women's oppression have argued that liberals fail to see that capitalism and the negative stereotyping of women causes even educated and economically secure women to be at the mercy of sexist practices and traditions.

The critics of liberalism have also argued that liberalism places too much emphasis upon individuality and thus the theory fails to recognize how our conceptions of who we are, and what we see as valuable, are tied to our social relations. They insist that we are not alone in shaping who we are and in defining our possibilities. Society, according to these critics, plays a more extensive role than liberals are willing to admit.

Although liberals have recognized the alienation that people experience in modern society, their individual-rights framework has not readily lent itself to an in-depth analysis of this phenomenon. I disagree, however, with the critics of liberalism when they contend that the individual-rights framework is inadequate to describe the nature of alienation. I shall attempt to show that liberals can describe the nature of alienation in capitalist society even though the theory is inadequate when it comes to addressing what the liberals must admit to be a violation of important rights.

Liberal theorists might characterize this new form of alienation in terms of a denial of the rights to such things as autonomy and self-determination and claim that these denials rob persons of their freedom. Alienation on their account is just another way of saying that people are unfree and, further, that they don't appreciate that this is so. But if the liberal response is to be helpful, we need to know more precisely in what sense alienation is a denial of important rights, e.g., the right to be free.

In what sense is the alienated person unfree? Can a person be alienated even if she has basic constitutional rights, material success, and a job that calls upon her abilities and talents in interesting ways? Some theorists think so. If alienation is a lack of freedom as the liberal theory suggests, in what sense are the people who have constitutional rights and material well-being unfree? The liberal theorist Joel Feinberg has discussed the lack of freedom in terms of constraints.[8] If we define alienation as constraint, then alienated persons are unfairly constrained in the ways that they can conceive of themselves in a culture that defines them in stereotypical terms. But what are these constraints? To borrow Feinberg's terminology, are these constraints external or internal? According to Feinberg, "external constraints are those that come from outside a person's body-cum-mind, and all other constraints, whether sore muscles, headaches, or refractory 'lower' desires, are internal to him."[9]

If we employ the language of constraints to understand alienation as a kind of unfreedom, should we view this unfreedom in terms of external or internal constraints or both? On a liberal reading of DuBois's and Ellison's characterizations of the African-American experience, this experience is characterized by a denial of opportunities because of a morally irrelevant characteristic, a person's race. It is plausible to interpret them in this way because this is clearly one of the consequences of a system of racial discrimination. However, I believe that they had much more in mind. The focus on the denial of opportunities is the standard liberal way of understanding the consequences of racial injustice. This is why you find liberal writers like Feinberg discussing freedom in terms of the absence of constraints and John Rawls concentrating on designing social institutions such that offices and positions are open to all under conditions of self-respect.[10] The focus by liberals has been primarily on what goes on outside of the body-cum-mind.

This is not to say that they completely ignore such psychological harms as self-doubt and a lack of self-respect that can result from injustice. In fact, Feinberg notes that things like sickness can create internal constraints which serve to limit a person's freedom.[11] Rawls, as well, appreciates the impact that injustice can have on a person's psyche. Thus he spends some time expounding on the connection between justice and a healthy self-concept.[12] He argues that in a just society social institutions should not be designed in ways that prevent people from having the social bases for self-respect. So both Feinberg and Rawls recognize that such things as freedom and justice go beyond removing inappropriate external constraints. But, nonetheless, I don't think that Feinberg and Rawls can fully capture the insight offered by DuBois and Ellison because their emphasis on the external constraints causes them to underestimate the internal ways that people can be prevented from experiencing freedom.

Since Isaiah Berlin's distinction between positive and negative freedom, liberals have recognized that such things as ignorance and poverty can limit a person's freedom.[13] Recognition of the limitations caused by internal constraints has led some liberals to argue that a society cannot be just if it does not address internal constraints on people's freedom. Such liberals would be open to the idea that an examination of the African-American experience would reveal the obvious and subtle ways that a lack of education and material well-being can lead to a sense of estrangement, a lack of self-respect. They would argue that this is true even when formal equality of opportunity can be said to exist. On their view, the real problem is not the lack of laws that guarantee equality under the law, but finding ways to make real these guarantees. For them it is not so much how African-Americans are viewed by the rest of society, but rather that they should be treated in ways that make it possible for them to act and choose as free persons. According to this view, things are just even if people are hated by the rest of the community, provided that they are guaranteed equal protection under the law and steps are taken to ensure real equality of opportunity. These liberals insist that there is a large area of human affairs that should escape government scrutiny. In these areas, people should be able to pursue their own conceptions of the good provided that they don't cause direct harm to others. I should add that these liberals also believe that those who fail to provide such necessities as food and education, to those who are in need of them, cause direct harm by failing to do so.

However, some communitarian critics of liberalism have argued that this way of understanding the requirements of justice underestimates the importance of how we form a healthy self-concept in a community.[14] They emphasize the importance of being seen and treated as a full member of society as opposed to a person who must be tolerated. They question the wisdom and usefulness of attempting to find impartial norms that will guarantee each person the right to pursue his or her own unique conception of the good constrained by an account of the right defined by impartial reasoning. This concern has led some communitarians to reject the search for impartial ideals of justice in favor of a method of forging a consensus about justice through a process of democratically working across differences through open dialogue. According to this view, we will not be able to put aside our partialities, but we can confront them through discourse.

Communitarians would contend that African-Americans or any minority group that has been despised and subjugated will feel estranged from the dominant society if they are merely tolerated and not accepted and valued for their contributions. They believe that the liberalism of Feinberg, Rawls, and Nozick can at best produce toleration, but not acceptance. But this view, of course, assumes that we can identify some common goods (ends) to serve as the foundation for our theory of justice. This is something that liberals who give priority to the right over the good deny.

The communitarians, whether they realize it or not, have pointed to a persistent problem for African-Americans – the problem of recognition. How do African-Americans become visible in a society that refuses to see them other than through stereotypical images? One need only turn to the history of African-American social and political thought to see that African-Americans have wrestled with the question of what the appropriate means are for obtaining recognition and respect for a people who were enslaved and then treated as second-class citizens. Some argued that emigration was the only answer, while others maintained that less radical forms of separation from white society would do. Others contended that blacks could obtain recognition only if they assimilated or fully integrated into white society.[15] Neither of these approaches so far have been fully tested, so it is hard to say whether either approach can adequately address the problem of the lack of recognition for African-Americans in a white racist society.

The new alienation theorists believe that liberals cannot adequately describe or eliminate the kind of estrangement experienced by African-Americans and other oppressed racial groups. Is this so? Yes and no. I shall argue that liberals can describe the experience of estrangement using the vocabulary of rights and opportunities, but I don't think that they can eliminate this experience and stay faithful to their liberal methodology.

Typically when we think of a person being denied rights or opportunities we think of rather specific individuals and specific actions which serve as the causes of these denials. For example, we might think of a specific employer refusing to hire a person because he or she is African-American. The African-American, in this case, is denied job-related rights and opportunities by a specific person. But even if we changed our example to involve groups rather than individuals, the new alienation theorists would maintain that the experience of estrangement they describe goes beyond such a description. According to their account, African-Americans who have their rights respected and don't suffer from material scarcity are still estranged in a way that their white counterparts are not.

Are these theorists correct or do prosperous and highly regarded middle-class and wealthy African-Americans serve as counter-examples to the above claim? Don't such persons enjoy their rights and opportunities? If not, what rights and opportunities are they being denied? I believe that rights and opportunities are being denied, but it is more difficult to see what they are in such cases. I think that liberals can contend that middle-class and wealthy African-Americans are still alienated because they are denied their right to equal concern and respect in a white racist society. Even though they may be able to vote, to live in the neighborhood of their choice, and to send their children to good schools, they are still perceived as less worthy because of their race. The dominant attitude in their society is that they are less worthy than whites. The pervasive attitude is not benign. It acts as an affront to the self-concepts of African-Americans and it causes them to expend energy that they could expend in more constructive ways. The philosopher Laurence Thomas graphically described this experience in a letter to the *New York Times*.[16] For example, African-Americans are too aware of the harm caused by being perceived by the typical white as thieves no matter what their economic and social standing might be. African-Americans, because of the dominant negative attitudes against them as a group, are denied equal concern and respect.

It is difficult to see that this attitude of disrespect is a denial of rights because we most often associate political rights with actions and not with attitudes. In fact, it sounds awkward to say that I have a right that you not have a certain attitude towards me. This statement seems to strike at the very heart of liberalism, but in reality it does not. Liberals can and do say that human beings should be accorded such things as dignity and respect, and they believe that this entails taking a certain attitude or having dispositions towards others as well as acting or refraining from acting in particular ways. So, it is not that they cannot account for the particular estrangement that African-Americans experience because of the attitude of disrespect generated by the dominant society, but that they don't seem to have the theoretical wherewithal to resolve the problem.

Since liberals assign great weight to individual liberty, they are reluctant to interfere with actions that cause indirect harm to others. So even though they recognize that living in a society that has an attitude of disrespect towards African-Americans can constitute a harm, and a harm caused by others, they are reluctant to interfere with people's private lives in order to eliminate these harms.

How can liberals change white attitudes in a way that is consistent with their theory? They could mount an educational program to combat false or racist beliefs. Liberals have tried this, but given their strong commitment to things like freedom of thought and expression, and the fact that power and privilege is attached to seeing nonwhites as less worthy, educational programs have only had modest success in changing white attitudes. Critics of such educational programs argue that these programs can never succeed until racism is seen as unprofitable.

Let us assume that the critics are correct. Can liberals make racism unprofitable and respect individual liberty, one of the cornerstones of their theory? There are two basic approaches available to liberals: they can place sanctions on all harmful racist attitudes or they can provide people with incentives to change their racist attitudes. But in a democracy, the will of the majority is to prevail. If the attitude of disrespect towards African-Americans is as pervasive as the new alienation theorists suggest, then it is doubtful there will be the general will to seriously take either of the approaches. I don't think that liberals can eliminate harmful racist attitudes without adopting means that would be judged by the white majority as unjustified coercion. However, they can adequately describe the alienation that African-Americans experience even if they cannot eliminate it.

## The Marxist Account

The Marxist explanation of the African-American condition assumes that the problems experienced by this group can be traced to their class position. Capitalism is seen as the cause of such things as black alienation. For the Marxist, a class analysis of American society and its problems provides both a necessary and a sufficient understanding of these things. According to the Marxist, alienation be it black or white is grounded in the labor process. Alienated labor, in all of its forms, is based in private property and the division of labor. On this account, if we eliminate a system of private property and the division of labor, we will eliminate those things that make alienated relations possible.

The Marxist does recognize that political and ideological relations can and do exist in capitalist societies, and that these relations do appear to have the autonomy and power to shape our thinking and cause certain behaviors. But, for the Marxist, these relations only appear to be fundamental when in reality they are not. They can always be reduced or explained by reference to a particular mode of production. Racism is ideological; an idea that dominates across class lines. However, class divisions explain racial antagonisms, it is not the other way around.[17] But Marxists don't stop here. They also contend that in order to eliminate racism, we must eliminate class divisions where class is defined in terms of one's relationship to the means of production.

Classical Marxists would oppose the new account of alienation advanced by recent theorists. The classical Marxists would insist that all forms of alienation, no matter how debilitating or destructive, can be explained in terms of the mode of production in which people are required to satisfy their needs. For them, it is not a matter of changing the way African-Americans and whites think about each other or the way African-Americans think of themselves because ideas don't change our material reality, relationships with others, or our self-conceptions. Our material conditions (mode of production) shape our ideas and our behavior.

On this account, African-Americans are estranged from themselves because of their laboring activity or lack of it. They view themselves in hostile terms because they are defined by a mode of production that stultifies their truly human capacities and reduces them to human tools to be used by those who have power and influence. This all sounds good, but many black theorists (liberal and progressive) have been skeptical of this account of the causes and remedy for black alienation and oppression. They argue that the conditions of black workers and white workers are different and that this difference is not merely a difference in terms of things like income and social and political status or class position. The difference cuts much deeper. In a white racist society, African-Americans (workers and capitalists) are caused to have a hostile attitude towards their very being that is not found in whites. The new alienation theorists contend that the classical Marxist explanation of African-American alienation is too limiting. It fails to recognize that alienation occurs in relationships apart from the labor process. W. E. B. DuBois, although a dedicated Marxist, claimed that the major problem of the twentieth century was race and not class. Some theorists have contended that Marxists are too quick in dismissing the significance of race consciousness.[18] I think the facts support their conclusion. In the next section, I will focus directly on this issue of African-American alienation.

## African-Americans and Alienation

I believe that the atmosphere of hostility created against African-Americans by our white racist society does amount to a serious assault on the material and psychological well-being of its African-American victims, but I also believe that this assault can, and in some cases does, lead to the types of alienation discussed above. However, I disagree with those who conclude that most or all African-Americans suffer from a debilitating form of alienation that causes them to be estranged and divided in the ways described in the new account of alienation. I also reject the implication that most or all African-Americans are powerless, as individuals, to change their condition. The implication is that group action as opposed to individual effort is required to combat this form of alienation. There is also the implication that revolution and not reform is required in order to eliminate this form of alienation.

I don't wish to be misunderstood here. It is not my contention that capitalism is superior to socialism, but only that it is possible for African-Americans to combat or overcome this form of alienation described by recent writers without overthrowing capitalism.

Are African-Americans, as a group, alienated or estranged from themselves? I don't think so. Clearly there are some African-Americans who have experienced such alienation, but I don't think this characterizes the group as a whole. African-Americans do suffer because of a lack of recognition in American society, but a lack of recognition does not always lead to alienation. Even though African-Americans have experienced hostility, racial discrimination, and poverty, they still have been able to construct and draw upon institutions like the family, church, and community to foster and maintain a healthy sense of self in spite of the obstacles that they have faced.

Although African-Americans have been the victims of a vicious assault on their humanity and self-respect, they have been able to form their own supportive communities in the midst of a hostile environment. During the long period of slavery in the United States, African-Americans were clearly in an extremely hostile environment. If there ever was a time a group could be said to be the victims of the assault caused by white racism, slavery was such a time.

Slaves were denied the most basic rights because they were defined and treated as chattel. Some scholars, like Stanley Elkins, even argued that slavery caused African-Americans as a group to become less than healthy human beings.[19] On the other hand, there is a group of scholars who argue that slaves and their descendants were able to maintain healthy self-concepts through acts of resistance and communal nourishment.[20] I tend to side with this latter group of scholars.

What is crucial for the truth of their position is the belief that within a larger hostile environment supportive communities can form that can serve to blunt the assault of a hostile racist social order. This, of course, is not to say that these communities provide their members with all that is necessary for them to flourish under conditions of justice, but only that they provide enough support to create the space necessary for them to avoid the deeply divided and estranged selves described in some recent work on alienation.

The history and literature of African-Americans is rich with examples of how communities have formed to provide the social and moral basis for African-Americans to have self-respect even though they were in the midst of a society that devalued their worth. Once again, I think it bears repeating. I don't deny that a hostile racist society creates the kind of assault that can lead to alienation, but only claim that this assault can be and has been softened by supportive African-American communities.

The sociologist Orlando Patterson disagrees. Patterson has argued that African-Americans are alienated because slavery cut them off from their African culture and heritage and denied them real participation in American culture and heritage. He character-izes this phenomenon as "natal alienation."[21] African-Americans, on Patterson's account, feel estranged because they don't believe that they belong. They are not Africans, but they also are not Americans. One might argue that the present move from "black American" to "African-American" is an attempt to address the phenomenon of natal alienation. According to Patterson, the past provides us with crucial insight into the present psyches of African-Americans. In his view, the fact of slavery helps to explain the present condition and behavior of African-Americans, includ-ing the present underclass phenomenon.[22]

I disagree with Patterson's conclusions. He falls prey to the same shortcoming that plagues the liberal and the Marxist accounts of the African-American experience. They all fail to appreciate the role of ethnic communities in the lives of individuals and groups. Although DuBois never played down the horrors and harms of racism, he refused to see the masses of black people as a people who were estranged or alienated from themselves. In fact, in his *Dusk of Dawn*, DuBois describes how black people have been able to draw strength from each other as members of a community with shared traditions, values, and impulses.[23] Being anchored in a community allows people to address and not just cope with things like oppression and racism.

The work of the historian John Blassingame can also be used to call into question Patterson's natal alienation thesis and it also provides some support for the importance of community in the lives of African-Americans. Blassingame argued that even during the period of slavery, there was still a slave community that served to provide a sense of self-worth and social cohesiveness for slaves. In my own examination of slave narratives, first-hand accounts by slaves and former slaves of their slave experiences, I found that all slaves did not suffer from a form of moral and social death.[24] By moral and social death, I mean the inability to choose and act as autonomous moral and social agents. Of course this is not to deny that slavery was a brutal and dehumanizing institution, but rather that slaves developed supportive institutions and defense mechanisms that allowed them to remain moral and social agents.

But what about the presence of today's so-called black underclass? Does this group (which has been defined as a group that is not only poor, poorly educated, and victimized by crime, but also as a group suffering from a breakdown of family and moral values) squarely raise the issue of black alienation or estrangement? Some people think so. They argue that Patterson's natal alienation thesis is extremely informative when it comes to understanding this class. Others reject the natal alienation thesis, but remain sympathetic to the idea that where there once was a black community or institutions that served to prevent the erosion of black pride and values, these structures no longer exist to the degree necessary to ward off the harms of racism and oppression.

In *The Truly Disadvantaged*, William J. Wilson argues that large urban African-American communities are lacking in the material and human resources to deal with the problems brought on by structural changes and the flight of the middle class.[25] According to Wilson, these communities, unlike communities in the past, lack the wherewithal to overcome problems that are present to an extent in all other poor communities. If Wilson is correct, the resources may not exist in present-day African-American communities to ward off the assault of a hostile racist society. I am not totally convinced by Wilson's argument, but I think his work, and the work of the supporters of the new account of alienation, make it clear that there needs to be further work which compares African-American communities before the development of the so-called "black underclass" with urban African-American communities today.

At this juncture, I wish to distinguish my claim that supportive African-American communities have helped to combat the effects of a racist society from the claims of black neoconservatives like Shelby Steele. In *The Content of Our Characters*,[26] Steele argues that African-Americans must confront and prosper in spite of racism. Steele's recommendations have a strong individualist tone. He argues, like Booker T. Washington, that racism does exist but that African-Americans who are prudent must recognize that if they are to progress, they must prosper in spite of it. In fact, Steele even makes a stronger claim. He argues that African-Americans have become accustomed to a "victims status" and use racism as an excuse for failing to succeed even when opportunities do exist.

I reject Steele's conclusions. First, I don't think that individual African-Americans acting alone can overcome racism. Individual blacks who succeed do so because of the struggles and sacrifices of others, and these others always extend beyond family members and friends. Next, I reject Steele's claim that the lack of progress by disadvantaged African-Americans is due in any significant way to their perception of themselves as helpless victims. Such a claim depends upon a failure to appreciate the serious obstacles that African-Americans encounter because of their race. Even if it is true that African-American advancement is contingent on African-Americans helping themselves, it does not follow that African-Americans should be criticized for failing to adopt dehumanizing means because they are necessary for their economic advancement.

African-Americans should not be viewed as inferior to other groups, but they should also not be seen as superior. Racial injustice negatively impacts the motivational levels of all people. African-Americans are not an exception. Steele makes it seem as if poor and uneducated African-Americans lack the appropriate values to succeed. He contends that the opportunities exist, but that too many African-Americans fail to take advantage of them because they cannot break out of the victim's mentality. I reject this line of reasoning. As I have argued elsewhere,[27] this way of thinking erroneously assumes that most disadvantages result from a lack of motivation. In reality, it would take exceptional motivational levels to overcome the injustices that African-Americans experience. Because some African-Americans can rise to these levels, it would be unreasonable to think that all could. Steele underestimates the work that must be done to provide real opportunities to members of the so-called black underclass who struggle with racism on a daily basis.

I would like to forestall any misunderstandings about my emphasis on the role that supportive communities play in the lives of oppressed groups. I am not maintaining that African-Americans don't experience alienation because they are able to draw strength from supportive communities. My point is that supportive communities can, in some cases, minimize the damaging effects caused by a racist society. Nor is it my intention to deny that African-Americans and other groups must constantly struggle to maintain a healthy sense of self in a hostile society that causes them to experience self-doubt and a range of other negative states.

## Notes

1  Liberal thinkers tend to argue that alienation results when human beings can no longer see themselves as being in control of or comfortable in their social environment, and they contend that this discomfort occurs when crucial rights are violated, e.g., the right to autonomy. In an interesting twist on the liberal position, Bruce A. Ackerman argues in *Social Justice and the Liberal State* (New Haven, Conn.: Yale University Press, 1980), esp. 346–7, that the right to mutual dialogue is necessary to protect the autonomy of individuals in a community.

2  See, e.g., John Elster, ed., *Karl Marx: A Reader* (Cambridge: Cambridge University Press, 1986), ch. 11; Bertell Ollman, *Alienation* (Cambridge: Cambridge University Press, 1976), part III; Robert C. Tucker, ed., *The Marx–Engels Reader* (New York: W. W. Norton & Co., 1978), 73, 75, 77–8, 252–6, 292–3.

3   See Frantz Fanon, *Black Skin/White Masks* (New York: Grove Press, 1967), ch. 1; June Jordan, "Report From the Bahamas," *On Call* (Boston: South End Press, 1985), 39–50.

4   The famous speech delivered by Martin L. King, Jr. at the March on Washington, D.C., August 1963.

5   See Howard Brotz, ed., *Negro Social and Political Thought 1850–1920* (New York: Basic Books, 1966).

6   Ralph Ellison, *The Invisible Man* (New York: New American Library, 1953).

7   W. E. B. DuBois, *The Souls of Black Folk* (New York: New American Library, 1969), 45.

8   Joel Feinberg, *Social Philosophy* (Englewood Cliffs, NJ: Prentice-Hall, Inc., 1973), ch. 1.

9   Feinberg, *Social Philosophy*, 13.

10  John Rawls, *A Theory of Justice* (Cambridge, MA: Harvard University Press, 1971), Section 67.

11  Feinberg, *Social Philosophy*, 13.

12  Rawls, *A Theory of Justice*, 440–6.

13  Isaiah Berlin, *Two Concepts of Liberty* (Oxford: Clarendon Press, 1961).

14  See Alasdair MacIntyre, *After Virtue* (Notre Dame, Ind.: University of Notre Dame Press, 1981), ch. 17; Michael Sandel, *Liberalism and the Limits of Justice* (Cambridge: Cambridge University Press, 1982), 59–65, 173–5.

15  Howard McGary, Jr., "Racial Integration and Racial Separatism: Conceptual Clarifications," in Leonard Harris, ed., *Philosophy Born of Struggle* (Dubuque, Iowa: Kendall/Hunt Publishing Co., 1983), 199–211.

16  Laurence Thomas, in *The New York Times*, August 13, 1990.

17  See Bernard Boxill, "The Race and Class Question," in Harris, *Philosophy Born of Struggle*, 107–16.

18  See, e.g., Howard McGary, Jr., "The Nature of Race and Class Exploitation," in A. Zegeye, L. Harris, and J. Maxted, eds, *Exploitation and Exclusion* (London: Hans Zell Publishers, 1991), 14–27; and Richard Schmitt, "A New Hypothesis About the Relations of Class, Race and Gender: Capitalism as a Dependent System," *Social Theory and Practice*, 14, 3 (1988), 345–65.

19  Stanley Elkins, *Slavery: A Problem in American Institutional and Intellectual Life* (Chicago: University of Chicago Press, 1976).

20  John Blassingame, *The Slave Community: Plantation Life in the Antebellum South* (New York: Oxford University Press, 1972), 200–16.

21  Orlando Patterson, *Slavery and Social Death* (Cambridge, MA: Harvard University Press, 1982).

22  Orlando Patterson, "Towards a Future that Has No Past: Reflections on the Fate of Blacks in America," *The Public Interest*, 27 (1972).

23  W. E. B. DuBois, *Dusk of Dawn* (New Brunswick, NJ: Transaction Books, 1987), esp. ch. 7.

24  See Howard McGary and Bill E. Lawson, *Between Slavery and Freedom: Philosophy and American Slavery* (Bloomington: Indiana University Press, 1992).

25  William J. Wilson, *The Truly Disadvantaged* (Chicago: University of Chicago Press, 1987).

26  Shelby Steele, *The Content of Our Characters: A New Vision of Race in America* (New York: St. Martin's Press, 1990), esp. chs 3 and 4.

27  Howard McGary, "The Black Underclass and the Question of Values," in William Lawson, ed., *The Underclass Question* (Philadelphia: Temple University Press, 1992), 57–70.

# 2

# Race and Class Exploitation

The term "exploitation" is used to describe the condition of numerous individuals and groups. We often hear the terms class exploitation, race exploitation and the exploitation of women tossed about in discussions about equality and justice. All these uses of the term "exploitation" are thought to denote a negative or unacceptable state of affairs, but it is not obvious that they all refer to the same thing. Some activists and social critics have assumed that to be exploited is a terrible thing and that it serves no useful purpose to attempt to distinguish, say, class, racial or sexual exploitation. For them, such efforts only prove to be divisive and contribute to the lack of solidarity exhibited by exploited groups. I disagree. A thoughtful analysis of the different forms of exploitation may serve to provide the conditions for solidarity rather than disunity. It may also put us in a better position when it comes to eliminating the causes of the different types of exploitation.

In a short chapter, I cannot examine all the various modifiers that have been attached to the term "exploitation." Instead, I shall examine the concept of exploitation with an eye towards determining whether or not there are any significant differences between exploitation based upon class and exploitation based upon race. In my discussion, when I refer to racial exploitation I will mean the exploitation of people based upon claims about the distinct natures of groups of people according to supposed inherited unique mental or physical traits. These physical traits are thought to play a causal role in the formulation of the personal attributes of members of the group.

Furthermore, these traits are thought to figure largely in the shaping of cultures. However, it should be noted that the alleged scientific evidence in support of these two claims is suspect. There is little, if any, scientific support for biological or genetic accounts of race. Nonetheless people from all walks of life still insist that the notion has some biological or genetic foundation. This religious-like commitment to the biological or genetic conception of race and races has strong political, psychological and sociological consequences. People are categorized, identified, and mistreated because they are thought to be members of certain racial groups. It is also true that racial identification has become one of the most common means of self-identification. So, even though it is correct to emphasize that in a physical sense races do not exist, in a social sense they do because the myth of race has created a reality unto itself.[1]

Some people argue that race, in itself, can be a benign notion. It is only when some racial groups are thought to be superior to others that the problems arise.[2] Others maintain that the very existence of racial groups is harmful.[3] I shall not enter this debate, but I mention it here because some people argue that the only way to stop racial exploitation is to down play the importance of races, while others contend that we can still classify people on the basis of race and assign importance to a person's race, but not exploit them because of their race.

Before we begin, two points of clarification are in order. When I use the term race, I acknowledge that racial classifications have been employed in different ways in response to different economic, historical, and social conditions. So one's group membership can be, in part, effected by these influences, but at the core there are still ontological claims about the physical nature of the being that determine racial identification. Secondly, we must be aware that members of the same racial group can exhibit "racist-like" attitudes and behavior against members of their own group. But we should be careful to distinguish something that is racist from something that is "racist-like." For example, Charles Dickens in describing the English working class employs language that is similar to the language employed by racist white Southerners to describe African-Americans, but I shall suggest a reason why this language and the treatment of the white working class was deplorable, but not racist.[4]

I do not intend to imply by these remarks that racial exploitation can occur only when races are defined in terms of obvious physical characteristics like a person's skin coloring. In my view, it is possible for people with the same skin coloring and national origins to divide into different racial groups and thus it is not impossible for racial exploitation to occur towards members of a subgroup with the same skin coloring.

In this chapter I focus on the relationship between African-Americans and whites, but I in no way intend to suggest that other racially defined groups are not exploited. Much of what I have to say about the exploitation of African-Americans can be extended to other racially defined groups.

In the first section, I lay out what have now become standard accounts of the general concept of exploitation. These accounts are drawn from the work of both progressive and liberal authors. In the second section, I construct progressive accounts of race and class exploitation. In the final section, I describe and defend my own accounts of racial and class exploitation in the light of my discussion of the standard accounts.

## Standard Accounts of Exploitation

In this section, I briefly spell out three interpretations of Marx's concept of exploitation criticized by Allen Buchanan in his book *Marx and Justice*[5] and present Buchanan's own interpretation of Marx's notion of exploitation. I then discuss Robert Nozick's[6] critique of the Marxist account of exploitation and the challenges he raises for a Marxist interpretation of exploitation.

Buchanan examines, and eventually rejects, three popular interpretations of Marx's concept of exploitation. He argues that these interpretations are plausible, but in the final analysis do not accurately capture the important relationship between Marx's concept of exploitation and his theory of alienation. Buchanan argues that this connection is more intimate than scholars have realized.

Now let me briefly state the three interpretations of Marx's concept of exploitation that Buchanan criticizes. The first interpretation of Marx's concept of exploitation is based upon the wage-labor process in the capitalist mode of production. According to this interpretation, the worker in a capitalist mode of production is exploited because his labor is forced, he is deprived of the surplus value that results from his labor and does not control the product that results from his labor.

The second interpretation also focuses on the three conditions listed in the first interpretation, but claims that modes of production other than capitalism can generate these states of affairs, for example, oriental despotism, ancient slave-holding societies, and feudalism.

The third interpretation of Marx's account of exploitation is more general and goes beyond the wage-labor process. According to this interpretation, bourgeois human relations in general are exploitive because they utilize persons as one would a tool or a natural resource. This utilization harms the person being so used, and its benefits accrue to the user rather than the person being used.[7]

Buchanan is sympathetic to some of the reasons why scholars have interpreted Marx's concept of exploitation in the three ways described above. There is textual support for all three interpretations; they are all faithful to Marx's radical critique of capitalism and are consistent with his call for revolution by the working class. Nonetheless, Buchanan believes that the first two interpretations are too narrow and restrictive and the third interpretation lacks content or substance because it fails to provide a systematic classification of the ways in which human beings are utilized and the specific forms of hardship that this utilization inflicts upon them.

Buchanan's own interpretation of Marx's notion of exploitation builds upon the third interpretation, but he attempts to give substance to what it means for a person to be utilized, by drawing upon Marx's theory of alienation. By alienation, Marx basically meant that a person is treated as an alien being, not as a fellow human being with human capacities which must be nurtured if they are to develop. Buchanan cites the following passage from

"On the Jewish Question"[8] to support his contention that we cannot truly understand Marx's notion of alienation without recognizing the intimate connection between Marx's notion of exploitation and his theory of alienation:

> Selling is the practice of externalization . . . Man thereby converts his nature into an alien, illusory being, so under the domination of egoistic needs he can only act practically, only practically produce objects by subordinating both his products and his activity to the dominion of an alien being, the capitalists, bestowing upon them the significance of an alien entity – money.

Buchanan recognizes that any viable interpretation of the concept of exploitation must have a normative component. Marx's account of exploitation is no exception. Buchanan rejects all interpretations of Marx's account of exploitation which claim that Marx was only doing descriptive or "scientific" work.

Clearly he is correct. How can one give an adequate account of exploitation without an evaluative or normative component? However, both Marxists and non-Marxists face the problem of supplying this normative content. Non-Marxists have appealed to moral or religious principle in their attempts to supply this normative content. Unfortunately, given the received interpretations of Marx's views on morality and religion, it is doubtful that Marxists can appeal to morality or religion to supply the normative content to their accounts of exploitation.[9]

If they cannot appeal to morality or religion, how can this normative content be supplied? There appear to be two principal strategies that Marxists might take. It could be supplied by a theory of practical rationality that would make it rational for agents to prefer a mode of production that did not utilize them as alien beings over one that did, or by adopting a theory of human nature that would show that human beings desire, as a matter of their natures, relationships where they are not treated as alien beings.

However, these strategies would not explain why exploitation is wrong or unjust. They can only give us reasons why people prefer or desire not to be exploited. But we should remember that people can desire or prefer things that are unjust or wrong. So even though capitalist society treats certain of its members as alien beings, and these persons do not prefer to be treated in this way, we should not conclude that they are being treated unjustly or wrongly unless we have a sound argument in support of this normative conclusion.

Marxists might attempt to explain why exploitation is wrong by appealing to some utilitarian-like standards that measure the rightness and wrongness by the maximization or satisfaction of undistorted individual desires or preferences. On the other hand, they could appeal to an ideal person or community that is not reducible to the undistorted desires and preferences of individuals. Buchanan believes that a consistent Marxist account of exploitation that is able to supply the normative component will do so by appealing to a set of distinct normative ideals of persons and community. According to Buchanan, the support for such ideals is one of the principal tasks of Marxist scholarship, and this work will draw Marxist scholars into some of the traditional problems in moral philosophy. So, for Buchanan, Marxists cannot define exploitation in purely descriptive or scientific terms. They must do so by an appeal to moral concepts.

On the other end of the political spectrum, we find the supporters of individualism and capitalism maintaining that capitalism is not an exploitive system and that the wage-labor process is not necessarily exploitive. Of course, these theorists have their own definitions of exploitation. I cannot consider each of these accounts, but I will consider one such account that is fairly representative of this way of thinking.

Robert Nozick argues against the Marxist account of exploitation because he believes that such accounts violate the moral rights that we all have to be free. In his view, Marxist accounts of exploitation are incompatible with our right to individual freedom. Although capitalism may allow or even encourage people to take advantage of the lack of abilities or insights of others, it is not unjust for Nozick. Since Nozick believes that to exploit another is to do something unjust, he refuses to define capitalism as an exploitive system because he does not think that it is inherently unjust. Capitalism may allow for certain immoral acts, but for Nozick, this is one of the acceptable consequences of respecting an individual's right to individual freedom. Nozick refuses to define justice in terms of egalitarian, communitarian, perfectionist or welfarist principles.[10]

The concept of "coercion" is crucial to Nozick's and other liberal ways of understanding exploitation. For them, one is exploited only if one is forced to do or refrain from doing something that is permissible for one to do or refrain from doing. For example, people who are captured and forcibly sold into slavery are exploited, whereas people in dire circumstances who agree to work for a low wage because they believe it will enhance their life prospects are not exploited. Of course, there are heated debates over when a person is coerced and when a market exchange is voluntary. But my point is that these accounts refuse to say that a person is exploited simply because that person is down and out or that they do not fair well because of the just choices of others. Given what I have said above, a viable Marxist account of exploitation will rest on a theory of alienation and non-liberal principles of morality. While a viable liberal account of exploitation will rest on the defense of a legalistic account of individual freedom and a theory of coercion, i.e. an account of when a person is forced to do something.

## Race and Class Exploitation

What is race and class exploitation? Let us first look at the Marxist response. The classical response by many Marxists has been to deny that there are any significant differences between race and class exploitation. Some Marxists contend that race exploitation is simply class exploitation. The supporters of this reductionist position are not simply making a claim about what is the best approach to take if one wants to eliminate all forms of exploitation, they see themselves as describing the nature of exploitation. For them racial exploitation is a species of class exploitation, but they do not believe that the converse is true. In other words, we can describe racial exploitation in terms of class exploitation, but we cannot describe class exploitation in terms of racial exploitation.

How are we to understand "exploitation" in multicultural, gender conscious, capitalist societies? According to the reductionist position above, we just have to explore more thoroughly the class analysis of such societies and by so doing will come to see that we do not have to abandon a properly worked out class analysis or amend such an analysis in fundamental ways in order to describe accurately the nature of the various other forms of exploitation experienced in multiracial, gender conscious, capitalist societies like the United States.

Bernard Boxill correctly points out, in his article "The Race and Class Question," that supporters of the reductionist position do not mean that we can define race in terms of class.[11] They would admit that these two things are distinct and would require different analyses. There is also no need for them to contend that racial exploitation is always less objectionable. In fact, they could even believe that, morally speaking, things like racial and sexual exploitation are more objectionable than class exploitation, yet still maintain class exploitation is the fundamental category. Finally, they could admit that we cannot eliminate exploitation if we ignore such things as a person's race or sex, yet still insist that in the final analysis other forms of exploitation are reducible to class exploitation.

How should we understand this reduction? Boxill interprets the reductionist position as follows: "the claim that race is subsidiary to class means that it is the class struggle that is the cause, condition, or explanation of racial antagonisms, not racial antagonisms that are the cause, condition, or explanation of class struggle."[12] According to Boxill, if the Marxists simply mean that a theory of racial antagonism can be deduced, with the appropriate transitional principles, from a theory of Marxist class struggle, then they may be right. What Boxill objects to is the Marxist's claim that class struggle is the cause, condition, and explanation of the transcendence of racial antagonisms in multiracial capitalist societies. So his worry is not with the claim that class analysis is the more fundamental theory if we are to correctly understand exploitation, but with the claim that class analysis is the only viable analysis for explaining how a society overcomes racial antagonisms.

But perhaps Boxill is premature in accepting the position that class analysis is more fundamental when it comes to explaining various types of exploitation. I would like to explore this possibility.

Does racial exploitation reduce to class exploitation? Perhaps it has been thought to do so because of the belief by many that exploitation must be defined in purely economic terms. In other words, people are exploited because of their relationship to the labor process. On this reading, a person's race may be useful in helping us to understand why certain people are exploited, but it cannot explain what counts as exploitation. Remember, for the Marxists, exploitation is directly related to where a person stands in the means of production. So, according to this view, there is no conceptual confusion involved in saying that someone is black but not exploited, or white and exploited. Even though the overwhelming majority of African-Americans may be exploited on this reading, it is because of where they stand in relation to the means of production and this condition is not defined in racial or genetic terms.

If we recall our earlier discussion, Buchanan argues that we should not understand Marx's account of exploitation solely in economic terms. Remember he rejects accounts of exploitation that are defined solely in terms of the labor process. For Buchanan, these accounts depend upon the discredited labor theory of value and thus fall prey to some of the criticisms mounted against this theory. Finally, he believes that these accounts tend to treat exploitation as a purely distributive matter and, by so doing, commit Marx to a dependency upon a notion of distributive justice, something that Marx clearly rejects.

What if we move to the general account of exploitation defended by Buchanan? Does his interpretation of Marx's account of exploitation entail that class exploitation is the most fundamental form of exploitation? In answering this question, we should remember that, according to this interpretation, people can be exploited in systems with various modes of production even though they occupy positions of relative privilege within that social and economic system. On this account, slaves, serfs and workers can all count amongst the exploited. Buchanan's interpretation of Marx's general account of exploitation does not connect exploitation narrowly to the capitalist labor process, but this interpretation does flatly deny that persons in a capitalist system can sell their labor to other persons for wages and not be exploited. Highly skilled as well as unskilled workers are exploited, according to

Buchanan's interpretation. So, this account of exploitation has a material as well as a psychological component. Remember that, according to Buchanan's expanded interpretation of exploitation, in class societies all the members of the society are exploited because they are used as tools for the ends of others.

Liberals, unlike Marxists, define exploitation as coercing someone to serve the ends of another or as coercing someone to serve their own ends (paternalism). Liberals, be they political conservatives, libertarians, or welfarists, play down the importance of class exploitation. They reject the view that workers are exploited in virtue of living in a class-structured society. According to them, exploitation can be found in capitalist societies, but it need not exist. But communist societies are judged to be necessarily exploitive because they allow state coercion in a manner that violates individual liberty.

Although liberals deny that there is any such thing as class exploitation in the Marxist sense of the concept, they do recognize (sometimes reluctantly) that there can be race exploitation in capitalist as well as communist societies. So, for liberals, racial exploitation cannot reduce to class exploitation because class exploitation in the Marxist sense does not exist.

We should be careful here and notice that liberals are not maintaining that only racial groups can be exploited. Their point is simply that we should not confuse a social group with a class defined in Marxist terms. They reject the view that all workers as a class are used as unwilling tools to satisfy the ends of owners. However, they do admit that some people are used as tools because they are members of certain historically despised groups.

## A New Look at Race and Class Exploitation

What should we conclude from the seeming impasse between the liberal and Marxist accounts of exploitation? Are their positions mutually exclusive? I think that they are, but we need not deny the existence of class exploitation in order to show that racial exploitation is different in a fundamental way from class exploitation.

We can discern the differences between race and class exploitation by focusing more clearly on what it means to be used as a tool or to be treated like an alien being in society. Unfortunately, Marxists and capitalists tend to interpret racism in either material or psychological terms. In other words, they focus on the material things that people are denied by virtue of their racial identification or the psychological problems they experience relative to their self-concepts. The focus on one or the other obscures a fundamental difference between class and race exploitation.

The fundamental difference, as I see it, is that when a person is treated as an alien being or used as a tool because of class membership, then she is accorded personhood even though she is deprived of the fruits of her labor with all that this entails. But when a person is used as a tool in virute of his race, he is thought by the prevailing ideology of the society to be less than a person and treated accordingly. The denial of personhood means a lack of membership in the moral community rather than a lack of full membership.

Full membership in the moral community means that the being has rights that others are bound to respect and there are things that members can demand as opposed to request as a matter of privilege. But we should not assume that denial of full membership will entail that such beings will experience material deprivation. Those who are denied full membership may have their needs (and even their desires) met, but these needs and desires are met subject to the will of others. Some domestic pets live quite comfortable existences, without being accorded the status of full members in the moral community.

An important part of racial exploitation (defined here as treating persons as non-person tools) is the fact that members of the racially exploited groups are thought to be naturally incapable of satisfying the conditions of personhood. Racists believe that a biological or genetic barrier prevents certain beings from ever becoming persons, even though they may be capable of doing the things that would normally qualify beings for personhood. The evidence in favor of personhood is discounted for what are often the most unconvincing reasons. However, it may be presumptuous to expect that rationality will always force the racist to abandon his racist views. Racists are strongly driven by their emotions or sentiments even though they may employ ingenious schemes to rationalize their feelings and sentiments about certain groups. The Scottish philosopher and famous sceptic, David Hume, was a classic example of a well educated person who took great pride in being rational, but who nonetheless held and expounded racist views.[13]

Much of my argument about the differences between race and class exploitation hinges on being able to draw a meaningful distinction between full membership and a lack of membership in the moral community. Ralph Ellison draws graphic attention to what it means not to be seen as a bona fide member of the community.[14] He describes the phenomenon for blacks in terms of invisibility. In other words, he described how blacks in America were beings who were not seen as authentic human beings with all that this implies.

We also find Cornel West, in his book *Prophesy Deliverance: An Afro-American Revolutionary Christianity*, contending that regarding African-Americans as human beings is a relatively new discovery in the modern West. He asserts that

the modern world has been shaped first and foremost by the doctrine of white supremacy, which is embodied in institutional practices and enacted in everyday folkways under varying circumstances and evolving conditions.[15]

In a similar vein, Richard Popkin in an excellent series of articles, clearly demonstrates that the eighteenth century was the watershed of modern racial theories that saw blacks and American Indians as inferior human beings.[16]

However, none of these authors clearly assert that blacks were perceived by whites not to have any moral status, though it is clear that they believed that blacks were not assigned full moral status with whites.

By full moral status, I mean acknowledging and treating a being as having a natural right to having intrinsic value assigned to her well-being and freedom.[17] Furthermore, this being is entitled to demand to be conceived of and treated accordingly. So, in my view, having less than full membership means that you do not have a right to have intrinsic value assigned to your well-being and free-dom, though your well-being and freedom is not seen as un-important. However non-membership in the moral community means that your pain and well-being are unimportant and do not have to be considered; this applies, for example, to weeds or cer-tain insects. This is tantamount to treating livings things as objects.

The denial of personhood to members of certain groups and the rationalizations that accompany these denials are intensified by the difficulties we encounter when we attempt to give necessary and sufficient conditions for being a person. We all think that we know what it means to be a person, but our knowledge is called into question when we are forced to explain the concept. In writing on the morality of abortion, Mary Ann Warren offers the following traits as central to the concept of personhood: consciousness, reas-oning, self-motivated activity, the capacity to communicate, and the presence of self-concepts.[18] However, she is quick to admit that there are numerous problems involved in formulating a precise definition of personhood, let alone in developing behavioral cri-teria for deciding when the concept applies.

Racists who seek to rationalize their racist beliefs and deeds take great comfort in this uncertainty about personhood. By this I do not mean to imply that this uncertainty gives validity to their rationalizations, but it is a way of masking the inconsistency and wrongness of their views about why members of one group should be treated differently in virtue of their group membership.

The debates over American slavery clearly illustrated this point. Some people objected to slavery on the grounds that it singled out black people for such treatment. But slavery was not abhorrent because it singled out blacks for such treatment, it was wrong because it treated persons as non-persons. Slavery would have been wrong if slave masters were equal opportunity enslavers.

Critics of my account of racial exploitation might respond by claiming that at one time in American history African-Americans were viewed as non-persons by the dominant society, but surely as a society we are long past this point.[19] We may be tempted to accept this reply until we recognize that we should not confuse law with morality and theory with practice. There is a good case to be made that laws in the US acknowledge the personhood of African-

Americans and other racial minorities, but even if this is true, it does not follow that the moral outlook in the US is one that accords the status of persons to African-Americans. There is plenty of room in everyday practice for African-Americans to be viewed and used as non-person-like tools even if formally the law prohibits certain treatment in certain defined areas.

Another objection can be put in the following way: surely in our everyday lives we have come to accept people of all races as fellow human beings and, as such, persons. Unfortunately, even if we agree that people have come to recognize each other as genetic human beings, it does not follow that they acknowledge all genetic human beings as persons. Moral debates over abortion and euthanasia have shown us that being genetically human does not obviously imply personhood.

Earlier, when I denied that white English workers were treated as non-persons, I did not mean to suggest they were allowed to achieve their full human potential. I firmly believed that they were not. This also can be said about white wage-laborers today. My point is simply that they were considered to be persons, even if it was thought to be highly unlikely that they could ever become the owners of the means of production.

African-Americans, on the other hand, have been perceived as non-persons by the prevailing ideology of society. This perception has made it possible for them to be viewed and used as tools. However, my position does not commit me to the view that people must organize on the basis of race to eliminate racial exploitation. Nor do I contend that each and every white person conceives of African-Americans as non-persons. Oddly enough, it even allows for African-Americans to view themselves because they are also affected by racist ideology. A sad fact of American life is that none of us are immune to racist ideology. There needs to be a great deal more work done on the psychology and sociology of racism and more frank interaction between members of different races if the damaging consequences of racism are to be mitigated.

## Notes

1 Ashley Montagu, *The Concept of Race* (London: Collier-Macmillan, 1969).

2 Lucius Outlaw, *On Race and Philosophy* (New York: Routledge, 1996), esp. 157.

3 Kwame Anthony Appiah, "Racisms," in David Theo Goldberg, ed., *Anatomy of Racism* (Minneapolis: University of Minnesota Press, 1990), 3–17.

4 Charles Dickens, *A Tale of Two Cities* (New York: Random House, 1990).

5 Allen E. Buchanan, *Marx and Justice: The Radical Critique of Liberalism* (New York: Rowman and Littlefield, 1982).

6 Robert Nozick, *Anarchy, State and Utopia* (New York: Basic Books, 1975).

7 Buchanan, *Marx and Justice*, ch. 3.

8 Karl Marx, "On the Jewish Question," in L. Easton and K. Guddhat, eds, *Writings of the Young Marx on Philosophy* (New York: Doubleday Publishers, 1976), 248.

9 See, e.g., Robert Tucker, *The Marxian Revolutionary Idea* (New York: Norton Publishing Company, 1969); and Allen Wood, "The Marxian Critique of Justice," *Philosophy and Public Affairs*, 1 (1972).

10 Nozick, *Anarchy, State and Utopia*, ch. 7.

11 Bernard Boxill, "The Race and Class Question," in L. Harris, *Philosophy Born of Struggle* (Iowa: Iowa University Press, 1983), 107–16.

12 Boxill, "The Race and Class Question," 108–9.

13 See Richard Popkin, "Hume's Racism," *The Philosophical Forum*, 9 (1977–8), 211–26, and "Hume's Racism Reconsidered," *The Journal*, 1 (1984): 61–71.

14 Ralph Ellison, *The Invisible Man* (New York: New American Library, 1953).

15 Cornel West, *Prophesy Deliverance: An Afro-American Revolutionary Experience* (Philadelphia: The Westminister Press, 1982), 47.

16 Popkin, "Hume's Racism," and "Hume's Racism Reconsidered."

17 See Bernard Williams, "The Idea of Equality," in P. Laslett and W. G. Runciman, eds, *Philosophy, Politics and Society*, 2 (Oxford: Blackwell, 1962); Gregory Vlastos, "Justice and Equality," and Richard Wasserstrom, "Rights, Human Rights, and Racial Discrimination," in A. I. Meldin, ed., *Human Rights* (Belmont: Wadsworth Publishing, 1970).

18 Mary Ann Warren, "On the Moral and Legal Status of Abortion," in R. Wasserstrom, ed., *Today's Moral Problems* (New York: Macmillan, 1985).

19 There are numerous publications that discuss the continued existence of racism and its consequences, e.g., David Theo Goldberg, *The Anatomy of Racism* (Minneapolis: University of Minnesota Press, 1990), and his *Racist Culture: Philosophy and the Politics of Meaning* (Oxford: Blackwell, 1993); Andrew Hacker, *Two Nations: Black and White, Separate, Hostile, Unequal* (New York: Scribner's, 1992); Robert Miles, *Racism* (London: Routledge, 1989); Paula Rothenberg, *Racism and Sexism: An Integrated Study* (New York: St. Martin's Press, 1988).

# 3

# Racial Integration and Racial Separatism: Conceptual Clarifications

African-Americans in the United States have endured economic powerlessness, second-class citizenship, problems of personal identity, and a lack of self-determination as a result of racial discrimination. African-American theorists in the US have proposed numerous approaches in their attempts to solve these problems. I shall focus on two conflicting approaches frequently tendered as solutions. The first is the racial separatist approach; the second is the racial integrationist approach. Both approaches take a variety of forms, and both have enjoyed support by African-Americans.

In what follows I will compare and contrast the integrationist thesis with the separatist thesis, but I shall not attempt to decide between them. Instead, I shall only attempt to clarify some of the conceptual issues and arguments that underlie the dispute and make some suggestions about how policy makers can benefit if they are clear about the conceptual issues involved in the dispute.

There is intense controversy as to what a race is. In fact, some have even argued that there are no races.[1] For the purpose of this chapter, I shall assume that there are races and, in particular, that there is a black race. I shall be exclusively concerned with the separation or the integration of the black race with the white race, but perhaps some of what I say can be naturally extended to the question of the integration or separation of any two races.

---

I

---

When we think of African-Americans who have advocated racial separatism as a way of eliminating or solving race related problems, we think of Edward W. Blyden, Martin R. Delany, Marcus M. Garvey, the early Malcolm X, the Nation of Islam under the leadership of Elijah Muhammad, and the Black Cultural Nationalist movements of the 1960s with figures like Maulana Ron Karenga and Imamu Amiri Baraka.[2] The rallying cry of these individuals and movements was that African-Americans were being contaminated and destroyed by the present economic arrangement and by an alien white culture and value system. For them complete or partial separation of the races was the most effective and morally acceptable means of halting the degradation that African-Americans faced.

We must be careful at this juncture and point out that although all the individuals and groups listed above shared the belief that the races must be separated in order to achieve well-being and self-determination for African-Americans, they differed in the specifics of how to achieve these ends. Garvey and the Nation of Islam stressed the importance of economic self-determination[3] whereas cultural separatists like Baraka and Karenga emphasized cultural identification.[4] When I say that they stressed different things, I do not mean that they completely ignored what the other group stressed.

Some separatists have been racial chauvinists, although it is possible for a person to support separation without advocating one race as being superior or unique. For example, one might merely believe that talent and abilities are correlated with racial groups, and that the abilities and talents possessed by all races are equally important, but that it would be prudent to separate the races in order to maximize human happiness. Then one must produce evidence that human happiness will, in fact, be promoted or is more likely to be promoted under such an arrangement.

Other separatists, like Garvey, have not been chauvinistic, but maintained that the races ought to be separate in every way. Garvey's argument was a consequentialist one because he believed that given the circumstances, the only practical means to achieve self-determination for African-Americans was through separation from whites. This consequentialist argument is popular amongst some separatists. But other separatists choose to justify their stance on deontological claims about the virtues of keeping the races pure. For example, the Nation of Islam, under the leadership of Elijah Muhammad, categorically supported the position that the races ought to separate in all areas of life.[5] This position is more controversial than a consequentialist position like Garvey's because it involves absolutist claims about differences between races and the things that may be correlated with these differences.

Cultural separatists, unlike separatists who stress the economic and political importance of keeping the races separate, place a great deal of emphasis on things like a person's self-concept. They believe that African-Americans suffer because they reject their black identity and by rejecting their identity and accepting integration or biological amalgamation they deny their own creative possibilities. The separatist believes that this leads to a life without a sense of meaning or purpose. Some cultural separatists see complete separation of races as a necessary but not a sufficient condition for blacks to achieve meaningful and purposeful lives, whereas others think that complete separation is unnecessary. For the latter, all that is required is that African-Americans be aware of their culture, take pride in it, and keep their cultural institutions separate from whites.

## II

Now that we have set out some of the various kinds of racial separatisms; let us examine arguments in favor of them. I shall not assess all the arguments that have been propounded, but those I scrutinize are representative.

Many African-Americans who have supported racial separatism to achieve economic self-determination appeal to statistics that compare the economic circumstances of African-Americans and whites. Numerous publications have made available the statistics that reveal the vast economic inequalities that exist between

African-Americans and whites. But these discouraging statistics nonetheless tend to underemphasize blacks' lack of control over industry, commerce, land, finance, communication, and the professions. Black separatists have claimed that the disparities in these areas are so great that African-Americans could never become full participants in such an economic system.

This claim seems to be based upon the practical failure of economic integration in America. The claim is questionable. Merely because African-Americans have a history of economic inequality in this country, one cannot conclude that in a racially mixed society one could never resolve the economic inequalities that exist between African-Americans and whites. Since no concerted effort has been advanced, one may not conclude that such an effort could never be successful.

Does the separatist claim that in a society consisting of one racial group there will be no disparities in incomes? If he does, then his claim is obviously false. Japan is a capitalistic society consisting of primarily one racial group, yet large disparities in incomes and economic powerlessness of individuals exist. Although the existence of economic disparities is relevant, it does not, by itself support the separatists' thesis, but the economic inequalities of our society do have a bearing on the subject.

One of the most compelling economic arguments for separatism concentrates on the problems one faces in trying to upgrade a previously excluded group. Proponents of this argument usually articulate their intuitions regarding these problems in an uncritical manner. They, and their opponents, tend to be overly emotional and fail to examine the vital points in question. Still the discussions are not entirely unreasonable. For example, when the black separatist remarks:

It is crazy to think that blacks can integrate in the areas of jobs and education. White people can't make the commitments necessary to insure equal opportunity, which are necessary if economic racial integration is to be taken seriously.

The black separatist believes that whites will not make the necessary commitments because: (1) some are malevolent; (2) some will feel that it is against their interests; and (3) others feel integration will harm various American institutions. Professor Sidney Hook articulated the latter view with regard to government affirmative action programs. Hook claimed that when the Department of Health, Education and Welfare requires from universities actual evidence of their efforts to equalize employment opportunities for minorities, the result is adverse to quality education at our universities.[6]

Worries like Hook's reflect the enormous moral and legal problems associated with achieving racial equality. So far, issues such as compensatory education for African-Americans and other racially oppressed groups and the preferential hiring of African-Americans are still hotly debated. I am not suggesting that settling these issues will bring about racial equality, but rather that they bear directly on it. However, the worries articulated above will not serve to vindicate the conclusion that racial separatism is required to eliminate the problems that African-Americans face.

The two claims examined above – that past and present inequalities suggest the impossibility of equality in the future and that whites lack the commitment needed to create equality – are reservations advanced by separatists against integrationist policies. Perhaps the economic difficulties can be avoided if the society is willing to redistribute wealth and take certain compensatory measures. There is an argument, however, for the claim that the integration of the races deprives people of culture and self-worth. If this argument is sound, it is a more formidable criticism than the two economic reservations.

### III

Leroi Jones (Amiri Baraka) and Maulana Ron Karenga at one time advanced the view that racial integration would deprive African-Americans of culture and self-worth.[7] They felt that racial integration deprives African-American people of a culture that they already have or that they ought to regain, because it involves the grafting of African-Americans onto the white culture. They felt that when this is done African-Americans will be forced to accept a culture that developed in western Europe, one that ignores black art forms and black values. Jones and Karenga concluded that African-Americans must recover and maintain the positive aspects of their culture.

Before we can evaluate the cultural separatist position, we must have a clear understanding of what separatists have meant by culture. The term "culture" has been used interchangeably by separatists with terms like ethnicity and race. According to many sociologists, this is a mistake. For example, Orlando Patterson feels that we should distinguish cultural groups from ethnic groups. He defines an ethnic group in terms of how symbolic objects are used to " maintain group cohesiveness, sustain and enhance identity, and establish social networks and communicative patterns that are important for the group's optimization of its social and economic position in the society."[8] For Patterson, "a cultural group is simply any group of people who share an identifiable complex of meanings, symbols, values and norms."[9] Patterson also stipulates that there need not be any conscious awareness of belonging to a culture in order to be a member of a cultural group.

Space prevents us from getting embroiled in a discussion of the differences between cultural and ethnic groups. In my examination of the literature by black cultural separatists, I have found that they have taken "culture" to mean more than the sometimes conscious and sometimes unconscious sharing of symbols, values, and norms. The cultural separatist operates with a concept of culture that includes Patterson's definition of ethnicity.

There is, of course, an obvious objection that might be raised against the position that integration deprives African-Americans of their culture. The objection is this: surely one cannot argue that some African-Americans don't willingly participate in, study, and cherish various aspects of white culture. Furthermore, these African-Americans might derive satisfaction and, in some cases, economic gain from this activity.

Is such an objection persuasive? I think not. Because some African-Americans receive financial and social benefits at a high cost, it is not good reasoning to assume that other African-Americans should be willing to pay these costs. The black cultural separatists believe that the game is rigged because the major cultural and economic institutions are set up to guarantee that African-Americans cannot fully participate unless they are willing to forgo their own culture in order to benefit from American institutions. A National Broadcasting Company white paper on race relations in America pointed out that many blacks who are economically secure are still extremely dissatisfied. This dissatisfaction, according to the separatist, can be traced to the fact that in American institutional settings African-Americans are forced to adopt a culture other than their own.

If such a reply is to be compelling, we must have a clear idea of the things African-Americans must forgo in order to benefit from American cultural and economic institutions. What are they? One thing that has often been mentioned is self-respect. As I interpret the position of the cultural separatists, they are maintaining that in the past all forms of racial integration have amounted to the elimination of the cultural identity of African-Americans and that this has damaged and continues to damage the self-concept of African-Americans. When we talk about our self-concept, two concepts come to mind: self-respect and self-esteem. Writers have sometimes proceeded as if these two concepts are synonymous. This is a mistake. Although there are important similarities between the two concepts, there are important differences. In order to adequately assess their position we should now take note of an important difference between the two concepts.

We esteem a person in reference to his abilities and talents as compared with the abilities and talents of others. A crucial aspect of self-esteem is the fact that the opinions of others are crucial to a person's assessment of whether or not he feels that he is worthy of esteem. Self-respect on the other hand, does not necessarily depend upon the assessment of others. In fact, the person who stands steadfast in spite of the negative assessment of others might be thought, under appropriate conditions, to epitomize the self-respecting person.

An important feature of self-respect is that one tragic or disgusting episode late in a person's life can justify our describing the person as lacking in self-respect, irrespective of his abilities and talents. There are certain acts that the self-respecting person will not do and, when possible, allow to be done to him. The racial separatist believes that to acquiesce in the denial of one's culture is one such act. One might question whether this is true. I doubt that it is always the case that failing to protest a serious wrong serves to undermine a person's self-respect. For there certainly are cases where it is in one's interest or the interest of one's loved ones to acquiesce in a wrong or injustice. If this is so, African-Americans may not go along with the denial of their culture simply for the sake of doing it, but rather to obtain goods that are necessary for their survival. In such cases, it is not clear that in doing so they undermine their self-respect.

The cultural separatists could grant that such cases do exist and that it is sometimes morally preferable to place great value on other things like saving the lives of one's loved ones, but that the price for such deeds may be our self-respect. Consider the case of an African-American worker, in a white environment, who is required to minimize or give up her identification with her culture in order to care for and protect her children. She does so willingly, but she still detests what she has to do. Even though her actions do not flow from a defective character, they nonetheless are her actions, therefore, she must accept some responsibility for them. In such cases, the separatist might argue that a person's self-respect is still undermined.

If this particular line of argument is not compelling, then there is a similar argument that may be more supportive of the separatist position. In the argument stated above the cultural separatist concentrates on the self-respect of African-Americans. There is another aspect of the black experience that illustrates the separatist point. This aspect is revealed graphically by Marcus Garvey. Garvey wrote:

The only wise thing for us . . . Negros to do, is to organize the world over, and build up for the race a mighty nation of our own in Africa. And this race of ours that cannot get recognition and respect in the country where we were slaves, by using our ability, power and genius, would develop for ourselves a nation that would get as much respect as . . . any other . . . [10]

Garvey is focusing on self-esteem because he feels that African-Americans receive very little recognition from most US whites for their deeds and accomplishments. Recognition by others plays an important role in developing good self-esteem. William James put the point this way:

A man's social "me" is the recognition which he gets from his mates . . . no more fiendish punishment could be devised than that one should be turned loose in society and remain absolutely unnoticed by all the members thereof.[11]

The separatist claims that African-Americans are not generally recognized by many of the cultural and economic institutions of our society because African-Americans are thought to be expendable or of little consequence in the realization of the basic goals and values of these institutions. Garvey proposes that African-Americans expend their energies developing their own institutions rather than attempting to modify institutions controlled by whites. His solution is the total separation of both races, but all separatists need not take such an extreme position. The moderate separatist could argue that African-Americans should strive to control some institutions, but not to exclude whites from participating in these institutions. In doing so, African-Americans can gain recognition and legitimation for African-American achievements. Of course, recognition is a necessary but not a sufficient condition for African-Americans to develop a healthy self-concept. The communication of respect by one's peers is also necessary, but the separatist believes that this will occur when African-Americans separate from whites and begin to support each other.

Another argument frequently advanced by separatists has as one of its important premises the fact that African-Americans, unlike any other group, were brought to this country and brutally stripped of their culture, language, and religion. Black separatists, of all varieties, have argued that this caused African-Americans to lose important traditions and values and that this has contributed to people other than African-Americans having too much influence on the shaping of black lives. Given these things, separatists feel that African-Americans must (1) realize that it is absolutely necessary that they decide their own destinies and (2) be aware that this could entail a radical departure from Anglo-American traditions and values.

Integrationists and separatists accept the fact that black slaves were robbed of their African heritage, but they disagree over the truth of (1) and (2) above. Integrationists have granted that African-Americans and whites are different, but not so different that they cannot be integrated into American society. For this reason, integrationists believe that there is no need for African-Americans to adopt things like traditional African values or to stress the differences that exist between blacks and whites. Because they don't accept these things, they don't put stress on African-American self-determination, but on things like class viability. Separatists, on the other hand, have felt that the racial, the ethnic or the cultural question is more fundamental because of its importance to self-determination, therefore it must be addressed before questions of class inequities.

The above arguments by the extreme or the moderate separatists are persuasive if we accept the following claims:

(1) that white racism is endemic in white American society, that it is central to the culture and economic interest of the white majority;
(2) that racial identification is functional from the standpoint of economic, psychological, and social development;
(3) that racial separatism can be a democratic solution to the race problem; and
(4) that a supportive bond can/does exist between African-Americans.

The empirical evidence needed to support these claims is sparse. Although I do not feel that racial separatists of any variety have shown that racial separatism is the best or only solution to the race problem in the United States, perhaps they have cast doubt on integration as a solution. But before drawing any conclusions, one should look carefully at the integrationist position.

---

## IV

---

The major figures and movements within the integrationist camp include: Frederick Douglass, Booker T. Washington, Martin Luther

King, Jr., the National Association for the Advancement of Colored People, the Southern Christian Leadership Conference, and the National Urban League.[12] The basic underlying assumption of the black integrationist position is that American institutions can be designed so that blacks can enjoy, along with whites, economic, political, and social security as well as self-respect.

Integrationists reject the black separatist contention that white racism is so deeply woven into the fiber of American institutions that it cannot be unwoven. The major advocates of the integrationist position thus reject the separatist proposal as unwarranted. They also feel that separatism is immoral because it stresses the differences between human beings rather than their similarities. However, it should be noted that even though Douglass, Washington, and King all supported the idea of African-Americans becoming completely integrated into all areas of American life, they did not advocate or feel that this would entail biological or cultural amalgamation. Whether or not they are right or wrong depends upon whether or not any numerical minority can integrate into a culture different from their own and still maintain their own cultural or ethnic identity.

The term "integration" has been used by different people to mean different things. Some people have taken this fact as proof that the term cannot be defined. For example, Malcolm X in his *Autobiography* wrote: "The word has no real meaning. I ask you: in the racial sense in which it's used so much today, whatever 'integration' is supposed to mean, can it precisely be defined?"[13] Such a conclusion is incorrect. The word can be defined.

Unfortunately most attempts to define "racial integration" have been unsuccessful. This, in large part, is due to a failure to derive a definition from the experiences and ideas of black and white Americans. Instead people have tried to define the term "integration" in general (or in the abstract) and then placed "racial" in front of it. Understood in this way, it is impossible to have a useful working definition of "racial integration."

On the other hand, when we examine some of the writings of black and white Americans we discover several definitions of the term. One proposed definition of racial integration does not preclude separatism. According to this definition, racial integration refers to the condition where an individual of any race can safely make the maximum number of voluntary contacts with others. If racial integration in this sense were to be achieved, all racial barriers to association would be eliminated except those based on ability, taste, and personal preference. This position is advanced by those who give weight to the freedom of the individual.

Despite the apparent comparability of integration and separatism, when integration is interpreted in this manner, most of the planning for integration is based on racial integration interpreted as racial balance. According to the racial balance account, individuals of each racial group should be distributed in a manner such that the desirable areas of life contain a representative cross-section of the population. This appears to be the position adopted by the National Association for the Advancement of Colored People and other civil rights groups.

Needless to say, efforts to achieve racial balance have been fraught with practical difficulties. Some of these difficulties were mentioned in section II, so there is no need to rehash them here. However, it is worth noting that most efforts to strike racial balance have concentrated on how to desegregate African-Americans rather than on how to desegregate whites. The consequence of such efforts has been to adopt methods and goals that may not correspond to the interest of the African-American masses. This objection must be addressed by those who equate racial integration with racial balance.

In theory, integration allows for the coexistence of racial identities within a single socioeconomic framework. Amalgamation, on the other hand, requires that the different racial identities become absorbed into one body. In theory, this distinction is clear, but in reality, racial integration often becomes interpreted as racial amalgamation. Both racial amalgamation and racial balance have the following consequence: they both assume that members of the races in question should not have the complete freedom to separate on the basis of racial preference. Thus the critics of integration have argued that both approaches violate something that we give great weight; namely individual liberty. Their objection is that if we respect people's choices or preferences then it is doubtful that there is a morally acceptable way to move to a racially amalgamated or a racially balanced society.

The integrationist position depends upon the following basic assumptions for its validity: (1) that there are not unresolvable differences between African-Americans and whites, and (2) that problems confronting African-Americans have as their root cause biased or unjust institutional design or they are the consequence of a systematic failing.

Whether or not these assumptions are true is still a matter of much discussion. We cannot settle these issues here. What I want to do now is to extract what I take to be some of the valuable points that emerge from the debate between the integrationists and the separatists.

## V

In order to appreciate and assess the points raised by the integrationists and separatists, we must discuss ends. One might assume that the ends of the integrationist and the black separatist are identical. Historically both sought to eliminate the problems confronting African-Americans, but they differed radically on how to achieve this end and in their respective interpretations of the problems that blacks face. Although some integrationists and separatists believe that they share the same ends, not all do.

Most integrationists have sought to integrate African-Americans into the white culture rather than vice versa. This, on the surface, appeared to be acceptable because most whites enjoyed advantages and opportunities that African-Americans did not enjoy. So, by making African-Americans more like whites, they felt that they could eliminate the disadvantages and inequalities that African-Americans faced. Cultural and economic separatists vigorously opposed such a solution, even though they too wanted to eliminate these disadvantages and inequalities. But they did not feel that African-Americans could achieve these things by integrating into white society, Carmichael and Hamilton declare this position:

Clearly "integration" – even if it would solve the educational problem – has not proved feasible. The alternative presented is usually the large scale transfer of black children to schools in white neighborhoods . . . Implicit is the idea that the closer you get to whiteness, the better you are.[14]

Carmichael and Hamilton are echoing the separatist rejection of the assumption that the white Anglo-Saxon ideal is the best for defining social arrangements and providing solutions to the problems that African-Americans experience.

Another important difference, in terms of ideals, between the integrationists and separatists of all varieties is the belief by the integrationist that he is entitled to judge what is best for all people (black and white). Malcolm X asserts this point quite clearly in response to a question asked by a white person in the audience at a meeting before his death: "What contributions can youth, especially students who are disgusted with racism, make to the black struggle for freedom?" Malcolm X's response was: "Whites who are sincere should organize among themselves and figure out some strategy to break down prejudice that exists in white communities . . . this has never been done."[15]

The separatist does not feel entitled or obligated to define what strategies are appropriate for races other than his own. It does not follow that he wishes ill on other groups. His point is simply that he does not have the information or shared experiences to know what other groups need and how their needs ought to be met. If the separatist advocates a strong notion of group self-interest, then to be concerned only for the interest of one's own group may entail the violation of the interest of other groups. This would be something that the separatist would have to live with if she is to be consistent.

When we look closer we discover other differences in ideals. The separatist rejects the ideal of individualism, and endorses collectivism. He feels that one of a person's primary, if not ultimate, obligations is to the race of which he is a part. The cultural separatist Ron Karenga wrote:

There is no such thing as individualism, we're all black. The only thing that saved us from being lynched like Emmett Till or shot down like Medger Evens was not our economic or social status, but our absence.[16]

All racial or cultural separatists put the interest of African-Americans as a cultural and racial group before their own personal welfare and, of course, before the welfare of other groups. One might interpret the separatist as denying individual freedom. In other words, individual African-Americans, under the separatist ideal, are not free to adopt other racial identities. The separatist would reply that the sense of individual liberty being employed in this type of objection is an illusion. For all separatists the social realities are such that it is impossible for an African-American person to adopt a racial identity other than his own, unless his physical appearance allows him to pass for white. But even then, he must be on guard to prevent his heredity from being discovered. If his identity is revealed, he will be identified as African-American irrespective of his physical appearance or temperament and thereby subjected to the indignities that all blacks face regardless of their socioeconomic standing. One drop of black makes the person black, but many drops of white blood does not suffice to make the person white.

The ideals of the biological and cultural amalgamationists and the proponents of racial integration as racial balance come under attack from those who value personal freedom. Given the present social realities, in order to achieve either of these ideals a society would be forced to disrespect the preferences of its members who choose to retain distinct racial identities and establish social institutions that excluded people with racial identities different from their own. This is an attack on personal autonomy. Unlike the racial separatists' rejection of individual preferences, this rejection is done in spite of the social realities rather than because of them.

## VI

Where does all of this leave us? What I think our discussion suggests is that activists and policy makers are going to have to further clarify their goals. This will involve paying close attention to the aspirations and values of those who will be affected by their policies. To date much of their efforts have been expended on the means to achieve vague ideals. If they are to clarify their ideals, they must learn from the integrationists and the separatists.

African-American and white communities are a reality everywhere in the United States. The policy maker should not ignore this reality. It has not been demonstrated that equality, fairness, or justice require that we eliminate these communities. In the past, policy makers have sought to meet the immediate needs of the disadvantaged, rather than expanding the resources of the disadvantaged, so that they can be in a position to interpret and meet their own needs. The black separatist stresses the importance of African-Americans having a healthy self-concept, which involves having certain resources which will give them control over their own lives.

The key term here is "resources." What I mean by resources is the control that individuals and groups have over issues and objects that are in their interest. The assumption is that the more control a person has over things that matter to him the better off he will be, other things being equal. Rational self-interested people thus try to maximize their control over things that matter most to them. It might also involve striking alliances with people with different interests in order to gain control where individually one is weak.

African-Americans having control over their own lives is a theme that runs through all of the black separatist literature. Yet you do not find this theme stressed in the integrationist literature. The integrationist places emphasis on the welfare of African-Americans rather than on control or group autonomy. Integrationists appear to believe that there is no point in having control if this does not promote one's welfare in regard to the basic necessities of life. The integrationists feel that this is the case with African-Americans, and they concentrate on promoting welfare rather than control. For them, as long as welfare is achieved, whose efforts produce it is secondary. Although the separatist is not indifferent to the welfare of African-Americans, he does not believe that the welfare or good self-esteem of African-Americans can be fully secured unless African-Americans have control over their lives.

This point can be illustrated by focusing on the issue of forced school busing. What are the goals of forced busing? Hopefully not to simply have African-Americans and white children sitting together in the same classroom, but to produce quality education for all and to contribute to better race relations. Some policy makers have clearly failed to see this. The lesson to be learned from the dispute between integrationists and separatists is that rather than expending energy and money to force people to integrate or separate, we should start with the social realities as they are and provide members of all groups with the opportunity and resources to shape their own lives. Given social realities, would not a voucher system for the financing of public education create better education for all and give African-Americans parents and children more control over their education? Have black policy makers fully explored this possibility?

The separatist, as we have seen, focuses on controlling one's resources and the need to avoid being deprived of one's culture. Although not all of the separatist arguments are cogent, these two points deserve further consideration. Policy makers must not ignore these two points. They should seek to determine the proper relationship between controlling one's resources and satisfying one's wants and needs. They should also examine, in a very comprehensive way, the relationship between race and culture.

The integrationist arguments are not totally persuasive either, but they do reveal some compelling points. For example, their stress on improving the welfare of the African-Americans rather than on group self-determination is a point that warrants careful scrutiny.

Policy makers must determine whether the emphasis on welfare rather than self-determination will eliminate the subjugation of African-Americans and promote better race relations. In doing this, they will need to decide whether or not group self-determination is a necessary condition for individual African-Americans to enjoy certain basic rights that are taken for granted by most white Americans. They will also need to decide whether or not trying to eliminate racial distinctions altogether or keeping them and playing down their importance is the best way to promote good race relations.

There are no simple answers or solutions to the complex questions and problems raised above. However, becoming clear about the nature of the question or problem is an indispensable first step towards an answer or a resolution. If we are to adequately address the problems above, we must also work closely with people from all branches of human inquiry and attempt to bridge the gap between the framers of policy, the practitioners, and the political and social theorists.

## Notes

I wish to thank the New York Society for the Study of Black Philosophy, Brian McLaughlin, and the late Irving Thalberg for their comments on an earlier draft of this chapter. I also thank Rutgers University for a Minority Faculty Development Grant that provided partial support for this project.

1  See Ashley Montagu, *Man's Most Dangerous Myth: The Fallacy of Race* (New York: Oxford University Press, 1974), and Ashley Montagu, *Race, Science, and Humanity* (New York: Van Nostrand Reinhold, 1963). For recent discussions of the nature and validity of racial identities see: Kwame Anthony Appiah, *In My Father's House: Africa in the Philosophy of Culture* (New York: Oxford University Press, 1992); J. L. A. Garcia, "The Heart of Racism," *Journal of Social Philosophy*, 27, (1996): 5–45; Lucius T. Outlaw, Jr., *On Race and Philosophy* (New York: Routledge, 1996).

2  See Edward W. Blyden, "The African Problem and the Method of its Solution," and Martin R. Delany, "The Condition, Elevation, Emigration, and Destiny of the Colored People of the United States" (abridged), in *Negro Social and Political Thought 1850–1920*, ed. Howard Brotz (New York: Basic Books, Inc., 1966); Marcus Garvey, *Philosophy and Opinions of Marcus Garvey on Africa for the Africans* (London: Frank Cass, 1923); Tony Martin, *Race First* (Westport, Conn.: Greenwood Press, 1976); Malcolm X (with assistance of Alex Haley), *The Autobiography of Malcolm X* (New York: Grove Press, 1965); Elijah Muhammad, *Message to the Black Man in America* (Chicago: Muhammad Mosque of Islam No. 2, 1965); Leroi Jones, "The Need for a Cultural Base to Civil Rights and B Power Movements," in *The Black Power Revolt*, ed. Floyd B. Barbour (New York: Collier Books, 1968), 136–44; and Maulana Karenga, *The Quotable Karenga* (copyright by US Organization, 1967), 1–7 and 9–14.

3   Garvey, *Philosophy*, 49–50, and Muhammad, *Message to the Black Man.*

4   Jones, "The Need for a Cultural Base," 136–44, and Karenga, *The Quotable Karenga*, 1–7.

5   Muhammad, *Message to the Black Man.*

6   Sidney Hook, "Discrimination Against the Qualified," *New York Times,* opposite editorial page, November 5, 1971.

7   Jones, "The Need for a Cultural Base," 140–4, and Karenga, *The Quotable Karenga*, 1–7 and 9–14.

8   Orlando Patterson, *Ethnic Chauvinism: The Reactionary Impulse* (New York: Stein and Day, 1977), 102.

9   Ibid., 104–5.

10  Garvey, *Philosophy*, 42–3, emphasis added.

11  William James, *Psychology: The Brief Course,* ed. Gordon Allport (New York: Harper and Row, 1961).

12  See, Brotz, note 2 above, 203–331 and 356–71, and Martin L. King, Jr., "I Have a Dream," *Negro History Bulletin* (1968): 16–17.

13  Malcolm X, *The Autobiography*, 275.

14  Stokely Carmichael and Charles V. Hamilton, *Black Power: The Politics of Liberation in America* (New York: Random House, 1967), 157.

15  Malcolm X, *Malcolm X Speaks*, ed. G. Breitman (New York: Grove Press, 1966), 221.

16  Maulana Ron Karenga, "From the Quotable Karenga," in *The Black Power Revolt,* ed. Floyd B. Barbour (New York: Collier Books, 1968), 190.

# 4

# The African-American Underclass and the Question of Values

The African-American underclass is said to be poor, badly educated, directly related to crime either as perpetrators or victims, and typically young. Data indicate that, unlike the African-American urban poor in the recent past, the underclass also appears to be locked into a cycle of poverty. If these data are accurate, then the crucial question is "Why are members of the underclass locked into their underclass status?" A debate rages between conservatives and liberals about how to answer this question. Conservatives maintain that the key to solving the problem is altering the values of the African-American underclass so that it might better participate in the capitalist market economy.[1] Conservatives also typically add that the state should eliminate many of the burdensome regulations that they believe work to the detriment of people at the bottom rungs of the socioeconomic ladder, for example, minimum wage laws. Liberals, on the other hand, assert that the state must play an active role in solving the problems of the African-American underclass. The state, in their view, should create laws and programs that provide state funds to educate and house those who are said to be locked into the African-American underclass.

The dispute between conservatives and liberals over the African-American underclass often occurs in the political arena, but it occurs in academic circles as well. William Julius Wilson in his book *The Truly Disadvantaged*[2] argues that liberals have failed to keep up their side of the debate in the dispute over the African-American underclass. He attributes this to a reluctance by liberals to examine some of the controversial data about members of the African-American underclass. Wilson believes that the sensitive nature of these data causes liberals to believe that if they examine the data they will be accused of "blaming the victims." They also fear that focusing on the inadequacies of this class will allow some to intensify the racism that exists in American society. Refusing to focus on the personal shortcomings of the members of the underclass, the liberals find fault instead with the design of social institutions.

In my view, both the conservative and liberal solutions involve doctrinaire commitments that blind each approach to the virtues of the other's solution. Conservatives are right to focus on the mindset of members of the underclass, and liberals are correct when they maintain that we must focus on the social structure, but what they both fail to appreciate is just how much the design of social institutions influences the way people think. I argue that members of the underclass do suffer from an understandable but crippling resentment that is fostered by the unjust design of the basic structure of society.

My aim in this discussion is modest. I wish to suggest a possible reason why both conservatives and liberals miss the point. In doing so, I take it as a postulate that it is possible to solve the problems of the African-American underclass without rejecting the capitalist mode of production. This is a big assumption, but one that conservatives and liberals usually accept. First, I describe what prominent liberal theorists have meant by full citizenship, especially in modern democratic societies. Second, I explain the kinds of things that can count as evidence that one has full citizenship. Third, I argue that members of the African-American underclass have good reason to doubt that they have full citizenship. I conclude by showing what effects having reasonable doubts about one's political status can have on people considered to be in the "underclass."

In Wilson's later work, he chooses to distance himself from the term "underclass." According to Wilson, the term has taken on too many meanings and has become the subject of heated debates between those on the right, who believe that members of the underclass cause their own predicament because of their unwillingness to work due to poor values, and by liberals, who claim that the underclass is caused by structural weaknesses in the economy. Wilson believes that the controversy surrounding this term may discourage serious scholars from doing conceptual and theoretical work on this group out of fear of becoming embroiled in a media and political controversy. In order not to discourage research in this area, Wilson suggests that the term "underclass" be replaced by the expression "ghetto poor."[3]

However, Wilson fails to see that it is not the name that causes the controversy, but the phenomenon itself. Even if we substitute the term "ghetto poor" for the term "underclass" people who believe that the behavior patterns of poor ghetto dwellers are caused by bad values will continue to do so in spite of the name change. Likewise, those who believe that the behavior patterns of this group are due to structural problems will continue to do so. Changing the name of those who are experiencing prolonged poverty and joblessness will do little to halt the political debate over what causes this phenomenon and how to remedy it. Wilson is correct in asserting that both sides of the debate have committed a fallacy by attempting to derive evaluative conclusions from his factual premises. However, I do not think that changing the name of the subjects of this debate will prevent people on both sides from making such invalid inferences. Nor will it reassure timid scholars who are reluctant to become a party to political controversy.

## The Nature of Full Citizenship

Individuals join together to form civil society for a variety of reasons, many of which have been discussed by political theorists. Some say that the only valid ground for state authority is the protection of the individual. Others maintain that it is for the promotion of the interests of those who form the social union. Those of a more collectivist sort claim that the promotion of the common good is the basis for civil society. I do not want to enter into this debate. My point is that in the liberal tradition a person who is said to be a citizen has the same basic rights as any other citizen. Of course, this does not mean everyone within the liberal tradition has defined the consequences of equal citizenship in the same way. For instance, some have been strong supporters of individual rights, while others have focused on the common good and have supported the rights of individuals only when doing so promotes the common good. However, the US Constitution vests rights in individuals, and modern theorists – be they contractarians, human rights theorists, or utilitarians – have been leery of any proposal that denies equal protection under the law to any citizen.

As Ronald Dworkin has said, equal citizenship requires each citizen to be treated with "equal concern and respect."[4] The belief that one is treated with equal concern and respect has an important impact on one's self-concept and plays a vital role in the formula for flourishing in a social context. By flourishing, I have in mind being able to construct one's life plan consistent with one's abilities and talents. Citizenship, in the liberal tradition, is thought to provide one with the opportunity to flourish by arranging society, such that its basic structure does not unfairly inhibit or prohibit one's pursuit of a chosen plan of life. The belief that one has a full citizenship also allows one to feel comfortable in supporting and defending what John Rawls has called the "basic structure of society." By basic structure Rawls means "the way in which the major social institutions distribute fundamental rights and duties and determine the division of advantages from social cooperation." Rawls goes on to define major social institutions as "the political constitution and the principal economic and social arrangements." The major institutions "define people's rights and duties and influence their life prospects."[5] Full citizenship certainly does not entail that one will get whatever one wants, but it does say that one will have the opportunity to satisfy one's needs and desires. When these things cannot be satisfied, it cannot be blamed on the basic structure of society.

According to this view, citizens are competitors in a game of life in which rules are not rigged in favor of any of the competitors. However, this view does not assume that people cannot be treated unfairly because of the unjust actions of individuals; it is clearly understood that the unfairness is not the result of the design of the basic structure of society. Persons who feel that they are full citizens believe that their rights are recognized and protected and that their failings can be traced to some personal shortcoming, individual act of injustice, or poor fate, but not to the design of the basic structure of society.

## Evidence of Full Citizenship

What things count as evidence in modern liberal democratic societies that one has full citizenship? The following list is not all-inclusive, but it does include many important indicators of full citizenship. Citizens have the right to participate in the political process. They have the right to earn a living without being forced to engage in activities that are degrading or exploitative. Citizens are not denied opportunities simply because of their race, sex, or religious affiliations. Citizens also have legal due process. Notice that I have not included in this list a right to a certain income. Liberals have disagreed over whether citizens' basic rights include welfare rights. However, citizens who languish in a permanent condition of poverty in a society that has plenty have to wonder about their equal citizenship status.

Having the secure conviction that one has the aforementioned rights and opportunities helps to foster the belief that one can succeed, but just as important, it allows one to believe that one is a legitimate member of a social community, and that the community interprets the common good in a manner that is consistent with one's own good. Of course, this does not mean that everything always goes one's way. Nor does it mean that some individuals cannot have more of societal good than others. However, to use Rawlsian terminology, it does mean that even the least-advantaged members of society will have a secure conviction that the basic structure of society is just.

## Laziness and the African-American Underclass

Wilson and others have defined the African-American underclass as young, poorly educated, intimately connected to crime either as perpetrators or as victims, and locked into a cycle of poverty. The important question is "Why is a certain segment of society plagued by these problems?" I said that both conservatives and liberals have their fingers on part of the answer. The liberals are correct in maintaining that there is still work to be done to guarantee equal opportunity to certain groups, particularly African-Americans. They are also correct in contending that the state must play some active role in this process. For example, because of their race African-Americans are still severely restricted when it comes to finding decent, inexpensive housing. This is true even for African-Americans who have been able to acquire middle-class status, but it is an especially acute problem for African-Americans who are members of the lower classes. A persistent worry for these people is finding and keeping a place to live.[6] As psychological studies have shown, this type of insecurity is very debilitating, especially for the young.

Conservatives, of course, argue that we have equal housing legislation on the books, so adding additional legislation will not solve the problem. Conservatives may be right that equal housing laws are on the books, but they are wrong if they mean that these laws are being enforced. In fact, during the Reagan years in which we have seen the emergence of the African-American underclass, the enforcement of equal housing laws has been virtually nonexistent. Therefore, I think the liberals are right that there is more work for the state to do, even if it is primarily the enforcement of civil rights laws already on the books.

But liberals may be wrong if they believe that at this point in the process enforcement of civil rights laws will solve the problems facing the underclass. Of course, few liberals have said that legislation alone will solve the problems. This is just a caricature of the liberal view advanced by some conservatives. However, I think it is fair to say that liberals have been reluctant publicly to declare that something about the people who make up the underclass may contribute to their underclass status.

Here we can learn from the conservatives, but they are not the only people who have asked African-Americans to examine themselves for a solution to their predicament. Black Muslims, for example, have consistently urged African-Americans people to examine their commitments, habits, and values and to fashion their own remedy to their problems rather than waiting for whites to solve them.[7] But, unlike the conservatives, the Muslims are quick to warn that the initial cause of African-American problems is white people. Black Muslims have attempted to provide an economic and social structure for African-Americans to enhance their self-esteem while providing them with the necessary resources for putting their life plans into action. Booker T. Washington also asked African-Americans to do some critical self-evaluation before fashioning their own programs for economic and social improvement.[8]

Clearly there has been progress over the years when it comes to race relations, and it is probably true that the significance of race is declining; nonetheless, race is still an important defining characteristic of people in our society. It is my contention that African-Americans in the underclass have been placed in an untenable position that makes it extremely difficult for them to evaluate their personal successes and failures. They have been told that racism no longer exists, and wealthy and middle-class African-Americans are pointed to as support for this claim. So, when poor African-Americans fail, people are quick to say that it is because of personal shortcomings and not systemic failings. Some African-American scholars have recently claimed that the values of the African-American underclass are the source of its predicament.[9] In other words, opportunities exist for these poor African-Americans, but the members of the underclass fail to take advantage of these opportunities because they are lazy, undisciplined, and too prone to satisfying their immediate desires. This view has become quite popular in some quarters.

Let us now examine this harsh critique of members of the African-American underclass. Being lazy means being resistant to work or disposed to idleness. Are all or most members of the African-American underclass lazy? I think not. First, it is not at all clear that African-Americans in the underclass are resistant to work. In order for someone to be properly described as being lazy, there must be a genuine opportunity for that person to engage in meaningful and nonexploitative work. For example, it would be wrong to call slaves lazy because they refused to work in the slavemaster's cotton fields. And it would be wrong to label as lazy someone who refused to prostitute his or her body for a wage. One thing is certainly clear. African-Americans in the underclass are not turning down good-paying, safe, and non-dead-end jobs. It is questionable whether enough gainful employment exists to successfully integrate members of the underclass into the broader economy. In fact, some economists have argued that integration of the underclass would require a rapid growth of the economy.[10] There is no guarantee that such growth will occur. Another question is whether it is rational for mothers heading single-family households to accept jobs that do not have health plans and child care services. Given the tremendous costs of health care and child care, the welfare system may be the only viable alternative for many underclass families. But what about those women who do work their way off the welfare rolls? Typically, these are people who have families to draw upon. Of course, a few women manage to secure low-paying entry-level jobs that do provide some modest health coverage; however, such jobs are the exception rather than the rule.

Those who criticize the members of the African-American underclass for lacking in values will sometimes admit that members of the African-American underclass face harsh conditions, but they quickly add that these persons have to be tough and do those things that will allow them to flourish. But is it fair to expect members of the African-American underclass to fight through these adversities? I do not deny that some do, but should this be expected of all members of this group? For example, suppose a person loses both legs because of some unjust act, and that the injustice goes uncompensated. Suppose further that this person goes on to accomplish a great deal in spite of her handicap. Should anyone in her circumstances be expected to act as she does? I think not. This person receives high praise because she stands apart from the norm. If her accomplishments were what the average person could be expected to do, then we would not hold her in such high regard. So, it would seem to be wrong or at least insensitive to condemn people for not being exceptional at overcoming serious adversities. However, I think this is just what is being expected of members of the African-American underclass.

I have attempted thus far to cast doubt on the claim that most members of the African-American underclass are lazy. Now I would like to buttress my rejection of this claim by looking carefully at the claim that members of this class are poorly motivated due to laziness. Such a view overlooks the relationship between being motivated and having the secure conviction that the rules or structure of society are not stacked against one. Living in a society in which one has good reason to believe that the basic structure is just does a lot for enhancing or at least sustaining one's motivational level. Members of the underclass lack good evidence that they live in such a society. When they look around their community, they see that its members lack the material things and opportunities that many other communities take for granted. This is especially devastating when we note that a large segment of the underclass are children. It is extremely difficult for children to understand that they must use modest opportunities and resources to fight against awful odds if they are to succeed, especially when they know that children in other communities do not face such an uphill struggle. They often see this as too much to ask of them, and this belief works against their being highly motivated. Is this a reasonable conclusion? I think so.

Rawls has persuasively argued that people do not deserve the benefits that result from the luck of the natural lottery.[11] Therefore, children in the African-American underclass do not deserve to be poor, nor do children born into affluent families deserve to be rich. The large number of children in the African-American underclass have a good reason for thinking that their situation is not something that they deserve. They are born into poor families and must work harder than people from more affluent families if they are to succeed. These beliefs have a negative impact on their motivational levels.

If what I have argued for so far is sound, then we have several reasons for doubting that members of the African-American underclass are lazy. Similar arguments would also seem to apply to the criticism that members of the African-American underclass are undisciplined and unable to defer gratification. Being disciplined and deferring gratification both depend upon having good evidence that the cards are not stacked against one. Exit studies for female and African-American students who have dropped out of graduate programs point to the difficulty of being disciplined when the environment in which one must operate is tainted by racism or sexism. Students in these studies report that it is difficult to separate their inadequacies from biased or unfair expectations. This uncertainty serves to impact negatively on their ability to gain strength through training. While in the process of growing and acquiring new skills, a time that is generally filled with self-doubt, they find it extremely taxing to separate the anguish and paranoia associated with a rigorous graduate program from the subtle forms of racism and sexism that still exist in institutions of higher learning. The underclass faces the same problem, but in more drastic circumstances. So, one should be cautious in such circumstances in condemning those who must deal with covert racism as suffering from a lack of discipline.

Of course, one could object that my argument is unsound because African-Americans in the past had to deal with racism and its effects, but nonetheless they were motivated to succeed and clearly did not suffer from "poor" values. However, such a response does not succeed when examined closely. First, the claim that African-Americans suffer because of poor values has existed since slavery. In fact, it was even offered as a justification for slavery. So, the idea that the downtrodden position of underclass African-Americans can be attributed to their poor values or lack of values is not new. What is new, though, is that we now have a chorus of African-American voices singing this tune. Unlike in the past, the increase in violent crime and the drug problem have caused many, including African-Americans, to search frantically for answers that may help to eliminate social problems that touch all of our lives. However, many critics might agree that the appeal to poor values was once a smoke screen, but that now this position has credibility.

Another explanation exists for why the effects of racism severely hamper members of the African-American underclass to a degree not experienced by blacks up until the 1960s. Several commentators, discussing the impact of integration on African-American communities in the United States, have pointed out that middle-class African-Americans have left these communities and taken with them the tax base and many of the things associated with stable communities. Large, urban African-American communities are now pretty much populated by people from the bottom rung of the economic ladder. Major institutions in these communities have been either destroyed or severely weakened by the flight of the black middle-class. One consequence of this flight is that people do not have the resources at their disposal to address many day-to-day problems. This may seem like a small point, but I assure you that it is not. It is one thing for a person from the outside to say that you can make it and another for someone who is struggling with the inadequate resources to do so. At one time, "making it" meant rising to the top in one's community; and as individuals progressed, so did the community. However, since the integration movement "making it" has meant escaping from one's community. This has the consequence of intensifying any antagonisms that exist between poor African-Americans and those who are better-off. Members of the so-called African-American underclass now face a society in which the basic structure is not just, intense competition for scarce resources, and abandonment by those best able to help ward off the effects of living in a society that is still plagued by racism.

Some may find my conclusion about laziness and the African-American underclass disturbing because they believe that it provides a convenient rationale for underclass African-Americans to acquiesce in their downtrodden position. Others may conclude that it supports the more disturbing position that African-Americans (especially healthy black males) should be excused for failing to do what is necessary in order to provide for their families. However, neither of these things follow from anything that I have said. It is not my contention that African-Americans should not go beyond what is expected of whites if they are to overcome the adversities that are so much a part of their daily lives. What I do say, however, is that those who cannot muster this strength should not be described as lazy. Many people in the African-American underclass are putting forth a gallant effort against bad odds to secure a living for their families. We must draw a line between what people are required to do as a matter of moral duty and supererogatory acts. People should not have to sacrifice their sense of self completely, even if doing so would serve some noble end, such as providing for the well-being of one's family. Of course, the morally good person is willing to make some sacrifice;

however, at some point we must draw the line. When we fail to do so, then we are too willing to accept false accusations, such as that all the members of the African-American underclass are lazy, because such accusations wrongly shift the focus from institutional design and social structure to the individual.

The line of argument advanced here does not deny that some members of the underclass are lazy. However, all classes within our society have some lazy members. But for the argument, that attributes underclass status to laziness, to succeed it must be the case that all, many, or most of the African-American underclass is lazy. There is no evidence available to support this strong evaluative claim.

## A Final Objection and Reply

One possible objection to the line of reasoning developed in this chapter can be stated as follows: past racism against African-Americans was so consuming and debilitating that it caused a segment of the African-American population to be unmotivated even in the face of opportunities. Supporters of this position might contend that these people have been reduced to this state by racism and deprivation. They could argue that they should not be accused of blaming the victims, because they are merely stating a psychological fact. They might go on to add that this is an unfortunate consequence of racism, but a consequence nonetheless. According to this view, denying or ignoring this consequence of racism will impede efforts to eliminate the so-called African-American underclass.

I would respond to such criticism in three ways. First, these critics are correct to think that African-Americans or any group who experienced systematic wrongdoing would be scared by the process. To think otherwise would be either to underestimate the horrors of racism or to romanticize the strength of African-American people. But one should be clear about what one takes to be the negative consequences of racism on the motivational structures of African-Americans. Second, it is one thing to say that genuine opportunities exist for African-Americans in the underclass and another thing to demonstrate their existence. It is extremely important to be precise about the nature of these opportunities. Third, even if we grant that in the face of opportunities some members of the underclass are unmotivated due to racism, it is not clear that these people should be characterized as having poor values.

When we scratch the surface of my first point, we will see that it is important to be as clear as possible about what the consequences of racism have been on the motivational levels of African-Americans. All too often people fail to realize that racism affects African-Americans in very different ways. (This is not to minimize or downplay the harmful effects by saying that they are different.) Undoubtedly, some people used the damaging effects of racism to become stronger persons. It made them have tough skins in the best sense of the term. On the other hand, others were consumed or destroyed by it. And, of course, there are various degrees in between these two extremes. If by scared my critics mean that most or many African-Americans in the underclass had their motivational structures completely destroyed, then of course laziness would be an issue. But African-American conservatives such as Glenn Loury, Shelby Steele,[12] and Thomas Sowell, who might identify with this line of criticism, cannot mean that the motivational structures of a large segment of the underclass have been destroyed. If this were true, their proposals for eliminating this class would not make sense. They do not think that these people are incapable of being motivated, but rather that they are not sufficiently motivated because they have become accustomed to handouts and because they fail to recognize viable opportunities for advancement.

This leads to my second point. When African-American conservatives talk about opportunities, they typically mean that there are jobs available. They claim that certain jobs are crying out to be filled, particularly jobs requiring highly specialized skills or those in the service industries that require minimal skills. This may be true, but a further question has to be asked: If employers are in such desperate need of these employees, why are they not doing more to train and recruit these people? Their lack of effort in these areas may cast some doubt on how desperate they are to fill these jobs. However, putting this issue aside, there is a more fundamental problem with the contention by African-American conservatives that ample opportunities exist for those who are willing to work. As we know, being positioned to take advantage of opportunities is conditioned by a number of things, for example, being properly educated or trained and having a work ethic. But several other things impinge on these two factors, for example, health care. All too often members of the underclass lack proper health care – not just health care in the narrow sense of being able to go to a doctor when one is very sick, but health care to the extent that pregnant women in this class can receive the proper prenatal care that is so crucial in preventing infants from experiencing physical and mental problems that will hamper their ability to learn. We also have to focus on environmental impediments such as the disproportionate number of persons from the underclass who are exposed to lead contamination, which can have disastrous effects on a developing child's ability to learn.

What these conservatives fail to see is that legitimate opportunities must be understood as more than whether or not there are jobs available. For example, in a number of large cities, such as Milwaukee, a number of jobs that underclass residents are qualified to fill have moved out of the inner cities to the suburbs, making transportation a major obstacle for people who would like to fill these positions. Furthermore, the cost of housing in the suburbs and housing discrimination prevent them from moving to where the jobs are. Once we see the obstacles that stand in the way of people who have few resources at their disposal, people who appear to lack motivation in the face of opportunity might really require motivational levels that would far exceed those of persons who we think are our most productive and successful citizens.

In light of this, is "lazy" or some other derogatory term the proper way to characterize members of the underclass? I think not. A number of people, including some liberals, are uneasy with my answer. They worry that such a response is a way of coddling people, of encouraging people to acquiesce in their misery. Very often these people will respond, "Surely you are not encouraging members of the underclass to prefer public assistance to earning their own living?" Nothing that I have said so far commits me to the view that members of the underclass should not attempt to help themselves. What I have tried to point out are some of the difficulties they encounter in trying to do so. However, if this question is posed to a member of the underclass who has had her motivational level damaged by racial discrimination and injustice, it is not clear that it would be unreasonable or immoral for such a person to prefer public assistance (which includes medical benefits) to a menial, low-paying, dead-end job without medical benefits. At first, this seems ridiculous because the model job we tend to use when analyzing such cases is one that draws on our abilities and talents in ways that we consider to be interesting or, if not, at least compensates such that the job is desirable even if it is uninteresting. If the job is low-paying and uninteresting, we might see it as a viable opportunity if it leads to a job that pays well or does draw on our abilities and talents in interesting ways. However, the question we must ask is, "Are members of the underclass being offered jobs that satisfy these conditions?" If the answer is yes, then clearly they should prefer working to public assistance. If the answer is no, I do not think that it is clearly rational to prefer a low-paying, uninteresting, dead-end job without medical benefits to public assistance that would provide one with the same income plus medical care.

Of course my critics would argue that I have excluded an important consideration, namely, the joy and satisfaction that a person receives from being self-reliant. In fact, Booker T. Washington, who some see as the father of the African-American conservative position, stressed the value of self-help in his famous "Atlanta Exposition Address." In this speech, Washington urged African-Americans to "Cast down your buckets where you are."[13] By this he meant that African-Americans should take any job, no matter how menial, as a first step on the road toward advancement. Clearly, self-reliance in most cases is a good thing, but even good things can be taken too far. It is clear that in some cases self-reliance can clash with rationality. Are the members of the underclass asked to be self-reliant at the expense of rationality?

Unfortunately, I think that in a large number of cases it is irrational for members of the underclass to choose self-reliance over public assistance. As I said earlier, adequate health care is an important component of any realistic appraisal of the opportunities available to members of the underclass. The United States is one of very few countries that do not provide some form of national health care. Health care in the United States is tied to certain jobs in the form of employee medical benefits. Given the high costs of medical care and the medical problems that correlate highly with poor people, adequate health care has to be a weighty consideration in the deliberations of members of the African-American underclass. Surely self-reliance ought to be given some weight by members of this class, but even if it is, it will lose out in their deliberations because being self-reliant would have the undesirable consequence of denying them adequate health care. In order to make self-reliance a rational choice for members of this group, there would have to be structural changes in the current welfare and health care systems.

To think that we can eliminate the problems faced by members of the underclass without altering some of our basic institutions and social policies is to look at the problem through rose-colored glasses.

## Notes

1 See Thomas Sowell, *Race and Economics* (New York: David McKay, 1975).

2 William Julius Wilson, *The Truly Disadvantaged* (Chicago: University of Chicago Press, 1987).

3 William Julius Wilson, "Studying Inner-City Social Dislocations: The Challenge of Public Agenda Research," American Sociological Review, 56, 1 (1991): 1–14.

4 Ronald Dworkin, *Taking Rights Seriously* (Cambridge, MA: Harvard University Press, 1977), 180–3.

5 John Rawls, *A Theory of Justice* (Cambridge, MA: Harvard University Press, 1971), sec. 2, 7–11.

6 See Herb Boyd, "The Crises in Affordable Housing," *Crisis Magazine*, 96, 5 (May 1989): 10–15.

7 Elijah Muhammad, *Message to the Black Man in America* (Chicago: Muhammad Mosque of Islam No. 2, 1965).

8 Booker T. Washington, *"The Intellectuals and the Boston Mob"* in *Negro Social and Political Thought, 1850–1920*, ed. Howard Brotz (New York: Basic Books, 1966).

9   See Glenn Loury, "The Moral Quandary of the Black Community," *Public Interest*, 79 (Spring 1985): 9–22.
10  William A. Lewis, *Race Conflict and Economic Development* (Cambridge, MA: Harvard University Press, 1985).
11  Rawls, *A Theory of Justice*, 12.
12  Shelby Steele, *The Content of Our Characters: A New Vision of Race in America* (New York: St. Martin's Press, 1990), esp. chs 3 and 4.
13  Booker T. Washington, "Atlanta Exposition Address," in *Negro Social and Political Thought, 1850–1920*, 357.

# PART II
## *The Response to Racism*

# 5
# Morality and Collective Liability

Discussions of pressing moral issues in the western world generally are based upon a morality that primarily is concerned with the relationships between individuals. This moral outlook focuses on the rights of individuals and the good society's role in protecting those rights. However, some writers believe there is a moral system that concentrates on the rights of groups and our responsibility to protect group rights.[1]

Critics of the position that we should focus on groups as well as individuals when we attribute moral liability believe that when we do so we adopt a form of tribalism.[2] Their reluctance to focus on groups is due partially to the fact that in the past people were unjustly discriminated against because they were considered to be members of a dangerous, inferior or undesirable group. The Fourteenth Amendment of the US Constitution is interpreted by these critics as endorsing the position that each individual should be judged exclusively on his own merits. In other words, it vests rights in individuals. With similar reasoning, these critics also conclude that concentrating on groups rather than individuals is inappropriate because it will cause the innocent members of groups to suffer and it will reopen the door to the kind of discrimination experienced by racial minorities and other oppressed groups.

Nonetheless, the system of morality that concentrates upon individuals rather than groups is now under siege from those groups who have been frustrated by a long history of oppression and injustice. Group demands and group solidarity on the part of racial minorities and women is, in part, a practical response to a continued discrimination against these groups. Racial minorities, women, and other groups have felt that in order to alleviate their problems as individuals, they also must press claims for their group. Sometimes the opponents of assigning moral concepts to groups associate group solidarity or group identification with separatist movements, be they feminist, racial, or religious, but they are often wrong when they do so because most of the demands of racial minorities and women are not separatist demands. Historically, the goals of these groups have been orientated towards integration into the socioeconomic system rather than separation. But even with this noted, there is still strong opposition against applying moral concepts like blame, praise, and liability to groups as a whole.

## I

The aspect of collective liability that has received a great deal of attention can be stated in terms of the following question: Can all the members, of a group be held morally liable if only some of it's members, actions have been faulty? There have been two responses by those who have defended collective liability. One group has argued that, under certain conditions, each member of a group may be held liable even if only some of the group's members' actions have been morally wrong or negligent. They believe that where some just or noble goal will be served by holding all the members of a group morally liable, we are warranted in doing so. According to these commentators, we should hold each or most members of the group in question liable even though the fit is not perfect between those members of the group who have wronged others, and those who actually are held to be morally liable. The imperfect fit is excused as an administrative convenience,[3] because attempts to improve the fit would involve drawbacks that would outweigh the good done.

Others have argued that simply being a member of a group can justify liability. In its most severe form, proponents of this position conclude from the judgment that S is a member of Group G that

S is morally liable for the faulty actions of any member of G. They see the fit as perfect.[4]

Both approaches and conclusions are inadequate. Judgments about the liability of individual members of a group are not logically deducible from judgments about the liability of the group as a whole.[5] It would take additional reasons to warrant such a judgment. It is also unjust to hold a person morally liable on the grounds of administrative convenience if the agent's, behavior was not faulty or negligent.

The problem of collective liability, as I see it, is to state and defend the conditions under which moral agents can be held morally liable for "practices" that they themselves did not directly engage in. I shall state and defend these conditions. I should stress that this chapter does not address the issue of whether or not, all things considered, restitution should be paid to those who are the victims of unjust practices. My aim is to show that moral liability exists in such cases and that a claim for restitution by the victims cannot be rejected simply on the ground that no moral liability exists.

On the account of collective liability I shall develop here, we will focus on "practices" rather than particular faulty individual or group actions. By a practice I shall mean a commonly accepted course of action that may be over time habitual in nature; a course of action that specifies certain forms of behavior as permissible and others as impermissible, with rewards and penalties assigned accordingly. An example of an unjust racial practice involving African-Americans and whites is blockbusting – a practice where a realtor sells a home in an all-white neighborhood to an African-American family at a price below market value because he knows that this will cause white families to move and allow him to sell their homes to African-Americans at a handsome profit.

I use the term practice in a way that a number of collective actions are practices, but it should be noted that not every practice is a collective action. This is so because in order for a set of actions to constitute a collective action there must be certain inter-relationships among the members of the set and this is not always the case with a practice.

My critics might object to a moral agent being morally liable for a practice, on the grounds that one cannot be liable for the practice itself since a practice is a type rather than a token.[6] I will agree if their point is that one cannot be morally liable for something that has no causal effects, but at the same time point out that a person can be morally liable for a practice in virtue of being morally liable for something that does have causal effects, i.e., instituting a practice, refraining from disassociating oneself from a practice, etc.

## II

When Joel Feinberg wrote his influential essay "Collective Responsibility," in 1968,[7] the United States was in the midst of the Civil Rights Movement and the Vietnam War. Some commentators believed that Americans as a whole should be held morally responsible for war atrocities and that southern whites, as a group, were responsible for the systematic discrimination suffered by African-Americans. After careful analysis, Feinberg concludes that there is no moral justification for collective responsibility as a form of collective liability in such cases.[8]

His discussion of collective responsibility is motivated by the belief that there are various kinds of responsibility; some of which don't entail any kind of official action or liability. He says "to be morally responsible for some thing or action is to be liable not to overt responses, but to a charging against one's record as a man."[9] This leads him to reject collective moral responsibility as a type of collective liability in the two cases above because some white southerners and some Americans can at most be described as responsible in the sense of a stain on their records as persons, but not in the sense of making them liable to overt responses.

He is right that given our present requirements for legal liability it is doubtful that all southern whites could be held legally liable for the negative consequences of racial discrimination in the south, and that all Americans could be held legally liable for disastrous effects of the Vietnam war. However, I disagree with his contention that there is no sense of moral liability that entails overt or official responses. Feinberg underestimates the role that moral norms play in shaping and directing human behavior. Moral norms that form our conventional morality may be followed for a variety of reasons, but I am sure that one of them is that people have come to see from childhood that following these norms is in their best interest.

Feinberg focuses on the differences between legal and moral liability, but there are some important similarities. For example, there are overt responses to violations of moral as well as legal norms; particularly when young people are given moral training. These overt responses are an integral part of their moral training. Even mature adults are subject to quite serious overt responses for violations of moral norms. We must recognize that not every overt response that has serious consequences on a person's life must be couched in legalistic terms. People are often held liable by withholding favors from them. The withholding of these favors is not ad hoc, it is done in direct response to violations of specific moral norms. Withholding these favors serves to coerce us, as do legal sanctions, to learn and support conventional norms. Being found morally liable is no trivial thing in a morally decent society. Doing so serves as more than a basis for self-punishment, remorse or pride.

For Feinberg, in order for there to be collective liability in the sense of being open to overt responses there must be (a) group solidarity, (b) prior notice to the liable party,[10] and (c) opportunity for control by the liable party. Feinberg rejects this sense of collective liability in our two controversial cases basically because he believes that condition (a) is not satisfied. Group solidarity exists when all members of a group share interests, feel pride when one of its members does something noteworthy, and feel shame when one of its members acts badly. On the other hand, if we reject Feinberg's account of group solidarity, a group may experience group solidarity although its members have minimal shared interests and feel no pride or shame when members of their group accomplish something noteworthy or act badly.

When a group is "loosely organized" and very large and diversified, not all of Feinberg's requirements for group solidarity are necessary. For example, residents of the State of California can experience group solidarity even though they individually may have little in common and varied interests. The poor Watts ghetto dweller may have little in common with the wealthy person who lives in Beverly Hills, but they can have group solidarity if they both rally around efforts to prevent needed water from being routed to some other state. Feinberg's rejection of collective moral liability rests on drawing a dichotomy between a group with solidarity and a random collection of individuals. Such a dichotomy is misleading. Of course, we would reject holding a person morally liable for the faulty actions of a collection of individuals of whom by the luck of circumstances he happened to be a part. But in our two cases above the groups in question are not a random collection of individuals. Members of these groups identify with the group even if they don't support all of the actions of its members. Racial and national identifications are quite strong. In fact, we are not fully conscious of how much we identify with these groups. Strong group identifications have served as a source of self-esteem and as a foundation for cultures. Solidarity, unlike group identification, requires a level of political and social consciousness. As, for example, when a worker begins to define himself as a member of the working class. Just being a worker is not sufficient to have a worker's consciousness. With racial and national identification there is perhaps not the level of political and social consciousness that would allow us to conclude that group solidarity exists, but there is enough group identification to warrant the judgment that the members of the group have chosen to identify with the group for the security and benefits that group membership provides.

We are certainly reluctant to accept the conclusion that all white southerners should be presumed to be liable for the unjust actions of some, but part of this reluctance can be overcome when we move from talking about actions to practices. However, we are still left uneasy about such a conclusion because we believe that people do not have control over such things as their race or sex, while they do have control over whether they will remain a racist or sexist. But people play very different roles in their dealings with one another. There are those who are oppressors and the direct beneficiaries of oppression, those who are nonparticipating beneficiaries of oppression, and those who appear to be innocent bystanders. The last two categories are what prompts Feinberg to conclude that holding southern whites, as a group, collectively liable to overt responses is unjustified. He believes that the contributory fault condition is absent or very weak in the case of some group members. Thus, for him, no such thing as collective responsibility as a type of collective legal liability exists in such cases. Feinberg is right. It would be unjust to hold a person legally liable for something he did not do because he is a member of a racial group whose actions have been faulty. Even if we add that this person benefitted because of the faulty action or practice, this, in itself, would not suffice to show that he is legally liable. Given the present requirements for legal liability, I don't think we can show legal liability for groups as a whole in such cases, but I do think we can show that a form of moral liability that carries with it serious non-legal constraints and sanctions is justified.

## III

The theory of collective moral liability that I advocate here assumes that the notion of community is crucial, community in the sense that each member of the society is serving her own interest by freely joining a group to carry on a common struggle for existence. According to my theory, no legal or moral demands should be placed on the individual such that the person who is subjected to them does not remain a free moral agent. My account of collective moral liability makes group members who fail to take certain steps morally liable for the negative consequences that result from their omissions. They have a moral duty to take these steps because it is a necessary part of their chosen strategy to insure that all members of society remain free moral agents, which is an integral part of their reason for joining the moral community in the first place.

Some philosophers have argued that a person who willingly commits an injustice is more blameworthy than a person who merely lets an injustice occur. My purposes here are not to question this admittedly controversial contention, but to grant it and argue that under certain conditions letting an injustice occur, perhaps less faulty than causing an injustice, is faulty enough, in a moral sense, to make a person morally liable.

The following are conditions under which moral agent X can be held morally liable for a faulty practice P:

(1) X knows or should have known about P.
(2) X identifies or has solidarity with those who engage in P or X does not sufficiently disassociate himself from P or X's failure to disassociate from P was not a part of a reasonable strategy to prevent further or greater harm.

When these conditions are satisfied, I hold we have a moral basis for liability. Let us now turn to a clarification and defense of these conditions.

## Condition (1)

Condition (1) refers to practices, not the individual or complex actions that occur between individuals. It is satisfied if a person knows that a practice exists even if he or she has not personally been a party to a particular act that is faulty. However, one further clarification is needed.

Often people will use ignorance of a fact or state of affairs as a reason for their not being held accountable. Sometimes such an excuse is valid, but there are many other cases where we believe that the ignorance excuse is inadequate. Imagine the case where a tour guide orders the members of his party to drink from a stream which, unbeknown to him, is contaminated. Should the guide not be held responsible for the illness or deaths of members of his party simply because he did not know that the stream was contaminated? We must answer no. He should have known. A part of his duty as a tour guide is to check such things, but we could modify our example in such a way that ignorance could relieve the guide of responsibility. Suppose the guide checked the stream for contaminants but did not test for some highly improbable bacteria that are rarely found in streams. In such a case, it would be wrong to hold him morally liable; he took all reasonable precautions. Where reasonable efforts have been made to become knowledgeable, ignorance can warrant the conclusion that the agent is not liable.

In cases of collective moral liability each member of the group will have duties that result from their simply being moral agents or citizens of some state. We can argue about the extent of such duties, but we can safely conclude that they do exist. Therefore, each person has the responsibility to know what his duties are and to know whether he is living up to his obligations. Pleading ignorance is no excuse unless one has made a reasonable effort to become knowledgeable.

## Condition (2)

The first part of condition (2) can be satisfied when those involved share some common interest; they need not feel pride or shame when a member of the group with which they share a common interest does something noteworthy or acts badly. A person can identify or have solidarity with a group even though he or she does not profit in a financial way from faulty practices engaged in or supported by the group. When this is the case, the person is liable because his emotional support for the group that engages in faulty practices enables the group to remain powerful and to continue its unjust practices. Even though the person does not financially profit, he will, at least, profit from the sense of emotional security that is attached to being a member of a powerful group. But this alone does not warrant liability. However, when the powerful group is oppressive and the emotional feelings of security that group members feel contribute to the disadvantage and oppression of members of other groups, it does.

The second disjunct of condition (2) requires disassociation where appropriate. Disassociation can involve publicly denouncing a practice, but only if that is all that one can do, and a refusal to accept any enrichment that occurs as a result of the faulty practice. But usually it will require direct action and a refusal to accept further enrichment. In either case, the moral agent is required to do something that separates him from the faulty practice. This may require complete disassociation from the group that he identifies with. Some people will be required to do more than others because of their power and influence, but this is as it should be. In advance we cannot say with great precision what sufficient disassociation entails because different factors are involved from case to case. Some of these factors include risk of harm, time, and opportunity for control; thus, liability will be contingent on these factors. Before I explain further what disassociation involves, one preliminary remark, about the morality of disassociating oneself from an injustice, is in order. I do not support the position that all people who disassociate themselves from injustice are doing so from attitudes that are morally commendable. My point simply is that there are cases where disassociation will serve to reduce the injustice, and if it does not, it can still be said to be morally commendable because the attitudes that are present are something other than self-righteousness.[11]

A crucial aspect of the disassociation condition is the avenues of action available for disassociation. The avenues of action will be political as well as legal. For example, when chattel slavery was legal in this country, there were laws that closed most of the legal avenues open to those people who opposed slavery, but there were still political avenues available, e.g., abolitionist movements. Some people took those avenues available to them and thus they succeeded in disassociating themselves from the horrible practice of slavery.

The third disjunction of condition (2) is necessary because there might be cases where a person collaborates with a tyrannical power in order not to blow his cover as an agent set on destroying it. In such cases, we certainly would not want to hold such persons morally liable. In fact, such a person's actions are morally commendable even though it may prove difficult to distinguish acts of resistance from mere collaboration.

My critics might object that it is physically or psychologically unrealistic to think that a person can be held morally liable because of a failure to disassociate from some unjust practice. Neither objection will suffice. First, the objection that it is physically unrealistic is unsatisfactory because the person is not required to travel great distances or to expend more than a modest sum of money to disassociate from an injustice. Given the present state of mass media and the varied organizations that allow for political participation, it would not be unrealistic to think, in cases involving serious unjust practices against groups, that these injustices could go unnoticed and that there would be no political avenues open to a person who wished to disassociate from them.

The objection that it would be psychologically unrealistic to expect people to disassociate themselves from unjust practices that they did not cause is not valid. If they mean that it would be unrealistic to expect people to be concerned with everyone else's problems, then I think they are correct. People have a difficult enough time keeping a handle on their own problems and the problems of their loved ones. However, this is not what is being required. We are not requiring an individual to be his brother's keeper, but to be aware that he can be held morally liable if he fails to disassociate from an unjust practice caused by a group that he identifies with. It is not my contention that people should widen or disregard their present loyalties, but I do deny that they are relieved of any moral liability, in certain cases, because they would be psychologically more content if they ignored these injustices and their consequences.

My theory differs from Feinberg's and others' because it recognizes the importance and role of moral liability in a good society. It also explains why group membership, in certain circumstances, can make one morally liable even though one does not personally cause or explicitly support the faulty practices engaged in by a group of which one is a part. The theory of collective liability that I have advanced is one that recognizes that we live in a world where we can no longer view ourselves as being detached from the actions of groups of which we are a part. We should be aware that efforts to achieve a morally good society for a time may bring about disharmony and social unrest. A morally decent society, in my judgment, is willing to pay these costs.

## Notes

This chapter was written with partial support by a Summer Fellowship from the Rutgers University Research Council.

1   See L.T. Hobhouse, *Morals in Evolution* (London: Chapman and Hill, 1951); Peter A. French, *Individual and Collective Responsibility: The Massacre at My Lai* (Cambridge: Schenkman, 1972), esp. 103–18 and 147–65.

2　For example, H. Gomperz, "Individual, Collective, and Social Responsibility," *Ethics*, 49 (1939): 329–42.

3　For instance, J.W. Nickel, "Classifications by Race in Compensatory Programs," *Ethics*, 84 (1974): 146–50, p. 147.

4　Bernard Boxill supports such a position in "The Morality of Reparation," *Social Theory and Practice*, 2 (1972): 113–22.

5　See May Brodbeck, "Methodological Individualism: Definition and Reduction," in May Brodbeck, *Readings in the Philosophy of the Social Sciences* (New York: Macmillan, 1968).

6　For a good discussion of the Act-type and Act-token distinction see Alvin I. Goldman, *A Theory of Human Action* (Englewood Cliffs, NJ: Prentice-Hall, 1970), 63–72.

7　Joel Feinberg, "Collective Responsibility," *The Journal of Philosophy*, 65 (1968): 674–88. Revised and reprinted in Feinberg's, *Doing and Deserving* (Princeton: Princeton University Press, 1970). All page references will be to *Doing and Deserving*.

8　Ibid., 247–8.

9　Joel Feinberg, "Problematic Responsibility in Law and Morals," in Feinberg, *Doing and Deserving*, 30 –1.

10　Feinberg, *Doing and Deserving*, 249.

11　For a fuller discussion of this point, see Thomas E. Hill, Jr., "Symbolic Protest and Calculated Silence," *Philosophy and Public Affairs*, 9 (1979): 83–102, pp. 99–102.

# 6

# Justice and Reparations

A question that confronts America today is: how do we make just a society that has been plagued by racist and sexist ideologies and by discriminatory institutions. This is a crucial question because of the enormous implications it has for public policy. It appears that any solution that we adopt will require that attitudes be changed, social goals be reexamined, and that some of our basic institutions be either altered or abandoned. In this chapter I will support the thesis that it is just reparation to afford preferential treatment in the areas of employment and higher education to African-Americans who are and have been the victims of institutional injustice.

James Foreman raised the issue of black reparations at New York's Riverside Church in May 1969.[1] During his interruption of the scheduled Riverside Church service, Foreman demanded $500 million as black reparations. Foreman said:

Fifteen dollars for every black brother and sister in the United States is only a beginning of a reparations due us as people who have been exploited and degraded, brutalized, killed and persecuted.[2]

This spectacular pronouncement by Foreman is now known as the Black Manifesto. Unfortunately, Foreman's tactics and not the manifesto received attention from the news media. The issue of black reparations was pushed into a corner and virtually nothing has been said about reparations as a concept of social justice. It is important for philosophers to analyze the concept of reparations if we are to become clear about the morality of such an issue.

The justification for reparations is basically a backward-looking enterprise. Reparations by definition are due only when a breach of justice has occurred. Typically, people who make demands for reparations do so on the ground that they have been unjustly treated in the past. If we consider African-American and colonial people who have made demands for reparations, their demands are based on documented injustices done to them in the past and, more importantly, an acknowledgment on the part of the transgressor's descendants that this is, in fact, true. In such cases, according to Locke and certain other social contract theorists, rectifications of past injustices are in order.[3]

## Compensation

Traditionally people who have been concerned with the justice of compensation have worried about placing the burden on the innocent or creating a distribution that is unfair. These feelings are enforced by the way we view theories of distributive justice. When we distribute something according to a principle we consider just, then we can't see any reason for a redistribution. For example, a person who is allotted three shares of some commodity according to some principle embraced by members of a society feels entitled to the three shares and is apprehensive of any redistribution that lessens his share.

The interesting thing about compensation seems to be that compensation might involve someone's being at fault or it might not. An important part of the right of compensation is the idea that we must ensure that each person has a right not to be hindered from arranging his life as he sees fit as long as it does not hinder others from doing the same.

## Justification for Black Reparations

I believe that the justification and intent of reparations is not the same as the justification and intent of compensation. In the case of reparation it is the case that someone is at fault. There are countless ways that the injustices might have occurred. The ways differ in detail, but they are all similar in one respect; namely that it is clear that an injustice has occurred.

The usual worry associated with the idea of giving reparations is not that one doesn't know that an injustice has occurred or who committed the injustice. This is merely a matter of fact. The difficult questions are: What are the ways that injustices have shaped present holdings? Do the beneficiaries of injustice who are not direct parties in the act of injustice have a duty of reparations? And what are permissible ways to rectify past injustices?[4]

Before we can answer these questions we must be clear in our thinking concerning the idea of a community paying reparations to a group. In order to do this, I shall analyze a less complicated case. Suppose a person X has the indisputable right to a certain watch. Let us further suppose that a person Y steals the watch from X. In this case, we can clearly see that Y owes X a watch and an admission of wrongdoing. If we complicate the example, we can get the following: after Y steals the watch from X he gives it to a person Z. This case has a pertinent similarity to the case of the demand for reparations by African-Americans, but they are different.

Now suppose Y steals the watch from X and Y dies; but before he dies, Y leaves a legal will that bequeaths the watch to his son W. In this case, we feel that W should return the watch to X and acknowledge the error by his father Y. This case is close, but not quite analogous to the demand for black reparations. In order for them to be analogous, both X and Y must die and both must have descendants. The debt of justice in this case involves the descendants of X and Y. We believe that W should return the watch to the legal heir of X. It is a lot harder in this case than in the other cases to see why the watch should be relinquished by W.

In our watch example we are able to trace the illegitimate holding transfer from person to person. Although this case has a pertinent similarity to the case of black reparations, they are not identical. In our watch example, the persons involved are individuals and the subject predicates would be either simple proper names like "John" or "Mary" or simple definite descriptions of the sort: the person who stole the watch from X at time t. The general principle that we follow in cases like our watch case appears to be: holdings that are illegitimately transferred insofar as possible should be returned to their rightful owners.

In the case for black reparations, unlike the watch case, reparations are not on an individual level, but involve groups. African-Americans, as a group, are demanding reparations from the white community. Bernard Boxill in his article "The Morality of Reparations" explains why African-Americans are owed reparations. Boxill says:

The slaves had an indisputable moral right to the product of their labor; these products were stolen from them by the slave masters who ultimately passed them on to their descendants; the slaves presumably have conferred their rights of ownership to the products of their labor to their descendants; thus, the descendants of slave masters are in possession of wealth to which the descendants of slaves have rights; hence, the descendants of slave masters must return this wealth to the descendants of slaves with a concession that they were not rightfully in possession of it.[5]

Boxill's explanation is in the right direction. But those who deny that these are good reasons for affording reparations to African-Americans would take issue with Boxill's views; and some who favor reparations would disagree with Boxill's formulation of the justification. An initially plausible objection against Boxill's line of reasoning can be stated in the following way: Why should I (a present-day white) pay for the injustices of malevolent whites in the past? I don't own any slaves and my parents and their parents didn't own any slaves. This is a challenging reply. But I think that Boxill anticipates this sort of objection by claiming that the descendants of slave masters have benefitted because of the unjust actions of their ancestors. This reply by itself is not enough to meet the force of this criticism. It can explain why the descendants of slave masters owe a debt of justice, but it fails to show how whites who are not the descendants of slave masters owe a debt of justice to African-Americans. In order to argue that the total white community owes the total African-American community reparations, we must present an argument that shows how all whites, even recent immigrants, benefitted from slavery and how all African-Americans felt its damaging effects.

Before we offer such an argument, we must be clear about what African-Americans are demanding as reparation. One of the most dramatic demands for black reparations can be found in James Foreman's Black Manifesto. This document is good in many respects and bad in at least one. Foreman's Manifesto was not meant as a justification or explanation of the concept of black reparations. Foreman's demand was just that: a demand, not a justification. When he asked for 500 million dollars in reparation from churches, people construed this to be repayment to African-Americans from whites for slavery. Such a conclusion is obviously false. Foreman had no such idea in mind. He realizes that to divide 500 million dollars among African-Americans in America would amount to about 15 dollars per person. This as reparation is an insult. Even if the money was invested on the behalf of all African-Americans, the resulting wealth would not be a proper reparation. Slavery and racial discrimination damaged African-Americans in ways and on levels that require more than a cash outlay. A mere cash outlay alone cannot bring about cultural respect and self-determination. I think if reparations as a means of rectifying past injustices is to be taken seriously, more than money must be involved.

I want to support the position that white Americans have received certain advantages over African-Americans because of the existence of slavery and other unjust discriminatory institutions in this country. Some of the advantages that whites enjoy are: access to better housing, better medical care, and better schools than the typical African-American has access to. Notice that it could be the case that because of slavery and racial discrimination, all Americans, including white Americans, have suffered. In this paper, I won't detail my reasons for thinking that whites enjoy certain advantages over blacks because of slavery and racial discrimination, but I believe that this claim, if true, supports my view that white Americans have a duty of reparations to African-Americans.

According to some people, this argument leads to undesirable consequences. They feel that this line of reasoning would justify poor whites paying reparations to African-Americans who have a better financial lot. Let us assume for the sake of argument that poor whites can have a duty of reparation to African-Americans who have a better financial lot. Are wealthy individuals like Bill Cosby, and Michael Jordan owed reparations? Their ancestors suffered the horrors of slavery, and they both suffered the sting of institutional racism. Because they have obtained financial success, does this make them ineligible for reparations?

Let us consider the following hypothetical case. Suppose John steals a car from Tom, and Tom is unaware that John stole the car. In this case, Tom can make no demands on John because he doesn't know John stole his car. Further suppose that Tom inherits an automobile dealership and then discovers that John stole his car. Tom can now demand that John return his car. This is true even if he now owns hundreds of new cars and John only has in possession the car he stole from Tom.

## Reparations to Groups as well as Individuals?

A persistent problem with giving reparations is trying to decide whether reparations should be made to groups as well as individuals. J. W. Nickel argues that reparations are owed to groups as well as individuals.[6] He argues that certain groups deserve reparations not because of any natural characteristics that make them a member of a group, but because they have suffered and still suffer because of those characteristics. In an earlier article, Nickel argues that African-Americans, as a group, deserve reparations because of injustices and not skin color.[7] However, in both of these short essays, Nickel fails to show why whites, as a group, have the duty of reparation to African-Americans.

## Justice and Reparations

Is it because of skin color? Of course not. Perhaps it is because of injustices. But has every white at some time acted unjustly toward some African-American? Here again we must answer no. Because we answer no to this question we should not conclude that whites, as a group, do not have a duty of reparation.[8] However, some argument is needed to justify this duty. In the second section of this

essay, I argued that because of unjust institutions and holding trans-
fers, such as bequests to children and inheritances, whites have
benefitted from injustices done to African-Americans even if they
did not personally perpetuate the injustice (See chapter 5).

Many will object to this claim because they are not aware of the
deep roots of racism in American institutions private and public.[9]
Numerous governmental reports and publications have pointed
out how racism pervades our society.[10] If these reports are accurate
then it is plausible to suppose that reparations can be made to
groups as well as individuals. What about the specific demand for
reparations by African-Americans as a group?

## The Demand for Black Reparations

People of varied political persuasions have argued that all people
must have power over their own destinies. They all agree that anything less is a violation of liberty. I too accept this conclusion and
feel that a black reparations program should serve this noble end.
But how can providing reparations to African-Americans serve to
give them power over their lives?

A comprehensive reparation should be forward looking. For this
reason, I suggested that a purely financial reparation might not
serve this forward-looking end.[11] A major source of the damages
that African-Americans suffered were the result of unjust institutions. These institutions are set up in ways that unjustly discriminate against African-Americans. Providing African-Americans
only with money to cover the financial damages done to them will
not suffice. There must be other things involved in the reparation.
For African-Americans, power to make decisions that affect their
lives is paramount. Preferential hiring and educational programs
might serve to give African-Americans this power.[12] There are
problems, both conceptual and technical, associated with such programs.[13] It is not the purpose of this essay to settle all these issues,
but I think there are good reasons to believe that such programs
will give African-Americans some of the means to obtain control
over their own lives.

James Foreman and others have realized that African-Americans lack political and economic power. The economic powerlessness of African-Americans in America is discouraging. Even with the hopeful trends that are beginning to develop in a few industries, African-Americans, as a group, still remain near the bottom of the social economic ladder.

John Rawls argues that a person needs primary social goods (like access to health care, decent income and social position) and fair equality of opportunity, for self-respect.[14] If Rawls is correct, and I think that he is, then many African-Americans in the country, lacking primary goods and fair equality of opportunity, lack two of the essential ingredients necessary for self-respect. A comprehensive preferential hiring and education program might give African-Americans this respect and control over their own destinies.

## Types of Reparation Programs

Above we suggested that a preferential hiring policy could count as proper reparations for African-Americans who have been the victims of injustice. Our argument depended upon the claims that (1) reparations can be made to a group as well as individuals and (2) that all whites gained specific advantages from slavery and racial discrimination and that all African-Americans have felt its damaging effects. This argument I will call the reparation argument for preferential treatment.

The argument for the preferential programs that I sketched above depends upon the following general principle: those who receive unfair advantages from Institution W have a duty to those who are unfairly disadvantaged by W. In our case for black reparations the subject predicates involved might be: persons put at a disadvantage by Institution W, the group of black Americans who are disadvantaged as a result of Jim Crow Laws, recent white immigrants who enjoy certain advantages over blacks as a direct result of racist institutions in America. These English subject predicates, unlike the ones in our watch example, connect the parties involved to some common institution or practice. We should also notice that in our watch example the holding in question is a material object.

It is clear in this case what must be returned, namely the watch. Even over time, returning the watch to its rightful owner presents very few problems. We either physically hand over the watch that was stolen or pay fair market value for the watch if it cannot be returned. The case we sketched concerning black reparations is not so simple. Here in a real sense there is no object or material holding (exactly) to be returned. What is at stake or in dispute is one person or group gaining an advantage in competitive situations involving institutions.

Do our intuitions tell us that applying our general principle brings about a just resolution in all cases? I think that if we follow our principle we can answer yes. Even the recent white immigrant, not void of contact with racist institutions, has received advantages that the typical African-American does not enjoy. The case of the recent immigrant, however, does raise the following bothersome questions: should those who have received greater advantages because of slavery and other racist institutions in this country share a greater portion of the burden of reparations? I feel that they should. However, it is no easy task to determine the logistics of the problem. I won't attempt here to solve this problem, but I feel that a satisfactory solution can be found.

Let us now review an argument that seeks to justify preferential programs not by looking to the past but on more forward-looking utilitarian grounds. This argument, although quite different from my own, nonetheless supports my belief that preferential hiring and educational programs are just. Many reasonable people are not convinced that my reparation argument demonstrates that a preferential hiring policy as a reparation is not unjust to those who fail to get the job or fail to get into law school because of preferential programs.[15] They usually present an argument similar to the argument put forth by Defunis in the famous case of *Defunis* v. *Odegaard and the University of Washington*.[16] Defunis argued that it was unjust and unconstitutional that African-American students be admitted to the University of Washington Law School with lower test scores than his.

Ronald Dworkin argues that Defunis' arguments are initially appealing, but in the last analysis, they are unsound. Dworkin claims that the faulty premise of Defunis' argument is his belief that law schools must use intelligence as the only criterion for admission to law school, and that he was denied fair equality of opportunity because the law school admitted African-Americans into the law school who had lower scores on tests that are claimed to measure intelligence and aptitude.[17]

Dworkin considers the argument that the LSAT tests, because they are culturally biased, don't accurately measure the capabilities of African-American applicants. He admits that this argument deserves consideration, but chooses to rest his case on a quite different line of reasoning. He contends that the Defunis argument rests on the faulty premise that test scores are the crucial factor for determining who should be admitted to law schools. Dworkin argues that law school entrance criteria should not be limited to tests of intellectual capacity, but should take into account other factors that will ensure that the best interest of the school and the community at large are maximized. In other words, the law schools weigh all factors that they feel will help bring about good social ends.

Many schools use a similar argument when they admit football players with lower entrance exam scores, with the justification that a competitive football team is an important part of college life. These arguments are similar, but not identical. They differ in that football players choose to be football players whereas people don't choose what racial group they will be members of. It is also true that people work to become football players, but people are born into racial groups. I realize that it is questionable whether or not football players should be given preferential treatment, but these cases give us a precedent for this sort of treatment.

Is this preferential treatment just? Can't we use Dworkin's utilitarian argument to justify actions that are clearly unreasonable? Dworkin cites the *Sweatt* v. *Painter*, 339 US 629, 70 S. Ct. 848 case involving an African-American man who was denied admission to a law school in Texas. Would not our utilitarian argument justify not admitting Sweatt to the Texas Law School on the grounds that it would not promote the public good. For example, racist alumni might not give contributions to the school if they admitted an African-American. Is the justification for not admitting Defunis the same as the one used by racists for not admitting Sweatt?

Dworkin very skillfully argues that they are not.

Dworkin's utilitarian argument does not rest on the old psychological utilitarianism of Bentham, but on the idea that the community's preferences should determine public policy. "If it can be discovered what each individual prefers, and how intensely, then it might be shown that a particular policy would satisfy more preferences, than alternative policies."[18] Reasoning in this manner the community's welfare is interpreted as that policy that satisfies the community's total collection of preferences better than any of the available alternatives, even though it fails to satisfy the preferences of some of its members.

Although law schools don't have a means for precisely evaluating the judgments about the preferences its admissions policies will effect, it is reasonable to believe that their judgments are plausible. This preference method appears to be fair to everyone to the extent everyone's preferences are considered. It appears that our utilitarian argument based on preferences gives each person the right to be treated equally.

However, when we look closer we discover that there are personal preferences and external preferences. Personal preferences are preferences for a person's own enjoyment of some goods or opportunities. External preferences are preferences for the assignment of goods to others. For example, a person might have a personal preference against educational policy because it will not enhance his own welfare. He might have external preferences against the policies because he hates African-Americans or disapproves of the mixing of the races. The point is simply that external preferences can reflect prejudiced attitudes or beliefs about a person or group.

Dworkin argues that basing public policy on the external preferences of the community causes some members of the community to be treated unjustly. This line of reasoning shows us why the justification for not admitting Defunis is not identical to the justification for not admitting Sweatt. Defunis was denied admission because a judgment was made by law school officials that such actions supported the public good. They also made a further judgment that the particular preferential admission policy in question would in fact achieve the public good determined by assessing the personal preferences of the community. While failing to admit Sweatt could only be interpreted as supporting the public good if we use external preferences as a measure of utility.

Dworkin's argument is compelling. If we conjoin my reparations argument with Dworkin's utilitarian argument, we are provided with good reasons for believing that preferential hiring and educational policies are just reparations.

## Black Reparations and the Law

In this section I will review a part of that body of legal literature that is directly related to the subject of reparations and consistent with the philosophical position that I gave above. Boris Bittker in his helpful book *The Case for Black Reparations* suggests that a proper way to justify affording reparations to African-Americans might be one that does not rest solely on damage done during slavery, but on those recent historical damages inflicted on African-Americans.[19] In the last century there have been countless harms and injustices inflicted against African-Americans. Many of them have been condoned by law. Bittker explores Section 1983 of Title 42 of the United States Code, which says:

Every person who, under color of any statute ... Of any State or Territory, subject ... to the deprivation of any rights ... Secured by the Constitution and Laws, shall be liable to the party injured in an action at law, suit in equity, or other proper proceedings for redress.[20]

According to Bittker, this statute's principal purpose was to deal with the terrorism perpetrated in the south by the Ku Klux Klan and similar terrorist groups. A question of great interest concerning Section 1983 is whether or not it provides a system of reparations for at least one form of discrimination. Before we look at Bittker's answer to this question, I should inform the reader that Section 1983 applies to liability for performance of official duties. The question is how should a citizen be compensated when a public official under law deprives him of his federal rights. On this question, Bittker concludes that:

> Where damages for past misconduct are at stake, however, to remit the plaintiff (person seeking compensation) to an action against individual officials would have the consequences of denying an effective remedy if they are impecunious. At most, the "essential governmental function" exemption ought to go no further than to relieve the state from vicarious liability for unauthorized torts of its employees.[21]

Section 1983 follows the traditional common-law approach to damages, that is, each plaintiff is treated as a discrete individual whose personal circumstances determine the amount he shall recover. This means that each African-American must file an individual suit for damages under Section 1983. Bittker also tells us that the government should not be held legally responsible for the unauthorized actions of its agents.

Bittker contends that Section 1983 serves as a useful starting point for supporters and non-supporters of black reparations. He feels that an examination of this section will lay bare the relevant questions concerning reparations. Some of those questions are: (1) Should reparations be made to individuals or groups? (2) Will it be necessary to promulgate an official code of racial classification to administer a reparation program? (3) Would it be unjust because it might divert funds that would otherwise be used to benefit the nation's poor? I won't explore Bittker's specific answers to these questions. However, I will recapitulate Bittker's answer to the relevant constitutional question – does the Constitution permit the federal government to establish and finance a program of reparations whose benefits would go to African-American citizens exclusively?

People who argue against programs that serve the ends of a particular group exclusively usually make reference to the Fifth Amendment's guarantee of due process of law or to the Fourteenth Amendment's guarantee of equal protection of the laws. Speaking as a lawyer, Bittker, after reviewing housing and school desegregation cases, says that he is not sure whether or not a black reparations program would be constitutional. He feels that some judicial verdict would have to be rendered on the constitutionality of such programs. However, he points out that a judicial verdict rejecting the program's constitutionality would not in itself be a judgment on its fairness or wisdom.[22]

If the constitution does not permit reparations programs, justice might require that we amend it to allow for such programs. If such programs are constitutional then we still must decide if it is just and wise to enact such programs. We must remember that to be legally responsible for injury is to be liable for damages or some official action. While, on the other hand, to be morally responsible does not necessarily entail any kind of official or unofficial action or liability. Feinberg writes:

> To be morally responsible for some thing or action is to be liable not to overt responses, but to a charging against one's record as a person. This record in turn can be used for any one of a variety of purposes as a basis for self-punishment, remorse, or pride, for example; but a person can avoid putting it to these further uses, leaving responsibility simply a matter of record.[23]

Feinberg suggests that when we speak of liability in cases of compensation and reparation, we must realize that each case has a different intent. According to Feinberg, the term "reparation" has the intent of redressing wrongful injury, while compensation serves to remedy losses which might not be anyone's fault. He also feels that reparation restores moral equilibrium, as would an apology or expression of remorse. The notion of compensation does not necessarily involve this idea. A result of reasoning along these lines is that it allows one to conclude that some grossly immoral act cannot be rectified.

Reasonable and intelligent people worry about the legal and moral difficulties associated with providing groups with reparations to rectify past injustices. Mr Justice Jackson of the US Supreme Court, in regards to the right of the Shoshone people to receive reparations, said:

> It is hard to see how any judicial decision under a jurisdiction act can much advance solution of the problem of the Shoshone Indians. Any judgment that we may render gives to these Indians neither their lands nor their money. We would not be second to any other in recognizing

that – judgment or no judgment – a moral obligation of a higher order rests upon this country to provide for decent shelter, clothing, education, and industrial advancement of the Indians. Nothing is gained by dwelling upon the unhappy conflicts that have prevailed between the Shoshones and the whites. The generation of Indians who have suffered have gone to the Happy Hunting Ground, and nothing that we can do can square this account with them.

Views like Justice Jackson's give some support to the claim that demands for reparations by oppressed members of our society such as African-Americans or Indians have no legal basis and that a duty of reparation or liability can't be established on moral arguments alone. I disagree with people who maintain that the demand for reparations by African-Americans has no legal basis. However, I do agree that some injustices are so gross and far-reaching in their damaging effects that moral equilibrium cannot be restored, but this does not mean that we should sit on our hands and not attempt to make some effort to eliminate in part the moral imbalance caused by past injustices. The idea of settling injustices that have placed a group at a disadvantage in a society by acknowledging remorse, but not taking any official steps to rectify the past injustices that have placed the group in question at a disadvantage, seems to be unjust.

In concluding, I would like to reiterate my defense against the charge that reparations, as here discussed, represents an injustice against those persons who are properly qualified for a position, but not selected because of preferential treatment. Aren't these people entitled to complain? I think that they are entitled to complain because there are not enough places at colleges and positions in businesses for capable and willing people, but not because some who have been the victims of injustices are selected over them. If everyone from the start had been treated fairly, the competition for present positions would even be more intense, making it more difficult for everyone. If nothing can be done to assure that all who are capable and willing receive positions, then this unhappiness should fall on everyone, not just on those who have historically been disadvantaged.

## Notes

1 Robert S. Lecky and H. E. Wright, *Black Manifesto: Religion, Racism and Reparations* (New York: Sheed and Ward, 1969), 114–26.

2 Borris Bittker, *The Case for Black Reparations* (New York: Random House, 1973), 168.

3 John Locke, *Two Treatises of Government*, edited by Peter Laslett (Cambridge: Cambridge University Press, 1967), ch. x.

4 Robert Nozick, *Anarchy, State and Utopia* (New York: Basic Books, 1974), 152.

5 Bernard Boxill, "The Morality of Reparations," *Social Theory and Practice*, 2, 1 (1972): 117.

6 James W. Nickel, "Should Reparations be to Groups or Individuals?" *Analysis*, 34, 5 (1973).

7 James W. Nickel, "Discrimination and Morally Relevant Characteristics," *Analysis*, 32, 4 (1972).

8 Boris Bittker, *The Case for Black Reparations*, ch. 8.

9 Randall Kennedy, *Race, Crime and the Law* (New York: Pantheon Books, 1997).

10 Gerald David Jaynes and Robert M. Williams, Jr., eds (for the Committee on the Status of Black Americans, Commission on Behavioral and Social Sciences and Education, National Research Council), *A Common Destiny: Blacks and American Society* (Washington, D.C.: National Academy Press, 1989).

11 Irving Thalberg, Jr., "Reverse Discrimination and the Future," *Philosophical Forum*, 5, 1–2 (1973–4).

12 Howard McGary, Jr., "Reparations and Inverse Discrimination," *Dialogue*, 17, 1 (1974): 10.

13 For a good discussion of some of these problems see: Gertrude Ezorsky, *Racism and Justice: The Case for Affirmative Action* (Ithaca: Cornell University Press, 1991), part II.

14 John Rawls, *A Theory of Justice* (Cambridge, MA: Harvard University Press, 1971), 440 –6.

15 Lisa H. Newton, "Reverse Discrimination as Unjustified," *Ethics*, 83, 4 (1973): 311.

16 *Defunis* v. *Odegaard*, 94 S. Ct. (1974).

17 Ronald Dworkin, *Taking Rights Seriously* (Cambridge, MA: Harvard University Press, 1977), ch. 9.

18 Ibid., 233.

19 Boris Bittker, *The Case for Black Reparations*, 9–11.

20  Ibid., 31.
21  Ibid., 58.
22  Ibid., 126.
23  Joel Feinberg, *Doing and Deserving* (Princeton: Princeton University Press, 1970), 76.

# 7

# Reparations, Self-Respect, and Public Policy

When we reflect on what should be the appropriate societal response to individuals and groups who have been the victims of unjust practices, a variety of considerations come to mind. For instance, we believe that any appropriate response should be in line with the constraints of justice, whatever they might be. We also believe that we should be concerned about things like the "public good." But it is difficult to determine what the appropriate constraints of justice are and whether a particular response is in accordance with these constraints. With regard to the "public good," there is a vast body of literature that attests to the fact that defining the "public good" and deciding when some policy or program is in the public interest is formidable.[1] But even with these difficulties noted, policy makers must still construct policies that serve as the society's response to the problems created by injustice.

Responses to injustice can be attitudal or behavioral. By attitudal I mean emotional responses like regret, remorse, resentment, and shame. When I say that they can be behavioral, I mean they may involve ceasing the unjust actions in question or they may involve the awarding of goods and services: (a) to make amends for the injustices inflicted, or (b) to promote things like the "public good." Policy makers have given great weight to considerations like "the greatest good for the greatest number," but such a consideration is ambiguous. They might mean the greatest total aggregate good or the greatest average good. But with either interpretation, critics have argued that giving great weight to this consideration can lead to morally unacceptable arrangements.

Although I do not wish to discuss the general validity of the principle of utility, I do want to point out what I take to be major problems with any teleological justification of policies that are viewed as a response to or remedy for injustice.[2] The principle of utility, for example, is not a deserts-based principle. As Joel Feinberg has argued, to say that S deserves X because giving it to him would promote the public good is to misuse the term "deserve."[3] He notes "that responsive attitudes are the things that people deserve and that 'modes of treatment' are deserved only in a derivative way, insofar as they are the natural or conventional means of expressing the morally fitting attitudes."[4] He warns that utilitarians are naive when they contend that utilitarian considerations can capture our responsive attitudes to injustice. Utilitarian considerations can only capture the public or conventional expression of these responsive attitudes.

I will argue that there are compelling reasons for appealing to rights-based arguments in a justification of policies that favor certain previously oppressed groups.[5] In my opinion, if we do not take into account these arguments, we will be unable to give all citizens what they are entitled to; namely, being full-fledged members of society. This entails that people not face "social institutions" that act as an affront to their self-respect simply because of such things as their race, religion, or sex.[6]

In the first section of this chapter, I note that it is important that the framers of public policies concentrate on material concerns like personal incomes or the reduction of poverty, but I argue that it is important for them to focus on the psychological response to injustice as a crucial aspect of social justice. I argue that because of past and present unjust institutional design, a deeply biased and harmful stereotypical attitude about certain groups persists in all aspects of society today, and that this negative stereotypical attitude towards these groups causes them to feel deep resentment, and this resentment acts as an affront to the self-respect of these group members.

In Section II, I illustrate the difficulties by focusing on Ronald Dworkin's[7] ingenious teleological defense of affirmative action such as preferential treatment for minorities and women. In the final section, I argue that even a mixed account of justice like that of John Rawls[8] will be teleological rather than rights-based; therefore, it is subject to the criticisms that I advanced against teleological accounts of the issue. This conclusion will be surprising to some because one would not suspect that a Rawlsian and a utilitarian would be in the same camp on this issue. For our purposes here, I adopt the position that there is a type of self-respect for people that does not depend upon their achievements or abilities, but on the recognition that as a person one is an authentic rights-holder worthy of all the rights that our moral law accords to individuals.

I

One way to show how faulty institutional design can lead to an affront to the self-concepts of all members of a group is through the following illustration. In a book entitled *Black Power*, Carmichael and Hamilton give the following definition of institutional white racism:

> Racism is both overt and covert. It takes two closely related forms: individual whites acting against individual blacks, and acts by the total white community against the black community. We call these individual and institutional racism. The first consists of overt acts by individuals, which cause death, injury or the violent destruction of property. This type can be reached by television cameras; it can frequently be observed in the process of commission. The second type is less overt, far more subtle, less identifiable in terms of individuals committing the acts. But it is no less destructive of human life. The second type originates in the operation of established and respected forces in the society, and thus receives far less condemnation than the first type.[9]

Individual and institutional racism are both morally repugnant; however, both can occur without bigotry. The toy store owner who feels that African-American children are in his store to steal and white children are there to purchase, and treats them accordingly, demonstrates individual racism. The toy store owner may not conceive of himself as being prejudiced and, in fact, may not be a bigot. The police department that uses a test that reflects a cultural bias may not intend their test to be racist, but the police department is pursuing a course which creates and supports institutional racism. When very few African-American candidates pass the tests, then something is said to be wrong with the black candidates rather than with the test. In the case of the store owner and the police officials, they would have us to believe that by a statistical inference we are warranted in concluding that their racial stereotyping is justified.

Institutions are stable social arrangements through which collective actions are taken. Institutions in our society that foster racism or sexism in a significant way can be found in the areas of economic life, education, and the administration of justice.[10] These institutions in some cases overtly discriminate, but in other cases the discrimination is covert. Knowles and Prewitt in their important work on institutional racism, describe how covert institutional racism works:

Maintenance of the basic racial controls is now less dependent upon specific discriminatory decisions. Such behavior has become so well institutionalized that the individual generally does not have to exercise a choice to operate in a racist manner. The rules and procedures of the large organizations have already prestructured the choice.[11]

In a covert manner those who are in control of American institutions display a negative stereotypical attitude towards racial minorities and women. They assume that members of these groups in general are like children who cannot be trusted with power and responsibility. Since institutions have the power to reward and penalize, institutions that embody these stereotypes place members of certain groups in a most unfortunate position. These group members must either reject these institutions, and the benefits that they bestow, because they act as an offense to them as self-respecting persons, or accept them and have them act as an affront to their self-respect.

My critics might retort that this analysis may apply to some, but certainly not to those group members who hold prestigious positions in society, which serves to prove that they are responsible, intelligent, and industrious individuals. They believe that this falsifies my claim that every group member is harmed because of the existence of things like institutional racism or sexism. One possible reply to this criticism would be to say that those group members who hold prestigious positions are harmed because fellow group members are harmed, but I will not adopt this defense because I suspect that the degree of solidarity necessary to substantiate something like vicarious harm in these cases does not exist.

A more realistic response to my critics would be one that does not depend upon vicarious harm, but a reply that shows how even those who hold prestigious positions actually are harmed because of biased institutional design. I take the following to be such a reply. Those group members who hold prestigious positions may be able to have high self-esteem because of the jobs or offices they hold in society, but yet they still experience an affront to their self-respect because they are still confronted by social institutions that have negative consequences in regard to their rights as persons, irrespective of their socioeconomic status. They have been forced to develop a thick skin so to speak. But because they have been able to do this, we should not conclude that they should and that this institutional design is acceptable. Although they are able to cope with this affront to human dignity,[12] they should rightly resent it.

Injustice can take a variety of forms and it can cause emotional as well as physical harm. However, we should not bunch all unjust acts together. Some unjust acts are due to such things as greed and temptation and do not necessarily involve an invidious denial of the equality and worth of the persons who are treated unjustly. On the other hand, there is a class of unjust acts that are motivated by a serious lack of respect for the equality and worth of the victims. Racist and sexist acts fall into this category. The victims of these types of injustice experience various feelings and emotions which range from anger to self-doubt, but one important emotion that should be present is resentment.

Resentment plays the crucial role of alerting us to the fact that we have been treated in a manner that we do not believe is appropriate or just.[13] We should be careful and not confuse resentment with envy. A person can be envious even though she does not believe that she has been treated unjustly or in an inappropriate manner. A just society need not be concerned with designing social institutions such that people are not envious of each other.

Now the depth of the resentment that people feel when they have been treated unjustly will vary depending on such factors as their maturity and their psychological and moral stability. It will also depend upon the nature of the injustice. If the injustice deprives them of their just deserts in terms of goods and services, then they certainly will and should resent it. But if the injustice cuts at their very right to be treated as bona fide members of the moral and legal communities, then this creates an even deeper resentment. When this resentment is allowed to fester it can lead to psychopathology or to a disrespect for the institutions and persons that caused or fail to prevent the injustice which led to the resentment.

Individuals who have been systematically denied full membership within our moral and legal communities for long periods of time because of characteristics like their race or sex will feel this deep resentment. All too often when we focus on the victims of this type of unjust discrimination, we tend to focus only on the material consequences of being treated unjustly. When we do this we fail to address the emotional damage that results from a prolonged systematic denial of basic moral and legal rights. To merely halt the unjust practice and to enhance the economic well-being of the victims is not enough to remove this rightful feeling of resentment. We should be careful here and note that there is certainly virtue in being able to forgive and forget; but as I have claimed, unjust practices that deny basic moral and legal rights on the ground that some members of society are less worthy than other members because of their race and sex are extremely difficult to forgive and forget because of the deep resentment such wrongs foster.

An important first step in forgiving and forgetting is putting the injustice behind one and getting on with one's life. However, in cases where one's moral status as a bona fide member of the community has been denied, an acknowledgment by the transgressors that they have wronged you when they treated you in this way is necessary as an affirmation that one has full moral and legal status. Orlando Patterson, in this connection, notes that when the slave stole from the slavemaster, this was an assertion by the slave of his moral worth; and when the slavemaster punished the slave for stealing, he implicitly admitted that the slave is a moral being.[14]

We can distinguish views with regard to the claim that certain people are not full-fledged members of the moral community. On one view, the people in question are believed to lack those attributes or characteristics that are necessary for membership in the community due to factors that are beyond their control. In other words, they are constitutionally capable of being members, but for whatever reason, fail to meet the requirements for full membership.

The other view presupposes that those who are denied membership are constitutionally ineligible. Both views have been used as the basis for the denial of basic rights to certain individuals and groups; but the latter view was usually employed as the rationale to justify the unjust discrimination against the members of racial groups.

Providing only goods and services to the victims when basic rights have been violated will not remove a deep-seated feeling of resentment. Perhaps the following example will help to make this idea explicit. Suppose person X borrows a sum of money S from person Y and promises to pay him back at time t, and when t arrives X claims that he does not owe S to Y, but that he will give S to Y anyway in order to promote harmony or good social consequences. I believe that Y will still feel resentful even though X is willing to give S to Y. Y feels resentful because there is the tacit implication or intimation that Y is getting something he does not deserve and that X's actions, although in some sense commendable, are done for the wrong reasons. By X not having to acknowledge his debt to Y, his actions leave the door open for his behavior to be interpreted as charity or a gift.

When we put this phenomenon in the larger societal context, we find that the resentment experienced by those who have been and still are the victims of systematic unjust discrimination is very deep. The psychological scars due to a systematic denial of basic moral rights are not so deep that they prevent most of the victims from functioning, but functioning with this resentment is not as healthy as ridding one's self of it. In order to remove this resentment in a rational person, one must provide the person with good reasons for believing that there is no longer adequate evidence to support the belief that he is not being treated as a full-fledged member of the moral community. If we fail to acknowledge that the person was treated in this terribly unjust way, and that the reason for the special treatment that this person now receives is to rectify this wrongdoing, we fail to provide the person with adequate evidence that he is a moral equal. Like our example involving the forgetful debtor, if the treatment accorded to this individual can be seen as flowing from motives such as kindness or sympathy, then such treatment does not serve as adequate evidence that the persons offering such treatment believe that the beneficiaries are their moral equals. People can show kindness and sympathy for animals and plants, yet most people do not believe that these living things are equal members of the moral community.

Policy makers must understand that from the point of view of justice, we must eliminate wrongful institutional design for the right reasons. This should not be done simply to maximize the average utility in society or to produce an equal distribution of the benefits that flow from these institutions, but to give people what they are entitled to as a matter of right as persons, and citizens. In my opinion, respecting the dignity and worth of those who were victimized by dehumanizing institutional design requires that our moral outlook be rights-based. However, because I characterize my approach to injustice as rights-based, it should not be assumed that I believe that social consequences are irrelevant.[15]

## II

One of the most eloquent defenses of preferential treatment for minorities and women is advanced by Ronald Dworkin. He supports the position that the greatest average utility and a noble social ideal will be achieved by adopting policies that favor minorities and women.[16] According to Dworkin, we have a right to be treated as equals under the law; but this does not entail that we have a legal right to equal treatment in every instance. In other words, there are cases where unequal treatment of citizens is justified providing that doing so promotes the greatest average utility for society as a whole and that it promotes a worthy social ideal.

Given Dworkin's argument in favor of preferential treatment, any group can be deserving of such treatment. Even if a group fell from the sky and had no history of discrimination but found themselves incapable of obtaining the desired social positions, preferential treatment of this group would be warranted. What Dworkin fails to see is that if he is committed to preferential policies to eliminate disadvantage irrespective of the nature of the actions that led to this state of affairs, he will fail to address the important emotional attitudes that are associated with a certain class of unjust acts.

Teleologists who argue that things should be changed by concentrating on the future rather than past injustices fail to consider the rightful resentment of those who are down and out and those who have overcome poverty and a lack of education, but continue to rightly believe that they are being wronged because they live in a society with a historical legacy that assigns an inferior stereotype to a person simply because he or she is a member of a certain group. A utilitarian could certainly argue that steps should be taken to eliminate this infectious resentment, but only if doing so brought about greater utility than not doing so. On the utilitarian account, it is conceivable that economically secure members of wronged groups would be asked to endure this debasing injustice for the good of society as a whole.

Once again we encounter the old deontological criticism that utilitarianism sacrifices or uses some people as means rather than ends in themselves. The teleologist, who is a utilitarian, could argue that if these stereotypes and feelings of resentment were so destructive, then removing them would have to raise the utility value in society.

This may be overly optimistic. As I stated above, eliminating injustice that has been in the making for hundreds of years, no matter if it is destructive, may decrease the total amount of utility in society. In any case, we have no guarantee that it will not. Simply proposing that we include these considerations in our utility calculations will not do. Since the utilitarian must give everyone's preferences equal weight, he cannot guarantee that people in a utilitarian society will not prefer social institutions that act as an affront to some minority group. The utilitarian must accept people's biased and prejudiced preferences unless he has some principled way of ruling them out. Dworkin's proposal of discounting external preferences and striving for some noble social ideal will not work unless we accept egalitarian, perfectionist, or welfarist goals.[17] Dworkin has not given us a convincing argument for accepting such goals. Hence, his argument for discounting external preferences is either ad hoc or it begs the question.

Let us now turn to a Rawlsian account. Remember Rawls claims to have captured the virtues of utilitarianism without falling prey to the frequent deontological criticism that utilitarianism forces us to unfairly use some members of society as means rather than ends. In the next section, I will explain why retreating to a Rawlsian position will not silence the rights-based critics who favor reparation arguments.

## III

Rawls provides us with a powerful theory with which we are supposed to be able to decide questions of distributive justice. Rawls' theory has been praised because it includes what many take to be the virtue of utilitarianism, namely promoting the public good while not falling prey to a Kantian criticism of utilitarianism: that it unfairly uses some people as means. However, my major criticism will be that Rawls does not go far enough in his deontological thinking. I employ Rawls' theory here for two reasons: first, it is a very well wrought account of distributive justice and, second, it appears that he might be sympathetic to both of the approaches that I described above.

Rawls' conception of justice can be characterized as a form of welfarism, but not obviously in the pejorative sense of a handout. One might expect that any supporter of reparations as a concept of social justice would find Rawls' conception of justice appealing. Historically, those who have been victimized usually find themselves occupying the least advantaged positions in society. However, this is a contingent truth; it is not necessarily this way. We can think of cases where individuals have overcome the burdens of oppression to occupy positions of advantage in society. In a society where people have become the advantaged members of society in spite of oppression, these people would be ignored by Rawls' theory, yet I feel they would be entitled, on grounds of justice, to reparation.

Rawls believes that some wrongs are not rectifiable. The best we can do in some cases is to cease the unjust actions and ensure against injustices of this sort in the future. We might have to forget trying to redistribute land or wealth in these cases. Can we forget gross injustices and yet maintain that we have an adequate account of justice? Is there justice when more advantaged members in society are owed a debt by members of society who are less fortunate? The answers to both of these questions is no. Rawls would disagree. According to Rawls, in a just society benefits should be distributed so that they are to the benefit of the least-advantaged members of society. This is his difference principle.[18] Because of this principle, Rawls would be hard pressed to justify many of the nonegalitarian measures that would be required to eliminate the destructive racial stereotyping in our society. I am sure that a strong egalitarian would not adopt measures that did not reduce the disparities between the haves and the have-nots, especially if those who benefit from the measures are not among the have-nots.

Above I said that a Rawlsian can justify, to a limited extent, certain kinds of reparation programs, but he would reject programs that would upset the (just) basic structure of society. He would oppose returning all lands taken unjustly from American Indians provided that we make present institutions just in terms of the distribution of goods and services and that we take steps to ensure fair equality of opportunity. To do otherwise would violate his difference principle. Remember, I said that Rawls does not allow rectification policies that create further inequalities. Will policies that favor members of oppressed groups create further inequalities? I think they might. They may take away a group's illegitimate advantages and create inequalities, but properly administered, they need not create further injustices.

In stressing the importance of reparations as a concept of social justice, I recognize that the problem of converting emotional injury to money or something material is very challenging. It would be difficult to calculate the aggregate amount that might be awarded if the nation undertook to compensate African-Americans for damage to their self-concepts. We cannot totally repay members of oppressed groups for all the injuries done to them. However, it is wrong to ignore the injuries done to them because they are not economically the least advantaged. Remember, it is not that being economically the disadvantaged is an affront to a person's self-respect but that they are not given what is owed to them. On my account, self-respect is a very important good that is theoretically prior to a right to reparation. The failure to rectify a wrong does not always result in an affront to a person's self-respect; but in cases where there have been prolonged wrongs against a group and the assignment of an unjust inferior status, demanding reparation is crucial to one's self-respect and thus one's psychological well-being.

I should stress that I am not claiming that a person has self-respect only if he always demands that he be treated fairly. Whether a person's toleration of unfair treatment signals a lack of self-respect depends upon what his reasons are for tolerating such treatment. For example, a slave who did not insist upon his right as a person to be treated fairly out of fear for his life could not be said to lack self-respect.[19]

Rawlsians and other teleologists want to eliminate the injustice faced by members of oppressed groups, but I am afraid that a purely teleological approach to remedying these injustices will not succeed. All people have the right to live in a society where they will not be wronged by social institutions simply because of things like their race or sex. In order to achieve this end, we must take note of past injustices to eliminate the legacy of racial and sexual injustice.

Purely teleological justifications of policies that favor certain oppressed groups are inadequate. A heavy moral and psychological cost is attached to letting one's right to have wrongs against one acknowledged and rectified be over-ridden by utilitarian, egalitar-

ian, or Rawlsian considerations. In my view, this right is a fundamental moral commodity that should be taken seriously.


## Notes

I read earlier versions of this chapter at Rutgers University and the
University of the District of Columbia. In addition to my colleagues
Martha Bolton and Peter Klein, a number of other people were kind
enough to offer comments. I thank the Rutgers Research Council for
support of this project.


1  For a good discussion of this issue see Brian Barry, "The Public
   Interest," *Proceedings of the Aristotelian Society*, Supp. Vol. 38 (1964):
   1–18.
2  The teleological approach says that an act is right if and only if it
   produces or will probably produce the greatest balance of good over
   evil. For examples of this approach involving preferential treatment
   of racial minorities and women, see Richard Wasserstrom's, "Racism,
   Sexism and Preferential Treatment: An Approach to the Topics,"
   *UCLA Law Review*, 24 (1977): 581–622; Thomas Nagel's "Equal
   Treatment and Compensatory Discrimination," *Philosophy and Public
   Affairs*, 2 (1973): 348–63; Ronald Dworkin's *Taking Rights Seriously*
   (Cambridge: Harvard University Press, 1977), ch. 9; and Irving
   Thalberg's "Reverse Discrimination and the Future," in *Women and
   Philosophy*, ed. by Carol Gould and Marx Wartofsky (New York: G.
   P. Putnam's Sons, 1976), 294–308.
3  Joel Feinberg, *Doing and Deserving* (Princeton: Princeton University
   Press, 1970).
4  Ibid., 82.
5  The demands for reparation by the victims of injustice is rights-
   based. By reparation, I mean the acknowledgment and redress of
   wrongdoing when it is known who is at fault. For examples of the
   reparations approach see: Judith Jarvis Thomson's "Preferential
   Hiring," *Philosophy and Public Affairs*, 2 (1973): 364–84; Graham
   Hughes, in "Reparations for Blacks," *The New York University Law
   Review*, 43 (1968): 1063–74; Bernard Boxill, "The Morality of
   Reparation," *Social Theory and Practice*, 2 (1972): 113–22; and Howard

McGary, Jr., "Justice and Reparations," *The Philosophical Forum*, 2–3 (1977–8): 250–63.

6  A "social institution" acts as an affront to a person's self-respect if the members of a group (e.g., racial, religious, sexual) are forced to view themselves in accordance with "social institutions" that define and treat members of their group as inferior or subhuman. I want to be careful to point out that I am only making the minimal claim that people have a right not to face "social institutions" that have embodied negative stereotypical attitudes about them. They do not have a right to force people in their private lives not to hold racist or sexist views. In my view, people have the right to dislike people for whatever reason they choose. However, a person's biased dislikes for certain groups should not be a part of "social institutions." Here I basically follow Rawls in defining social institutions as:

A public system of rules which defines offices and positions with their rights and duties, powers and immunities, and the like. These rules specify certain forms of action as permissible, others as forbidden; and they provide for certain penalties and defenses, and so on, when violations occur. (*A Theory of Justice*, 55)

7  Ronald Dworkin's *Taking Rights Seriously* (Cambridge, MA: Harvard University Press, 1977), ch. 9. All references to Dworkin will be to this work.

8  See John Rawls, *A Theory of Justice* (Cambridge, MA: Harvard University Press, 1971. All references to Rawls will be to this work.

9  Stokely Carmichael and Charles Hamilton, *Black Power: The Politics of Liberation in America* (New York: Vintage Books, 1967), 4.

10  See L. J. Barker and J. J. McCorry, Jr., *Black Americans in the Political System* (Cambridge: Winthrop Publishers, Inc., 1976); John F. Kain, *Race and Poverty* (Englewood Cliffs, NJ: Prentice-Hall, 1969); Marvin J. Levine, *The Urban Negro and Employment Equality* (Morristown, NJ: General Learning Corporation, 1972); *Report of the National Advisory Commission on Civil Disorders* (New York: Bantam Books, 1968); Lois B. Moreland, *White Racism and the Law* (Columbus, OH: Merrill Publishing Co., 1970).

11  Louis L. Knowles and Kenneth Prewitt, *Institutional Racism in America* (Englewood Cliffs, NJ: Prentice-Hall, 1969), 142–3.

12  For a good discussion of the relationship and human emotions, see Herbert Spiegelberg, "Human Dignity: A Challenge to Contemporary Philosophy," *Philosophy Forum*, 9 (1971): 39–64;

Michael S. Pritchard, "Human Dignity and Justice," *Ethics*, 82 (1971–2): 299–313; and I. A. Menkiti, "The Resentment of Injustice: Some Consequences of Institutional Racism," *Philosophical Forum*, 9 (1977–8): 227–49.

13  Rawls, *A Theory of Justice*, 533.

14  Orlando Patterson, "Towards a Future that Has No Past – Reflections on the Fate of Blacks in the Americas," *The Public Interest*, 27 (1972).

15  For a good defense of certain rights within a consequentialist theory of ethics see T. M. Scanlon, "Rights, Goals and Fairness," Stuart Hampshire, ed., *Public and Private Morality* (Cambridge: Cambridge University Press, 1978).

16  Dworkin, *Taking Rights Seriously*, 239.

17  For Dworkin's discussion of discounting external preferences, see ibid., 234–5.

18  Rawls, *A Theory of Justice*, 75–8.

19  For a complete discussion of this point see: Bernard Boxill, "Self-Respect and Protest," *Philosophy and Public Affairs*, 6 (1976): 58–69; Thomas Hill, "Servility and Self-Respect," *The Monist*, 57 (1973): 87–104; and Larry Thomas, "Morality and Our Self-Concept," *The Journal of Value Inquiry*, 12 (1978): 258–68.

# 8

# Affirmative Action: A Review and Commentary

Today many people would have us to believe that affirmative action programs in industry and institutions of higher learning are either counterproductive or unjust. Recently this view has been vigorously expressed by neo-conservatives, but neo-conservatives are not the only persons who are critical of affirmative action. Speaking about affirmative action, Michael Kinsley wrote in an article in *Harper's Magazine*: "No single development of the past fifteen years has turned more liberals into former liberals."[1] Kinsley's remarks are as true now as they were when he first made them over ten years ago.

In a recent collection of essays entitled *Affirmative Action and the University*, Steven M. Cahn claims that one might conclude that our society has reached a consensus about the legitimacy of affirmative action programs for racial minorities and women because affirmative action is not being discussed at academic conferences and in the pages of leading academic journals. According to Cahn, such a conclusion is far from the truth. He writes: "I believe the explanation for the unusual silence surrounding the issue lies not in widespread agreement, but in deep-seated, bitter disagreement, too painful to be exposed."[2]

If Cahn's remarks are true, then they are true only in modest or polite academic circles. For clearly there has not been a general silence about affirmative action by academics. A host of academics have been willing to speak out loudly against affirmative action. However, there is a grain of truth in Cahn's remark. Academics very often in face-to-face meetings don't have frank discussions about the merits of affirmative action as social policy. And I think Cahn is right to say many people have serious reservations about the wisdom of affirmative action. However, there are many people who support affirmative action and see it as a necessary means for achieving social justice. In fact, in a recent book entitled *Racism and Justice: The Case for Affirmative Action*, Gertrude Ezorsky argues forcefully in favor of affirmative action.[3]

In this chapter, I shall give a brief history of what affirmative action has actually meant in American society and then I shall state and comment on the various arguments that have been offered for and against affirmative action.

I

What is affirmative action? Affirmative action has taken on a variety of meanings in our society. Affirmative action is usually traced to the 1960s and the Great Society programs of Lyndon B. Johnson. Johnson noted that African-Americans, and members of other groups, were excluded from various institutions in American society. So affirmative action was a call for taking affirmative steps to include these excluded groups. But affirmative action defined as a stated commitment to the inclusion of previously excluded groups was not new. During the period of Reconstruction after the Civil War, Northerners called for the inclusion of African-Americans and they took some modest steps to bring about some inclusion. Clearly their efforts were not successful, but my point is that there was an official call and some efforts were made even though they could at best be described as minimal.

President Lyndon B. Johnson felt that passing laws prohibiting racial discrimination in employment and in educational institutions was not sufficient to bring about genuine inclusion. He argued that more affirmative steps needed to be taken. But what did the Johnson administration mean by inclusion? Did they mean proportional representation? By proportional representation, I mean having American institutions reflect the percentage of African-Americans in the population. Perhaps they meant equal opportunity but without setting any goals or quotas. I think it was the latter. But soon they discovered that it was extremely difficult to put teeth into efforts to achieve genuine equal opportunity for African-Americans without setting some goals. They tried to expand the pool of African-American applications with the hope that by increasing the pool one would increase the numbers of Africans in industry and higher education.

The primary method for increasing the pool was to take more affirmative steps to make African-Americans more aware of job opportunities. This meant placing announcements and advertisements in places that were more likely to be read by African-Americans. These efforts included very modest attempts to eliminate "old boy" networks. But neither of these practices did very much to change the character of American institutions. They remained predominantly white and male.

Given this sad fact, increasing demands were made to take more affirmative steps. However, supporters of the status quo rejected these demands because they believed members of certain groups lacked the qualifications to fill the positions, and that their lack of qualifications, and not racism, accounted for their conspicuous absence. But the supporters of affirmative action quickly responded that this historically has been the reason advanced to support a system of racial discrimination. The supporters of inclusion warned that affirmative action must mean much more. But exactly what should it mean?

It is at this point that racial preferences entered the debate. Initially the idea of preference meant that when the qualifications of minority and women applicants were equal to those of white males, the nod should be given to women and racial minorities. This amounts to giving a preference to these applicants, but the white applicants could not complain that the applicants who were selected had inferior qualifications. In theory, by adopting this procedure, American institutions could be made more inclusive. But in reality, the institutions still remained predominantly white and male and did not come close to being representative of the numbers of racial minorities and women in the population.

This type of preference did not provoke a great deal of controversy, but it had little chance of changing the character of institutions that had a long history of discrimination against members of certain groups. Philosophers, like Virginia Held, argued that more affirmative steps must be taken if we were to make reasonable progress in achieving social justice for racial minorities and women. In fact, she argued, to make less than reasonable progress would serve as an affront to the self-respect of members of these groups.[4] But what should count as reasonable progress? Held argued that racial minorities and women should not have to wait a hundred years for change.

The demand for reasonable progress led many of the supporters of affirmative action as a kind of preference to argue that even if there were some white males in the pool who had better measurable qualifications that we should still give a preference to racial minorities and women. The opponents of this idea objected on the grounds that this proposal violated the merit or the color-blind principles. Let me elucidate each of these objections.

The first objection claims that if we prefer racial minorities and women to white males who have better qualifications, then we violate an important principle, the merit principle.[5] The merit principle says that when we award goods in competitive situations under conditions of moderate scarcity then we are morally obliged to award these goods to those persons who have the highest merit. Some of the proponents of affirmative action did not disagree. They argued that a person's race or sex can be counted as a qualification under certain conditions. For example, some people used the role model argument as an illustration of this point.[6] According to the role model argument, having a teacher or authority figure of one's own race or sex can motivate one to strive to do better. This is thought to be true because the teacher or authority figure provides women and racial minorities with graphic evidence that people like them can succeed. So, on this view, the merit principle is not violated because race and sex, under certain conditions, can count as qualifications.

In a similar vein, some have argued that a person's race or sex is often correlated with certain important cultural traits and that it is important to have people from different cultures exposed to a wide variety of cultural experiences. This has been labeled the cultural pluralism argument in favor of affirmative action. According to this argument, we are justified in preferring racial minorities and women who might have lower test scores because when we count their cultural contributions their qualifications are better than those of some white males who have higher test scores.[7]

However, the role model and the cultural pluralism arguments have been challenged by many of the opponents of affirmative action and by some of its proponents. Some critics question the legitimacy of the alleged benefits that are said to result from achieving cultural pluralism in the work place or from having role models. Others admit that these things promote good consequences, but they believe they come about at the expense of the rights of white males. I will discuss this objection below, but first I want to explore the idea that affirmative action means hiring or admitting the less qualified.

Many of the supporters of affirmative action have resisted the characterization of racial minorities and women as less qualified. They vigorously challenge traditional measures of qualifications. However, in spite of their objections, the affirmative action debated in most circles continues to be interpreted as giving a preference to competent but less qualified individuals.

As a result, a great deal of the debate over affirmative action between academic philosophers during the 1980s focused on merit. The central question was: can we respect a principle of merit and depart from color-blind or sex-blind principles? The critics of affirmative action maintained that we could not.[8] They argued that to make a person's race or sex relevant is a kind of reverse discrimination. For them if it was wrong to use race or sex to oppress racial minorities and women, it is also wrong to use race or sex to help these groups. On their view, two wrongs don't make a right.[9]

On the other hand, the supporters of affirmative action have rejected the claim that affirmative action can in any way be identified with the wrongful discrimination that has occurred and continues to victimize members of certain groups. They claim that affirmative action, properly defined, is compatible with a merit principle and respectful of the rights of white males.[10] Who is right? In order to properly evaluate these positions we need to examine the principles upon which these positions are based.

## II

Two general approaches have been employed in providing justifications for affirmative action as preference. The first approach has
been described as the "backward-looking approach." This
approach has been defended by philosophers like Bernard Boxill,
Gertrude Ezorsky, and Judith Jarvis Thomson.[11] According to this
approach, what has happened in the past is a crucial part of our
justification for giving preferences to members of certain groups.
The two principles that are often appealed to in this approach are
the compensation and reparations principles.

The compensation principle says that since women and racial
minorities were discriminated against and excluded because of their
race and sex, they now deserve to have their race or sex taken into
account because it is the only reasonable way to compensate them
for the disadvantage they now experience. The aim of compensation, as Bernard Boxill puts it, is to eliminate present miseries that
result from past behavior. According to this view, the community
owes compensation to members of these groups for their present
exclusion and that the persons who should bear the burden of the
compensation are white males. White males should bear the burden
because they have benefitted from the present exclusion of these
groups. The compensation principle does not say that white males
must pay the compensation because they necessarily have acted in
some wrongful way, but because they have been the beneficiaries of
the discrimination against these groups. The idea is that when blacks
and women were unfairly excluded from the process, white males
had a better chance for success because members of these groups
were excluded from the competition. The aim of the compensation
principle is to eliminate present misery caused by past behavior.
This past behavior might include injustice, but it need not.[12]

The reparation principle, on the other hand, argues that racial
minorities and women are entitled to preferential treatment only
because they have been wronged; they have been unjustly deprived
of their property, labor, and the right to compete under fair conditions. According to the reparations argument, reparations are owed
because some transgression has occurred and the transgressor has a

duty to repair the damages that result because of his transgression.[13] Unlike the compensation argument, the reparations argument does depend upon identifying those who have been wronged as well as the wrongdoers. According to the reparation principle, those who have been wronged need not experience present miseries in order to be entitled to reparations. In fact, persons who are well off can be entitled to demand reparations from transgressors who are not as well off.

So, by way of review, according to the compensation argument, preferential treatment is justified because certain groups experience harmful exclusion because of past and present practices. Their present condition might be traced to wrongdoing as well as misfortune. While the reparation argument says that preferential treatment of certain groups is justified only because people's rights have been violated. Reparations are owed because these groups have experienced some wrongdoing.

The critics of the backward-looking approach have raised a number of objections. Some accept the general legitimacy of compensation and reparation principles, but wonder whether these principles can be applied to groups as well as individuals. They have argued that while individual African-Americans and women may be entitled to compensation or reparation, blacks and women as groups are not.[14] They conclude that the following inference is not valid: S is African-American or a woman, therefore S is entitled to compensation or reparation. Likewise they argue that because W is white and male it does not follow that all Ws have a duty to all Ss. There have been a number of articles written by philosophers discussing the validity of these inferences.

These articles centered on whether race (skin color) or sex are morally relevant characteristics. Richard Wasserstrom, in an often cited paper, argues that if we want to understand the meaning of race and sex we must recognize that we cannot do so without looking at these concepts in an actual social and historical context.[15] He argues that in the United States race and sex have different meanings than they have in other parts of the world. According to Wasserstrom, we cannot determine if a person's race or sex is a morally relevant characteristic without looking at the actual historical and social context.

But Wasserstrom's critics have maintained that even in context it is not the person's race or sex that is morally relevant, but things like discrimination or oppression. These critics resist making a person's race or sex a morally relevant characteristic because they believe that to do so would just repeat the way race and sex were used to deprive racial minorities and women of their rights. They don't question remedying discrimination or oppression, but they do reject the claim that because one is a member of a particular group then one has necessarily experienced discrimination or oppression. They insist that this remains true even if we restrict our discussion to a specific context like the United States.

Some of the supporters of providing preferences to groups respond by claiming we don't need a perfect fit between being African-Americans and being a woman and experiencing discrimination in order to conclude that all women and all African-Americans are entitled to preferential treatment. While other supporters insist that there is a perfect fit. Those who argue that the fit can be less than perfect have appealed to what has been described as the administrative convenience rationale. By this they mean that with any social policy there is rarely a perfect fit between those who are entitled to receive the benefits of such a policy and those who in fact receive these benefits. Therefore, given this fact, the supporters of preferential programs who use a person's race or sex for awarding benefits and burdens believe that this method is the only way to make reasonable progress towards changing the harmful exclusive nature of many American institutions. While their critics, on the other hand, have argued that the most effective way to combat this harmful exclusion is to use explicit needs-based criteria rather than a person's race or sex. This debate is still raging.

So far our discussion of the affirmative action controversy has focused on the recipients of preferential treatment. However, there still is a great deal of confusion over whether preferential programs that make a person's race or sex the relevant characteristics are fair to white males. Critics argue that even if all African-Americans and women are owed compensation or reparation as groups, it does not follow that being a white male is sufficient to establish that one has a duty of compensation or reparation to members of these groups.

Here it is especially important to call attention to the difference between the compensation and reparation principles. Supporters of the compensation argument who take race and sex to be morally relevant characteristics don't contend that all who are asked to bear the burden of the compensation have acted in some unjust or wrongful ways. But if it is not true that all white males are guilty of wrongdoing, then some white males who must shoulder the burden of the compensation are innocent. If this is true, then supporters of the compensation argument must explain why even those who are innocent must shoulder the burden of the compensation, especially since young white males are thought to bear a disproportionate share of the burden because they are not protected by tenure and seniority rules. This criticism has led Gertrude Ezorsky, a supporter of the backward-looking approach, to propose ways that the burden might be more equitably distributed.[16] Her critics, however, argue that this burden cannot be distributed fairly and that this is a persuasive reason for abandoning such programs.

The reparation argument in support of preferential treatment also faces this problem, but in a different way. Remember, according to this argument, only those who have acted unjustly must bear the burden. So the people who must bear the burden cannot be innocent. But even if all are guilty it seems reasonable to suppose that some may bear greater responsibility than others. If this is true, shouldn't the burden of the reparation be distributed in direct proportion to the nature of the person's wrongdoing? Would not a reparation principle require this? The supporters of the reparation argument have answered yes to this question, but they typically go on to argue that even though young white males may be less guilty, they are not totally innocent. Thus they conclude they do have a duty of reparation to those who have been wronged. Larry May and Stacey Hoffman have edited a recent collection of essays that discuss the theoretical problems associated with holding groups collectively responsible.[17]

Bernard Boxill, a supporter of the reparation argument, has discussed the other side of this problem.[18] He focuses on the argument that claims preferential programs are unjust because poor African-Americans don't benefit from such programs. Boxill argues that even if it is true that preferential programs provide greater advantages to middle-class African-Americans, it does not follow that middle-class African-Americans are not entitled to these benefits. He argues that one should not conclude because a person is better-off economically and socially that they have experienced less discrimination. Clearly this implication does not hold. But Boxill's critics would argue that they are making an empirical and not a conceptual point. They believe they can produce evidence to support their conclusion.

This criticism should not be taken lightly. It raises the important question of moral priorities. Do poor African-Americans have a greater moral claim than middle-class African-Americans to our society's efforts to remedy the effects of past discrimination? There are different points of view. One could argue that the fact that some African-Americans are worse off than others does not show that they have experienced greater discrimination. People who experience equal amounts of discrimination might handle it differently. If discrimination rather than need is the test for who should qualify for affirmative action, it is not clear that poor African-Americans have experienced greater discrimination. However, it does seem reasonable to conclude that discrimination directed at the poor might be greater because they are less able to ward it off.

But even if society has a more pressing obligation to remedy discrimination against poor people, it would not show that giving middle-class African-Americans affirmative action is unjust. It would only show that we should find a better means for remedying the effect of past discrimination. It would certainly not justify continuing the status quo.

But another important concern is brought to the surface by this discussion. It is clear that people who raise this as a criticism of affirmative action as preferential treatment are appealing to different arguments to support their position. Those who make this criticism very often believe that a person's needy condition justifies giving them a preference. This argument is quite different from a backward-looking reparations argument. The reparations argument does not rely on a person's material condition, but on the fact that their rights have been violated. According to the reparations argument, even people who are economically secure can still be described as victims with entitlements.

I will now turn to a discussion of an approach to preferential treatment which is quite different from the one taken by Boxill, Ezorsky, and Thomson. This approach is forward-looking in its appeal. It is very often attached to a very different conception of what a just society should look like in terms of race and sex.

According to the forward-looking approach, the present unacceptable condition of many African-Americans is morally undesirable and a good society should take aggressive or affirmative steps to change their condition because passive measures will only perpetuate these horrible conditions. On this view, unless affirmative steps, like giving Africans and women preferences, are taken far too many members of these groups will continue to lag behind white males.[19] Preferential programs are justified because they can make the future brighter for members of these groups. As I have argued elsewhere, if a group of persons fell from the sky and found themselves in a miserable condition, then a good society should take aggressive steps to eliminate this misery even though there was no history of discrimination against members of this group.[20] An often unstated assumption by the supporters of this approach is that a morally good society is one that works to create a society where a person's race or sex is something insignificant, certainly not something that is morally relevant.

The supporters of the forward-looking approach very often appeal to the principle of utility or some strong egalitarian principles to support their position. Ronald Dworkin has offered a good illustration of the utilitarian argument in support of affirmative action.[21] While Richard Wasserstrom has advanced an argument that is strongly egalitarian in its appeal.[22] Wasserstrom also makes it explicit that his goal is to achieve a racially and sexually assimilated society. By this he means a society that has the goal of eliminating race- and sex-based differences. A truly non-racist or non-sexist society for Wasserstrom would be one where the race or sex of an individual would be the functional equivalent of eye color in our society today. Of course some physiological differences would remain, but these differences would not have any significance for a person's sense of identity or how he or she is regarded by others. Although Wasserstrom is very clear in his endorsement of assimilation as the proper ideal of a good society, this is often an unstated premise in the arguments by those who take the forward-looking approach.

According to Dworkin's utilitarian argument, schools and other institutions can and should design their admissions and hiring policies by appeal to what promotes the greatest utility for society as a whole. If giving a preference to racial minorities and women serves to promote the greatest utility for society as a whole, then such programs are justified. Law schools have the right to use a person's race when admitting students if doing so will help to promote the good in a utilitarian sense.

There have been two basic criticisms of Dworkin's defense of preferential programs. The first is a standard criticism of utilitarianism. According to this criticism, utilitarians give an inadequate account of rights and justice in general, and the case of preferential treatment is a specific illustration of this failing. The second criticism challenges Dworkin's contention that such programs do, in fact, promote the greatest utility given all of the available alternatives. According to this criticism, the disutility caused by white resentment and the perceived negative consequences to the merit system override any utility that one might derive from the inclusion of members of previously excluded groups.

But perhaps the most serious objection that has been raised against Dworkin's defense of preferential programs is one that is similar to a criticism leveled against John Stuart Mill's distinction between higher and lower pleasures. Mill argued that certain pleasures counted more than others.[23] For example, an act that produces a smaller amount of a more valuable pleasure should be preferred to one that produces a larger amount of less valuable pleasure. Mill's critics have argued that the reasoning that Mill employs to support this distinction involves him in a contradiction. In a similar manner, Dworkin's critics challenge his distinction between internal and external preferences. Dworkin used this distinction to explain why in the past it did not promote the greatest utility for society as a whole for whites to use race to exclude African-Americans from law schools, but that using race to now include previously excluded groups does. Dworkin's distinction is drawn to allow us to discount racist preferences in the utility calculations. This troublesome distinction in Dworkin's argument has led some critics to question whether a utilitarian justification of preferential programs can ever be viable.

The derivative account of rights embodied in the utilitarian defense of affirmative action has also led some who favor the forward-looking approach to appeal to a strong right to equality to defend such programs. According to these egalitarians, even if these programs don't promote the greatest utility, and even if they force us to sometimes depart from a merit principle, such programs are justified because they bring us closer to the ideal of equality.

However, if one takes this stance, then one must show why a right to equality should take precedence over other rights like a right to liberty. The egalitarian defense of preferential treatment seeks to make the distribution of goods, opportunities, and resources in society more equal. But if this is the case, then why should a middle-class African-American receive a preference over a lower-class white male if our goal is to achieve equality. Perhaps, once again, the answer is that this is an unavoidable administrative convenience that we must tolerate if we are to achieve a more equal society. Bernard Boxill, although not a supporter of this way of justifying preferential programs, briefly addresses this criticism. He says the fact that middle-class African-Americans are competing with poor whites reveals the depth and nature of the racial inequality between blacks and whites in our society.[24] Boxill's point is that the gap between African-Americans and whites is so large that we will not be able to close it unless preferential programs are race specific. The assumption here is that group-based inequality should take precedence over individual inequality. However, this assumption is often difficult to accept by those who put stress on the individual rather than the group. But the supporters of preferential treatment, defended on egalitarian grounds, contend that we cannot hope to eliminate the vast economic and social differences in our society without eliminating group-based racial and sexual bias, and that we cannot eliminate these things without, for a time, focusing on groups.

The controversy over which principles should be employed to justify preferential programs still exists, but much of the recent literature has focused on the issue of self-respect. Black and white neo-conservatives and some liberals have claimed that preferential programs damage the self-respect of the recipients. The root idea here is that the recipients of such treatment will think less of themselves because they are getting something they are not entitled to have. According to this position, creating a more equal society through affirmative action will rob the recipients of their self-respect.

### III

Let us take a closer look at the claim that affirmative action as preference lowers the self-respect of African-Americans. What does this mean? One interpretation says that the self-respect of persons who receive a preference based on race or sex will be lowered because the recipients will rightfully believe that they are receiving something that they are not entitled to have. A second interpretation claims that the self-respect of these recipients will be lowered because they will not be able to compete on equal footing with the persons who have received their positions without a preference. The third and final interpretation claims that even if the recipients of these programs are justly entitled to receive preferences, white resentment is so great that it will cause them to think less of themselves because they are resented by the white majority.

Let us briefly explore each of these interpretations. The first interpretation assumes that preferential programs are unjustified and thus none of the rationales for these programs provide the recipients with a sufficient basis for a sense of entitlement. The idea is that people damage their self-respect if they willingly accept something they do not believe they deserve. The crucial word here is believe. If members of certain groups believe they deserve these preferences, then their self-concepts will not be damaged. The evidence seems to be clear that white males received unjust preferences when racial minorities and women were excluded from the competition for scarce positions. Did these white males think they were undeserving and thus lacked self-respect? There is little, if any evidence to suggest they did. Why didn't they? Was it because they rejected the idea people should get what they deserve or was it because they believed it was just to exclude women and people of color from the competition? I suspect it was probably the latter. But what about the recipients of affirmative action as preference? Is there any hard evidence that shows that most recipients of this preference believe they are getting something they do not deserve? I think not. What is offered as evidence takes the form of testimonials by black neoconservatives employed by conservative think tanks. This interpretation also assumes that there is no rational basis for believing that affirmative action programs are just. However, anyone who has carefully studied the literature, knows that this is far from true. If I am right, these particular critics of affirmative action do not have good reasons for concluding that affirmative action damages the self-respect of many or most of its recipients.

What about the second interpretation? This interpretation assumes that the recipients of this preference damage their self-respect because they cannot compete with those who don't receive preferences. Again, this is an empirical claim that needs to be supported. Is it true that affirmative action recipients have been unable to successfully compete with white males? The little evidence that does exist does not support this conclusion. However, when the critics of affirmative action are presented with statistics which show that women and racial minorities have been able to succeed in business and higher education, the critics shift their ground. They then begin to criticize affirmative action for things like grade inflation or the lowering of standards. But again there is no clear evidence that affirmative action is the cause of these things.[25]

The final interpretation claims that widespread white resentment serves to undermine the self-respect of all minority and women applicants, even those who have not received preferences.[26] This is a strange position. Why should African-Americans, for example, have their self-concepts damaged because many in the white majority are wrongfully resentful of something that African-Americans have good reasons to believe that they are entitled to have? White resentment should rightfully damage the self-respect of African-Americans only if this resentment is righteous resentment. Otherwise, Africans might have a host of rational reactions to white resentment, like anger, pity or disappointment, but viewing themselves as lacking in self-respect is not one of the reactions that would qualify as a rational response. Throughout history large numbers of whites have resented black progress, but clearly it does not follow from this that African-Americans should have less respect for themselves. I think it is true that some African-Americans do feel a lack of self-respect, but I would argue that this can be attributed to the negative picture that powerful people have been able to paint of efforts to change the status quo rather than to clear arguments which show racial minorities and women are receiving something they do not deserve.

## IV

In an interesting paper, "The Message of affirmative Action," Thomas E. Hill, Jr. argues that both the forward-looking and the backward-looking justifications of affirmative action do not fully reveal the purpose and value of carefully crafted affirmative action programs.[27] Hill claims that the backward-looking approach focuses on compensating the victims of past wrongdoing and the forward-looking approach focuses on the good societal consequences that will result from such programs. In Hill's words: "The main suggestion is that, ideally, a central purpose of affirmative action would be to communicate a much needed message sincerely and effectively. The message is called for not just as a means to future good relations or a dutiful payment incurred by our past. It is called for by the ideal of being related to other human beings, over time, so that our histories and biographies reflect the responses of those who deeply care about fair opportunity, mutual trust, and respect for all."[28]

Hill's conclusion about the message of affirmative action is quite sensible. As social policy, affirmative action should in some important way make the community a better place. Hill borrows this focus on community from the work of communitarian writers like Alasdair MacIntyre.[29] The idea being that Americans, be they black, white, red or brown, are part of a historical narrative that is still working itself out. As Americans, we share a common past; interests, goals, and problems, that we cannot fully appreciate if we simply take an ahistorical view of things. We, as a community, must look at where we have come from, where we are now, and where we want to be in the future. Assessments of our lives should not employ evaluative terms that are drawn strictly from economics, but also from narrative literature. In other words, we must recognize that we assess events in our lives not simply in terms of a balance sheet, but also in terms of character development, tragic disruptions, and comic interludes. Hill's point is clear. He thinks that we can learn a great deal from communitarian writers like MacIntyre and Michael Sandel, but he is reluctant to fully embrace the communitarian themes because he does not believe that the full implications of these themes have been developed.

But what does Hill mean by this? Communitarians like MacIntyre and Sandel have criticized liberal conceptions of justice for being ahistorical and too atomistic, but they have not developed, in a comprehensive way, their own alternative accounts of justice. If this is what Hill means, why should we embrace these communitarian themes before we understand the implications of doing so? The communitarian themes that Hill embraces certainly sound good, but if we adopt them, what are we committing ourselves to?

Will our concern for our own plans and projects have to take a backseat to community plans and projects if we approach things from a communitarian perspective? Who decides what our community plans and projects will be? Is the democratic process, as it now stands, sufficient for making such decisions? If not, can it be modified to do so?[30]

These are important questions. But in order to adequately answer them, we must be sensitive to what has transpired culturally and politically in American life in the last fifty years. At one point in our history, the melting pot ideal dominated our political and cultural thinking. The idea being that becoming an American means becoming assimilated into "the American way of life." But this way of thinking has been challenged and labeled elitist, racist, and sexist. Critics of the melting pot ideal reject this ideal in favor of cultural pluralism. By cultural pluralism they mean that each race or ethnic group has its own distinctive culture, different races and ethnic groups can express their distinctive cultures under conditions of justice in one nation-state, members of particular races or ethnic groups have special obligations to preserve and enhance their cultures, and that no culture is superior to any other culture.

Given that the cultural pluralism model now dominates our cultural and political thinking, how likely is it that a conception of morality that requires us to give priority to the good of community will be adopted by individuals who see their primary identifications in racial, ethnic, religious, and gender terms? This is especially true for racial minorities who have been forced as a matter of self-defense to see themselves in these terms.

Hill's way of understanding the message of affirmative action asks us to move beyond narrow individualistic and group thinking to evaluate social policies in a historical, holistic way. But if we examine our record of dealing with social policies that are intended to bring about equality of opportunity, we find that American society has not done well in this regard. The white majority has consistently been unwilling to value minority interests. This fact makes historically disadvantaged minorities reluctant to accept social policies that are supposed to serve the general good of the community because the general good has often been interpreted in ways that devalue minority interests.

Clearly Hill is right to emphasize the importance of community good in the adoption and framing of public policy. The tough question is how do we construct a sense of community good in a modern pluralistic society where cultural pluralism is accepted as a fact of life, and historically disadvantaged minorities struggle to overcome the vestiges of a system of racial and sexual discrimination under conditions of increasing scarcity?

I still have hopes that we can reach some democratic consensus about community good, but I am not very optimistic about this prospect. Thus, in the foreseeable future, I doubt that we, as a moral and political community, will be able to hear the message of affirmative action.

## Notes

1　Michael Kinsley, "Equal Lack of Opportunity," *Harper's* (1983): 8.
2　Steven M. Cahn, ed., *Affirmative Action and the University: A Philosophical Inquiry* (Philadelphia: Temple University Press, 1993), 4–5.
3　Gertrude Ezorsky, *Racism and Justice: The Case for Affirmative Action* (Ithaca: Cornell University Press, 1991).
4　Virginia Held, "Reasonable Progress and Self-Respect," *The Monist*, 57, 1 (1973).
5　Robert Fullinwider, *The Reverse Discrimination Controversy: A Moral and Legal Analysis* (Totowa: Rowman and Littlefield, 1980).
6　Anita L. Allen, "The Role Model Argument and Faculty Diversity," *Philosophical Forum*, 24, 1–3 (1992–3).
7　Richard Wasserstrom, "On Racism and Sexism" and "Preferential Treatment," both in R. Wasserstrom, ed., *Philosophy and Social Issues* (Notre Dame: Notre Dame University Press, 1980).
8　Alan Goldman, *Justice and Reverse Discrimination* (Princeton: Princeton University Press, 1979).
9　Lisa Newton, "Reverse Discrimination as Unjustified," *Ethics*, 83, 4 (1973).
10　See Bernard R. Boxill, "The Morality of Preferential Hiring," *Philosophy and Public Affairs*, 7, 3 (1978); and Ezorsky, *Racism and Justice: The Case for Affirmative Action*.
11　Bernard Boxill, "The Morality of Reparation," *Social Theory and Practice*, 2, 1 (1972); Ezorsky, *Racism and Justice: The Case for Affirmative Action*; Judith Jarvis Thomson, "Preferential Hiring," in M. Cohen, T. Nagel, and T. Scanlon, eds, *Equality and Preferential Treatment* (Princeton: Princeton University Press, 1977).
12　Boxill "The Morality of Reparation."
13　Boxill, "The Morality of Reparation"; and Howard McGary, Jr., "Justice and Reparations," *Philosophical Forum*, 9, 1–3 (1977–8).
14　Fullinwider, *The Reverse Discrimination Controversy: A Moral and Legal Analysis*; Goldman, *Justice and Reverse Discrimination*.
15　Wasserstrom, "On Racism and Sexism."
16　Ezorsky, *Racism and Justice: The Case for Affirmative Action*, 84–8.
17　Larry May and Stacey Hoffman, eds, *Collective Responsibility: Five Decades of Debate in Theoretical and Applied Ethics* (Savage: Rowman and Littlefield, 1991).
18　Boxill, "The Morality of Preferential Hiring," 246–61.
19　Ezorsky, *Racism and Justice: The Case for Affirmative Action*.

20   Howard McGary, Jr., "Reparations, Self-Respect, and Public Policy," in D. T. Goldberg, ed., *Ethical Theory and Social Issues* (New York: Holt, Rinehart and Winston, Inc., 1989).

21   Ronald Dworkin, *Taking Rights Seriously* (Cambridge, MA: Harvard University Press, 1977), ch. 9.

22   Wasserstrom, "Preferential Treatment."

23   John Stuart Mill, *Utilitarianism*, ed., Oskar Piest (Indianapolis: Bobbs-Merrill Company, Inc, 1957), 12–15.

24   Boxill, "The Morality of Preferential Hiring," 252.

25   Theodore L. Cross, "On Scapegoating Blacks for Grade Inflation," *The Journal of Blacks in Higher Education*, 1, 1 (1993).

26   Thomas Sowell, "Economics and Black People," *The Review of Black Political Economy* (1971), 18,19.

27   Thomas E. Hill, Jr., "The Message of Affirmative Action," in *Autonomy and Self-Respect* (Cambridge: Cambridge University Press, 1991).

28   Ibid., 209.

29   Alasdair MacIntyre, *After Virtue* (Notre Dame: University of Notre Dame Press, 1981).

30   Benjamin Barber, *Strong Democracy* (Berkeley: University of California Press, 1994).

# PART III
*Racism and its Remedies*

# 9

# The Race and IQ Controversy

Scientists and scientific communities have a great deal of power in most societies. In the United States, scientists have played a crucial role in events that have changed the course of history, e.g., Einstein's work on special relativity. The power of the individual scientist is especially amplified in liberal democratic societies with a strong commitment to such things as individual liberty and academic freedom. However, the power of these individual scientists and their respective communities is often overshadowed in the minds of the public by the power of politicians and the heads of industry. Nonetheless, we should not underestimate the power of research scientists. Scientists have tremendous impact on many aspects of our lives: the food we eat, the air we breathe, the medicines we use to cure our ills, and the weapons we have at our disposal to resolve conflicts. It is important to realize that power takes forms other than economic and political power.

Recognizing the abuses and potential abuses of power by business people and politicians, public interest groups and philosophers have proposed codes of ethics, guidelines, and regulations to ensure that the power of these groups stays within appropriate bounds. In some cases, laws have been passed to define and limit legally permissible uses of power. The concern that power not be used to harm innocent people has now been extended to professions in general, e.g., doctors, lawyers, etc. Although thoughtful people recognize the value of limiting the abuses of power, many people, particularly political libertarians, are still reluctant to adopt measures that appear to infringe upon the freedom of the individual. Libertarians warn of the dangers of using the power of the state to protect unsuspecting individuals from a variety of potential harms that might result from actions of powerful persons. They argue, for example, that we should deregulate the professions rather than adding additional regulations. They argue that the market should be used to weed out those persons who don't adhere to certain standards of decency. This is not to say that they believe that professionals can do whatever they choose, but rather that clear violations of people's rights, defined in the negative sense of rights that impose duties of non-interference on others, must occur before state intervention is warranted.

Although there are differences of opinion about the extent of the role of the state in these matters, there is general agreement that these persons have the personal responsibility to exercise a certain level of moral constraint. However, research scientists, for the most part, have escaped the attention of the watch dogs of abuses of power. Research scientists have been virtually free to engage in research of their own choosing provided that their work does not involve the direct misuse of subjects. But as we shall see, harm does not occur only to the subjects directly involved in the experimentation, it can also occur to innocent persons indirectly involved as a result of certain research projects and findings.

Richard J. Herrnstein and Charles Murray put the race and IQ debate back in the spotlight.[1] Gottfredson, an Americans, and Ruston, a Canadian,[2] are also scientists who contend that blacks as a group are less intelligent than whites and that blacks will thus fare poorly in any activity or task that requires a high degree of intelligence. They also conclude that it is poor reasoning to assume that, given the same opportunities, blacks and whites will do roughly the same in qualifying for careers or vocations that demand better than average intelligence.

The renewed interest in the race and IQ issue parallels the rise in racial hatred and violence in society in general, and on college campuses in particular. A climate of racial hatred and violence has historically fueled eugenics research. In this climate, it is not surprising to find a professor of philosophy, Michael Levin, in a letter to American Philosophical Association Proceedings, claiming that affirmative action programs in philosophy are unnecessary because few blacks are intelligent enough to be philosophers.[3] It is clear that race and IQ research is most often seen as significant in an atmosphere in which there are racial antagonisms and competition for scarce goods.

In the discussion that follows, my aims are modest. I wish to examine a common claim made by investigators of race and IQ that their research, even in the present climate of racial hostility and violence, does not reflect negatively on their characters. Some who hold this position claim that the search for truth is such an important value that it takes precedence over all other values, even the prevention of harm to innocent persons. On the other hand, researchers like Herrnstein and Murray reject giving such weight to the search for truth, but they still contend that their hands are morally clean when they engage in race and IQ research. My examination shall focus on this claim by members of the latter group.

I am not so naive as to think that all members of the second group are sincere when they make such a claim, but some may be. But what is even more important is that people of good will in general are inclined to be sympathetic to investigators if the moral nature of their actions is unclear. But if the investigators' actions are seen as morally suspect, then the general public will question the value of such investigations, even if performed with so-called good intentions. I would like to make it clear at the outset that my concern in this chapter is with moral and not legal issues, but I believe that moral disapproval can be quite effective in altering, directing, and shaping behavior.

Much of the criticism of race-related research constitutes a not-so-subtle indictment of the characters of the researchers but, specifics are seldom spelled out. I attempt to spell out one such criticism in this paper. In the first section I set out and criticize Noam Chomsky's argument that the moral dilemma vanishes once we see that the scientific significance and social utility of projects like race and IQ research are slight.[4] In the second section, I review the argument by Block and Dworkin that a scientist confronted with such a dilemma should voluntarily cease his investigations if they are likely to be used by others to cause serious harm.[5] Finally,

I construct and reject two arguments that might be used by decent but misguided scientists who wish to defend race and IQ research.

---

I

---

In *For Reasons of State*, Noam Chomsky makes the following claim:

> Turning to the question of race and intelligence, we grant too much to the contemporary investigator of this question when we see him faced with a conflict of values: scientific curiosity versus social consequences. Given the virtual certainty that even the undertaking of the inquiry will reinforce some of the most despicable features of our society, the seriousness of the presumed *moral dilemma* [emphasis added] depends critically on the scientific significance of the issue that he is choosing to investigate. Even if the scientific significance were immense, we should certainly question the seriousness of the dilemma, given the likely social consequences. But if the scientific interest of any possible finding is slight, then the dilemma vanishes.[6]

For some time Chomsky's remarks have troubled me. On the one hand, I share his reservations about scientists examining such hypotheses as "are whites more intelligent than blacks?" and "are blacks more intelligent than whites?" On the other hand, my allegiance to freedom of thought and expression and to the value of a person's sense of conscience leads me to doubt the validity of Chomsky's claim that once we see that the scientific significance of such examinations is slight, then the moral dilemma between scientific curiosity and social consequences vanishes.

Chomsky made his remarks about race and IQ research at a time when the views of Shockley and Jensen were receiving a great deal of attention.[7] However, over two decades later, the race and IQ controversy is still raging. Some researchers in this country and in other democratic nations are now maintaining that race and IQ research is morally defensible.[8] I should say at the outset that my sympathies lie with Chomsky's position, but unfortunately arguments in support of such a position have not been totally persuasive. The arguments are enthymematic because they fail to recognize some essential ingredients that must be made explicit if a Chomskian type argument is to succeed. My aim is to correct this shortcoming.

We should note that the race and IQ controversy should be distinguished from other cases in which the morality of certain research projects is an issue. For example, the reservations about nuclear science research are different from those about race and IQ research in terms of the magnitude of possible harm, the possible indiscriminate nature of the harm, and the proven benefits in spite of the possibility of great harm. As we shall see later in this chapter, the fact that race and IQ research involves the possibility of clearly defined groups being subjected to serious harm has a bearing on the morality of engaging in such research.

At this juncture, we should be clear about what the strong liberal position on freedom of thought and expression requires. Liberals, in the tradition of John Stuart Mill, would support the researcher's legal right to engage in the research of his choosing provided that it does not cause direct physical harm to others. We can certainly cite actual cases in which research has caused direct harm to others, so the liberal position, given Mill's harm principle, is to not allow all research unconditionally. It is also consistent with their position that researchers who engage in research that causes indirect or direct harm merit moral and social criticism. However, the liberal position is consistent with allowing people to legally engage in activities that are judged to be immoral, but not harmful to others.

On the other hand, against the liberal position, Marxists argue that individuals are not legally or morally at liberty to do things that destroy communalism. Respecting an individual's right to liberty does not license indirect physical or mental harm to others. We must be careful here and note that Chomsky is not recommending state censorship, be it from the right or the left. His point is that a scientist who engages in research that is likely to be used by others to cause indirect harm, faces no moral dilemma if the social significance of the research is slight.

The alleged dilemma that Chomsky examines can be represented as a complex constructive dilemma:

P1 If a scientist should cease potentially dangerous but insignificant research that may be used by others to cause harm, then the moral value that he assigns to individual and scientific freedom is violated.

P2 If racists get their hands on potentially dangerous findings, they will use the findings to cause harm.

P3 Either a scientist should not engage in potentially dangerous research if it is likely that his findings will be used by others to cause harm, or racists (and others) should have the potentially dangerous findings.

Therefore, either the moral value that the scientist assigns to individual and scientific freedom will be violated or racists will use his findings to cause serious harm.

Remember, Chomsky stipulates that if the race and IQ research has little or no value and the social consequences are negative, then the dilemma vanishes. He is probably right that if we take a current time slice, race and IQ research will be judged to be insignificant; but things that appear insignificant at one point may in the future prove quite significant. For example, Mendel's work on pea pods at the time was not considered to be scientifically or socially significant.[9] But as we know, his work has proven to be of great value.

In his discussion of psychology and ideology Chomsky writes:

imagine a psychologist in Hitler's Germany who thought he could show that Jews had a genetically determined tendency towards usury (like squirrels bred to collect too many nuts) or a drive towards antisocial conspiracy and domination, and so on. If he were criticized for even undertaking these studies, could he merely respond that the "fundamental issue" is whether inquiry shall (again) be shut off because someone thinks society is best left in ignorance?[10]

Such a response is odd in the context of Nazi censorship; the issue would be clearer in present-day United States or Canada. Nonetheless, Chomsky believes that the psychologist should not maintain that he is being wronged if he is criticized for undertaking such studies.

Chomsky begins his argument by stating that a conflict of values exists between scientific curiosity and social consequences. This conflict is similar to Mill's conflict between individual freedom and the demands of utilitarianism. In both cases a dilemma exists because of a conflict between the value that a person gives to individual freedom and the value that he assigns to the prevention of harm to innocent persons. But Chomsky is quick to point out that the seriousness of the dilemma will depend upon the seriousness of the hypothesis to be explored. According to Chomsky, it would be foolish to claim that society would be left in ignorance were it not for scientific research on insignificant matters of all sorts.

This response is inviting, but it may focus on the wrong issue. It is not the knowledge to be gained that is always crucial, but the value of the scientific process itself even if it does not bear fruit. So while Chomsky may be warranted in concluding that the particular hypothesis under examination has little or no scientific significance, he may not be justified in concluding that scientific methodology also has little significance. This is hard to see in the case of the psychologist in Hitler's Germany because scientific methodology was then used to support Nazism.

A further problem with Chomsky's response is his failure to specify who is to judge the scientific and social significance of the research in question. This is a complex matter. A number of groups and their interests need to be considered. These are the public, the scientific community, legislators, and possible victims. These groups and their interests are not necessarily mutually exclusive, but their interests can and do conflict. Unfortunately, Chomsky does not give us convincing reasons for making a determination about who should be the judge. Nonetheless, I would doubt that the judgment in such cases should be left exclusively to one individual.

If I am right that the judgment of the social significance of a dangerous research project should not be left to the individual researcher, then what about the scientific significance? Is Chomsky right that this judgment should not be made exclusively by the individual researcher? I think so. But suppose we accept a Kuhnian conception of science.[11] Then during a period of "normal science," a project might be judged to have little or no significance merely because the majority of the scientific community rejects it. Therefore, we would be wrong in such cases to claim that the researcher has a moral obligation to refrain from pursuing his project simply because it is judged to be insignificant by his peers. Who should decide the scientific significance of a research project is no simple matter, but even with the above objection, the scientific community must be consulted. As we can see, resting one's argument on the significance of the project has its shortcomings.

Chomsky's moral argument against insignificant research projects that lead to serious social harm is consequentialist in nature, but it is not utilitarian. He does not ask the moral agent to embrace the classical act-utilitarian position that each project should be judged as morally permissible only if it is likely to produce more happiness for all affected by it than alternative projects. Nor would Chomsky recommend that the moral agent adopt modern preference utilitarianism, which judges the permissibility of a project according to whether or not it satisfies the preferences of those affected. Instead, Chomsky seeks to promote or instantiate human dignity for all and for those things that support it. I suspect that he is willing to promote this end even if the general happiness in society is reduced or if the preferences of many of those affected by the promotion of this end are not satisfied.

There is an important question that must be answered if we are to accept a Chomskian outlook. How far should one be willing to go to defend the goal of human dignity for all? Chomsky would deny that curious scientists have a moral right to engage in insignificant research that threatens human dignity. For him it is highly unlikely that insignificant research of this nature will lead to optimal social arrangements. Thus, while his approach to the issue is not utilitarian, it is close enough that it still might fall prey to the deontological criticism that it disrespects the rights of the individual scientist – in particular what some take to be an important value and perhaps a fundamental right, the right to be free. Does the scientist who chooses to continue his insignificant investigations, which are likely to be used by others to cause serious harm, make a morally incorrect decision?

## II

Perhaps a better strategy for answering this question does not rest on the scientist's knowledge about the value of the research but focuses on whether the research, insignificant or not, creates directly harmful social consequences. The clear and present danger test in the law requires reliable evidence of a causal or statistical nature between the practice and social harm before the practice can be made illegal. In the race and IQ case, it is difficult to predict the actions of people who are given information of a biased or inflammatory nature; but sometimes we can be reasonably sure. When empirical evidence is available, even firm supporters of personal liberty like the American Civil Liberties Union (ACLU) have advocated limits on freedom of expression. Can we employ the reasoning in the clear and present danger test to give us some moral guidance? Will allowing research in the area of race and IQ create a clear and present danger?

Block and Dworkin, in their influential paper "Race, I.Q., and Inequality," state the conditions under which race and IQ research creates a clear and present danger. They write:

If one believes that the media of communication are biased, either because of political considerations or because of something in the nature of the media (*Time* magazine is not likely to be willing to devote the space to the necessary clarifications even if it desired to), and that one's results will be distorted in the direction of producing harmful consequences;

If one believes that the possibilities of countering such distortions are minimal (compare the force of a letter to the *Atlantic Monthly* with that of the original piece one is criticizing);

If one believes the kind of research in question is burdened with methodological problems, ambiguous implications, and open to a wide range of interpretations;

If one thinks it is unlikely that all sides in the disagreement will get equal access to the mass media or that, in any case, those in power will select from the ambiguous data the findings they need to rationalize their political and social programs;

If one believes that the likely benefits are minimal and the likely harms grave;

Then one has a responsibility to cease such investigations while the above circumstances obtain.[12]

Block and Dworkin appeal to consequentialist arguments as opposed to rights-based deontological ones. They believe that knowingly engaging in an activity that is likely to be used by others to cause serious harm to innocent persons is morally unjustified; on balance it creates a greater evil than renouncing the activity. But their approach and conclusions might be rejected by a scientist sympathetic to the position that there is a serious moral cost to abandoning certain strongly held values in order to promote better social consequences. The scientist who believes that she has a moral right to investigate whatever she chooses, irrespective of the consequences, is certainly engaging in a bit of fiction. Block and Dworkin make this clear, but their conditions fail to explain clearly why a scientist whose research does not cause direct harm to others has a moral obligation to cease his investigations; they obviously assume that the distinction between direct and indirect harm in these cases does not make much difference. Are they right?

Consider the scientist who wishes to engage in research that is likely to cause indirect harm. As a scientist, does he have certain moral obligations when it comes to indirect harm? Before we answer, we should be aware that the obligations of scientists vary from society to society depending upon such things as the level of technology, the abundance or scarcity of resources, and the form of government. But one thing is clear: a scientist, in any society, will have certain social obligations as a member of a particular social order. It is here that utilitarian considerations are applicable. However, as stated above, appeals to utility depend upon making judgments about the long-term consequences of research that could prove indirectly harmful. Unfortunately, these judgments are sometimes very difficult to support in a rigorous fashion. The evidence in support of indirect harm can point in opposite directions depending on how long or short the view that one takes.

An admittedly troublesome aspect of my position is the difficulty scientists face in determining when harm is to be considered "serious" harm. However, history can help us to see the serious harm that race and IQ research can cause. For example, in the early part of the twentieth century, there were a number of research projects that claimed that some white ethnic groups are naturally less intelligent than others.[13] These studies were used to justify immigration policies biased against certain ethnic groups. They also served as a rationale for policies that denied opportunities and needed services to members of certain ethnic groups. As you might guess, blacks were even more severely victimized because of this research. This harm was serious and quite obvious to even a casual observer. The conditions and attitudes that allowed it to occur have not changed very much, so a decent scientist has some basis for determining whether his research may be used by others to cause serious harm. The claim that a scientist must have absolute certainty in these matters is unreasonable. As Aristotle said, a discussion will be adequate if it achieves clarity within the limits of the subject matter.[14] In some cases scientists will run into difficulties in determining whether their work will be used by others to cause serious harm, but in spite of these difficulties, judgments must be made and used to determine the nature of our moral obligations.

Sometimes we foresee and intend the consequences of our actions, but other times we do not. Decent people believe that we should feel a sense of responsibility for the harmful consequences of our intended actions and for the consequences of some actions that we did not intend, but did foresee. Block and Dworkin share this belief. For them, a scientist who does not intend his research to cause harm, but is aware that his findings are likely to be used by others to inflict serious harm, is responsible because he has failed to cease such investigations even though he knew that it was probable that his findings would be used by others to cause serious harm. The root idea here is that in "powder keg" situations a morally decent person should exercise extreme caution and self-constraint. Good intentions alone will not free one of the moral responsibility for the resulting harm.

Is it always morally indecent to knowingly engage in research that is likely to be used by others to cause serious harm? Chomsky thinks so. In the case that Chomsky cites, the researcher cannot be excused on grounds of ignorance because he must realize that harm will result from a causal process of which he is a crucial part. According to Chomsky, by continuing his research, he is acting in a negligent manner; such conduct falls below the moral standard for the protection of others against unreasonable risk of harm. The crucial phrase here is "unreasonable risk."

As I have said, it is not always a simple matter to determine when risks are unreasonable, but in the race and IQ case Chomsky, Block, and Dworkin believe that we can speak with some certainty. Given this fact, should scientists engaging in race and IQ research, under the conditions described by Block and Dworkin, voluntarily cease their work because other human beings are subject to risk of harm? Some scientists are still unconvinced.

### III

These scientists may persist, even though their research may be used by others to cause harm, because they believe they don't have a duty to prevent harm to other people by curtailing activities that, in themselves, create no harm. To use terms employed by legal writers, they believe that they have a negative duty to refrain from harming others and a positive duty to aid others by protecting them from harm only if they have made some explicit or implicit agreement to do so. These scientists deny that by continuing their research they are in some indirect way morally responsible for the harm done to others. It is their opinion that even though certain negative consequences are foreseeable, this does not imply that the person who expects them and is capable of preventing them has a moral duty to do so.

Chomsky, I suspect, would reject this line of reasoning; he would claim that the scientist's belief that someone else in the causal process is morally capable of and responsible for preventing the harm is false. Chomsky does not believe that a rational person would depend upon racists in the race and IQ case to act in morally responsible ways.

Why does Chomsky believe that we cannot reasonably entrust material of a pernicious nature to racists? Are they mentally defective in a manner similar to persons who completely lack a conscience? It seems not. Of course, a complete answer to this question depends on an account of the agency or lack of agency of racists; lacking such an account, it would be premature to conclude that racists can never act in morally responsible ways when making decisions about the welfare of some racial groups. Thus, this would not be a position one would want to adopt even if one believes that a scientist should voluntarily cease his investigations if it is likely that his findings will be used by others (e.g., racists) to cause serious harm.

Since there is always the possibility that someone may use research findings that were intended to do good to cause pain and suffering, the scientist, as a moral agent, might maintain that it is unreasonable to hold a person responsible for these unintended consequences of his actions. Is this response correct? I think not. Perhaps a scientist would be right in claiming that he should not be held accountable for all of the unintended harmful consequences of his actions, but it is wrong to believe that he can, with good conscience, ignore entirely the unintended serious harmful consequences of his work.

Nevertheless, the idea that a person must directly cause harm in order to be responsible for the harm is a popular belief held by many concerned with legal as well as moral responsibility. Causing harm is thought to be an extension of doing harm.[15] So when there are extraneous or intervening forces that appear to break the causal chain between the agent's action and the harm done, then we must question whether agent A caused the harm. If A cannot be said to have caused the harm, then we are reluctant to conclude that A is responsible for the harm done. Writing about responsibility in the law and morals, Hart and Honore echo this point when they write:

A throws a lighted cigarette into the bracken, which catches fire. Just as the flames are about to flicker out, B, who is not acting in concert with A, deliberately pours petrol on them. The fire spreads and burns down the forest. A's action, whether or not he intended the forest fire, was not the cause of the fire: B's was.[16]

Can't the scientist, in our race and IQ case, argue that he is not responsible for any harm that results to African-Americans because he did not cause the harm? Remember, he does not use his findings to harm African-Americans. The harm is caused by those who misuse his findings. Is this not similar in relevant respects to the case discussed above by Hart and Honore? Could the scientist not argue that, like the case of the cigarette in the forest, his actions alone could not cause the harm?

Before we attempt to answer these questions, let us get a better picture of the moral principle that appears to lie at the heart of the scientist's reply. Let us call this principle P. Principle P says that, when another person's voluntary action intervenes with A's action and harm results because of the intervention, then A is not responsible for the harm. Does principle P justify the scientist's contention that it is morally permissible for him to engage in his research? Is this case similar enough in relevant respects to the cigarette example to make an analogy between the two plausible? Initially one might think so; however, if we explore further, we might think differently. It is true that in both cases the voluntary action of another alters the causal process such that, were it not for the interferences, the harm would never have occurred. In the words of Hart and Honore, "it reduces the earlier action and its immediate effects to the level of mere circumstances or part of the history" rather than a cause of the harmful action.[17] But if the two cases are indeed analogous, then we may be inclined to conclude that because the scientist did not cause the harm, he is not responsible for it.

However, before we assign responsibility for the harm in either case, we must understand the background conditions. If the smoker drops the match in a very dry forest where it is common knowledge that there are people in the forest who will pour petrol on untended lighted cigarettes, then we would be warranted in concluding that the smoker is responsible for the fire even if he did not directly cause it. Likewise we must understand the background knowledge the scientist has when he decides to do race and IQ research. To be analogous to the smoker example, the scientist must be unaware that his research will be used to cause serious harm.

But even if we say that A is not responsible for the harm, does it follow that A's action is morally permissible? The answer to this is not straightforward. Suppose a friend of mine has a watch that

he loves dearly; I also greatly admire the watch and would like to
have it. Let us further suppose that my friend runs into hard times
and needs money badly. If I offer to buy the watch when I could
easily lend my friend the money, is my behavior morally permissible? Remember, I have not in any way caused my friend's misfortune; at worst, I have taken advantage of it.

Before we answer this question, we should distinguish morally
decent behavior from good samaritanism. A good Samaritan is a
moral saint who goes beyond the requirements of duty, whereas a
morally decent person does what moral duty requires. People are
not required to be good Samaritans, but they are expected to do
their moral duty. Am I failing to do my moral duty when I refuse
to offer my friend a loan? Does friendship require this type of
behavior, or must some explicit agreement exist between friends
before an obligation can be said to exist? It seems that I have a
moral right not to loan the friend money even though it may seem
to be the wrong thing to do. Can people have a moral right to do
what is morally wrong? Some scientists may believe that they do
and that this justifies their research on projects like race and IQ

These scientists might attempt to refute the arguments by
Chomsky, Block, and Dworkin and justify their decision to continue potentially harmful research by claiming that the two propo-
sitions below are not contradictory:

1 S has a moral right to do A, where A is research on race and
  IQ, and
2 S's doing A is morally wrong.

In other words, the scientist believes that a person can have a moral
right to engage in his research even though it is morally wrong.
Intuitively this conclusion seems incorrect, but Jeremy Waldron has
argued that we should not let the linguistic awkwardness of the
assertion mask the truth of the proposition.[18] Waldron believes that
the following examples serve as cases in which a person can have
a moral right to do what is morally wrong:

Someone uses all the money he has won fairly in a lottery to buy race
horses and champagne and refuses to donate any of it to a desperately
deserving charity.

An individual joins or supports an organization which he knows has racist leanings, such as the National Front in the United Kingdom; he canvasses support for it among a credulous electorate, and he exercises his own vote in its favor.[19]

Waldron is careful to note that by a right he does not mean a legal right, but a moral right. For it is clear that we can have a legal right to do things that are morally wrong. According to Waldron, moral rights give rightholders the protection to make certain decisions when alternative courses of action are available. This protection of the individual's decision-making right is not moral justification for any particular decision.[20] He also argues that the alternative courses of action open to the rightholder as a decision-maker are not restricted to ones that are either correct from the moral point of view or morally indifferent. From this he concludes that the morality that gives rise to proposition 1 is distinct from the morality that gives rise to proposition 2 because they have different functions. The morality that gives rise to proposition 1 has as its function protecting choices, while the morality that gives rise to proposition 2 guides choices. If we recognize these two kinds of morality, we can see that moral rights can protect our decision to choose actions that are morally wrong.[21]

Suppose that Waldron is right. Is this finding of any use to the scientist who wishes to morally condone the continuation of research that is likely to be used by others to cause harm? By adopting Waldron's conclusion about the function of moral rights, the scientist might conclude that he has a moral right to continue his research even though doing so is likely to cause something that is morally wrong, namely, the causing of harm to innocent persons. But if the scientist believes that this moral right justifies his action from the moral point of view, he is mistaken. The scientist cannot defend his particular choice among a range of alternative actions by appeal to his moral rights, but only his protection to make such a choice. So, although the scientist may appeal to a morality that protects his right to choose, he is wrong to think that this morality serves to justify the particular choice that he makes. Thus, Chomsky can still maintain that the scientist, as a moral agent, should recognize that he faces no moral dilemma when it comes to choosing between continuing a research project that is not of great significance and causing serious indirect harm to innocent persons.

## Notes

I am grateful to Gerald Dworkin, Mary Gibson, Douglas Husak, Bill E. Lawson, Walton Johnson, and the late Irving Thalberg, Jr., for their comments and criticisms of earlier drafts of this chapter.

1  Richard J. Herrnstein and Charles Murray, *The Bell Curve: Intelligence and Class Structure in American Life* (New York: Free Press, 1994).
2  Linda S. Gottfredson is a Professor of Education Studies and J. Philippe Ruston a psychologist. They support the idea of a racial hierarchy in intelligence with Asians as the most intelligent race, whites next most intelligent, and blacks the least intelligent. It is worth noting that the research on race and IQ by Gottfredson, Ruston, and Shockley was all supported by the controversial Pioneer Fund. According to its charter, one purpose of the fund is to give financial support to "Children . . . descended predominately from persons who settled in the original 13 states prior to the adoption of the Constitution."
3  Proceedings and Addresses of the American Philosophical Association, 63, 5 (1990): 62–3.
4  Noam Chomsky, *For Reasons of State* (New York: Random House, 1973).
5  N. J. Block and Gerald Dworkin, "I.Q., Heritability, and Equality," in *The I.Q. Controversy*, ed. Block and Dworkin (New York: Random House, 1976), 410–540.
6  Ibid., 361.
7  See A. R. Jensen, *Genetics and Education* (New York: Harper & Row, 1972), 69–204, and "How Much Can We Boost IQ and Scholastic Achievement?" *Atlantic Monthly* (September 1971): 43–64; W. Shockley, "Dysgenics, Geneticity, Raceology: A Challenge to the Intellectual Responsibility of Educators," *Phi Delta Kappan* (January 1972): 297–307.
8  See, for example, Linda S. Gottfredson, "Societal Consequences of the g Factor in Employment," *Journal of Vocational Behavior*, 29, 3 (1986): 379–410; J. E. Hunter, "Cognitive Ability, Cognitive Attitudes, Job Knowledge, and Job Performance," *Journal of Vocational*

*Behavior,* 29, 3 (1986): 340 –62; A. R. Jensen, "g: Artifact or Reality?" *Journal of Vocational Behavior,* 29, 3 (1986): 301–31; R. L. Thorndike, "The Role of General Ability in Prediction," *Journal of Vocational Behavior,* 29, 3 (1986): 332–9.

9  Hugo Iltis, *Life of Mendel,* trans. Eden and Cedar Paul (New York: W. W. Norton and Co., 1932), esp. the preface and ch. 8.
10 Chomsky, *For Reasons of State,* 360.
11 Thomas Kuhn, "The Structure of Scientific Revolutions," *Foundations of the Unity of Science,* 2, 2 (1970).
12 Block and Dworkin, *The I.Q. Controversy.* 517–18.
13 Leon J. Kamin, "Heredity, Intelligence, Politics, and Psychology: II," in Block and Dworkin, *The I.Q. Controversy,* 376–81.
14 Aristotle, *Nicomachean Ethics,* trans. Martin Oswald (New York: Bobbs-Merrill Co., 1966), 1094b 13–14.
15 See Hart and Honore, *Causation in the Law,* 2nd edn (Oxford: Oxford University Press, 1985), 73.
16 Ibid., 74.
17 Ibid., 73.
18 Jeremy Waldron, "A Right to Do Wrong," *Ethics,* 92, 1 (1981): 21–39.
19 Ibid., 21.
20 Ibid., 35.
21 Ibid., 37.

# 10

# Police Discretion and Discrimination

The philosopher and legal scholar Ronald Dworkin gives the following account of discretion:

What does it mean in ordinary life to say that someone "has discretion"? The first thing to notice is that the concept is out of place in all but very special contexts. For example, you would not say that I either do or do not have discretion to choose a house for my family. It is not true that I have "no discretion" in making that choice, and yet it would be almost equally misleading to say that I do have discretion. The concept of discretion is at home in only one sort of context; when someone is in general charged with making decisions subject to standards set by a particular authority.[1]

Discretion is exercised at every level of police work, from the administration of justice by high police officials to the cop on the beat. Police administrators have the discretion to decide what policies should determine their duties. For example, they can decide to place greater emphasis on crime prevention than on the apprehension of criminals. Individual police officers also have a great deal of discretion, however, in the performance of their day-to-day activities. A. J. Reiss writes: "Most police officers work most of the time without direct supervision. Their discretionary decisions, thus, are not generally open to review by supervisors."[2]

Police officers have discretion in enforcing clearly stated laws, as well as the authority and discretion to settle disputes that do not clearly involve violations of the law. In this discussion I explore the following question: Can police discretion justify the use of a person's age, race, religion, and sex in determining who should be subjected to police authority? There is a popular belief that most police work is done strictly by the book. In other words, where there are clear laws and clear violations of these laws, police ticket or arrest those people who violate the laws. But even those people who have this rosy view of police work must reluctantly admit that sometimes police officers are uncertain about what the law requires and whether a particular individual has, in fact, violated the law.[3] There are also cases, however, where the police officer is certain that the law has been broken and knows who violated the law, but determines that more harm than good would be served by arresting the lawbreaker.

It is wishful thinking to believe that all police officers know the laws and mechanically apply them in a fair and impartial manner. This is an overly optimistic view of police work. In fact, I would go so far as to say that a very large percentage of police work is discretionary. If this is true, we can hope only that police discretion operates in accordance with the constraints of justice and the spirit of the law.

Let us begin our examination by considering the following case:

A police officer is parked on the side of a busy highway with a posted speed limit of fifty-five miles per hour. She observes a group of motorists who are exceeding the speed limit, but it is impossible for the officer to pull over all of the speeders. So she decides to pull over the violators that are close to her police vehicle.

Is this case of police discretion in line with the constraints of justice and the spirit of the law? The rule the officer appears to be following is: Ticket speeders who are nearest to the officer's vehicle. Given that the officer cannot apprehend all of the speeding motorists, and it would defeat the purpose of having speeding laws to let them all go, this rule of thumb employed by the officer seems fair and reasonable.

What about the motorists who are pulled over for speeding? Do they have a legitimate complaint? Is the officer using her discretionary powers properly or is she unjustly discriminating against this subgroup of speeders? Clearly on one level she is not. Members of the subgroup broke the law by speeding. Because they have broken the law, on a retributivist account of punishment they deserve to be ticketed. According to a retributivist, a person deserves punishment only if he or she is responsible or accountable for some illegal act.[4] So, on the retributivist account, one might argue that members of the subgroup of speeders are getting what they deserve even though they are singled out for ticketing.

But the officer could appeal to another principle of punishment to justify the use of her discretionary powers in this manner. She could adopt a utilitarian point of view. On this theory of punishment, we punish only if punishing promotes greater utility than any of the available alternatives.[5] Thus, people may be punished even when they are not responsible for their illegal acts. The officer could use this rationale to justify her decision to stop some, but not all, of the speeders if doing so promoted greater utility. But is it reasonable to think that the officer's decision to stop some, but not all, of the speeders promotes greater utility than letting them all go? I think so.

But the utilitarian and the retributivist justifications of punishment are not the only theories that we can employ to justify the officer's actions. We could also employ what the legal philosopher Joel Feinberg calls the notion of comparative justice.[6] According to the basic principle of comparative justice, "likes should be treated alike," so, in the context of punishment, when people commit like crimes they should be punished in a like manner.

If one embraces the notion of comparative justice, one could argue that we should stop either all of the speeders or none of the speeders. But I think Feinberg would say that this would be a premature conclusion. For the complete principle of comparative justice is: "Treat all men alike until it can be shown that there are relevant differences between them."[7]

The basic principle of comparative justice has a strong egalitarian element: the presumption that equals should be treated as equals. According to this principle, objective standards of justice are logically affected by comparisons between the parties. The critics of comparative justice, however, argue that justice does not require that we compare individuals with each other, only with objective standards. Thus, according to noncomparative justice, we do not treat individuals justly because we treat them alike, we treat them justly because we are following some objective standard.

Equal treatment does not necessarily entail justice. The former Green Bay Packers tackle, Henry Jordan, made the following remark about his coach, Vincent Lombardi: "He treated us all the same. 'Like dogs'." The critics of comparative justice warn us that this principle is at best a formal principle because it fails to specify what we should actually do when confronted with specific circumstances. In order to determine what we should do in specific circumstances, we must rely on some material principle that can tell us what to do in specific cases. In the case of our speeders, we might be on solid ground in stopping some, but not all, of them if we can show that there is some morally relevant reason for treating likes differently.

But what about more controversial cases? How should a conscientious police officer decide what to do in cases involving generalizations about race, sex, age, and so forth? There are two general approaches that I would like to explore briefly. The first is the Bayesian approach. According to this approach, a rational decision is one that is based on the maximization of expected utility. The Bayesian approach uses axioms that allow for the determination of subjective probabilities, and then uses these probabilities to calculate expected utility. This approach is not uncontroversial, even though it has a long history of application in normative and descriptive decision theory. A primary criticism of this approach has been that it is too comprehensive because most decisions, including rational ones, are made on the basis of less than complete information about the alternative courses of action available to agents.

In our case involving the police officer who wants to determine what her policy should be for pulling over speeding motorists, her primary aim is to select the lawbreakers from a given set of motorists. In some cases this is quite obvious. In other cases, the officer must make inferences about who, from the given set of motorists, are lawbreakers. But given that police officers in actual practice have some discretion about how and when to apply the law, they might employ the Bayesian approach in cases where there is no question in the officer's mind about who the lawbreakers are. My discussion of the use of police discretion in the first section of this essay assumes a Bayesian approach to decision making. At the end of the essay, I briefly consider how a contractarian approach might handle these issues.

The contractarian asks: What would rational self-interested parties agree to in real and hypothetical situations under conditions of uncertainty? The basic idea here is not what will maximize utility or promote the greatest happiness for all, but what rational self-interested parties would agree to. According to contractarians, their approach avoids a popular objection to the Bayesian approach, namely, that in its pursuit of the common good the Bayesian approach fails to respect the rights of individuals. In fact, the political philosopher John Rawls has forcefully argued that the right (the just) must be prior to the good. He endorses the Kantian idea that people should not be regarded as mere means.[8] A contractarian would argue that a just decision or procedure should not be based simply on how much social utility is expected to result from the decision, but on whether rational individuals, under conditions of fairness, would choose to harm or violate the rights of certain individuals in order to maximize social utility for all. Rawls and other contractarians insist that the contractarian approach respects the rights of individuals at the same time that it allows for an appropriate regard for the common good.[9]

## The Bayesian Approach

The police officer pulls some, but not all, of the speeders over for ticketing for what she considers morally relevant reasons. She calculates that ticketing some of the speeders is in line with an objective standard and that the reason offered for not holding all of the speeders to this standard is that it is not possible to do so. The speeders who are ticketed are not singled out because of something that is beyond their control. If they decide to speed again, they can change their relative position in the group of speeders. Where they are ticketed today for speeding, they might be spared tomorrow. The characteristics that are used to single out speeders are not thought to be "suspect." (Suspect characteristics are characteristics that are thought not to be within the actors' control, and they have a long history of being used as a basis for inflicting harm on innocent persons. Race and gender have been designated as clearly suspect characteristics in our society.) So, in our speeding case, the strong deterrent value of ticketing some speeders overrides the harm caused by not treating all the speeders in the same way.

But let us make a slight modification to our speeders case. Suppose the motorists who are singled out for ticketing are selected because they are members of a particular race or sex. Have they been unjustly discriminated against? Can the police officer provide a rationale that will allow her to employ suspect characteristics in her decision making? Is this a decision rule that the officer could reasonably adopt?

I do not think so. It is doubtful whether a rule that singles out speeders on the basis of their race or sex can be justified by reference to some objective standard of justice. Given the history of racism and sexism in this country, the disutility and unfairness created by such a rule would seem to outweigh any of the advantages to be derived from such a rule. But legal theory and practice does not categorically rule out the use of suspect characteristics. The law says that when these characteristics are employed in decision making, compelling state interests must be served by doing so. The worry is that in this case it is hard to see how some compelling interests are served by police officers following such a rule.

What if we add a further dimension to our case? Suppose the highway that our speeding motorists are traveling is known for drug trafficking. And let us further suppose that a particular racial group includes a high percentage of persons who have been arrested for drug offenses. Would these facts change our position about the use of race in deciding who should be pulled over for ticketing? I do not think they should. Yet some people have argued that we can and should use statistical arguments to draw inferences about what should be done to particular persons.[10] By the use of statistical reasoning, then, does the police officer have a morally relevant reason for pulling over motorists from only one racial group because there is a greater statistical probability that members of this group will be drug offenders?

Ours is a hypothetical case, but lawyers for nineteen minority motorists stopped for drug and weapons charges on the New Jersey Turnpike have argued that the state police use racial profiles to target African-American and Latino motorists. According to these lawyers, African-American motorists on the southernmost twenty-six-mile portion of the turnpike were five hundred percent more likely to be stopped by the state police than were white motorists. Although African-Americans represented only fifteen percent of all the motorists violating traffic laws, they represented forty-six percent of the motorists stopped between January 1988 and April 1991. The nineteen motorists claimed that such a practice violated their constitutional rights.[11]

This alleged discriminatory practice by state police is not restricted to New Jersey. A Hispanic man traveling on Route 84, just over the Connecticut border, was stopped for a cracked windshield and within minutes his vehicle was searched for drugs. Lawyers for the Hispanic motorist argued that Hispanics are illegally targeted for drug searches on Route 84, a major thoroughfare from New York to Boston. According to the attorneys, Hispanic motorists are stopped by the state police more often than other motorists and often they are interrogated and searched without cause.[12] In such cases, is a person's race ever a relevant characteristic for police stops and searches?

I don't think so. First, even if we assume that statistical arguments can be used to draw particular conclusions from general claims, it does not follow that in our specific example such an inference would be valid. Let us consider a slightly modified example taken from the work of the philosopher Laurence Thomas.[13] If we know that nine out of ten Acme cars are defective, then clearly it is rational to infer that it would be unwise to take the chance of buying an Acme automobile. So far so good. Doesn't our police officer employ similar reasoning when it comes to our speeding motorists? Suppose that ninety percent of known drug offenders are members of a particular racial group. Wouldn't this fact provide the officer with rational grounds for inferring that she is justified in pulling over only members of this racial group? I do not think that an objective noncomparative standard of justice would justify the officer's actions. But if we adopt the principle of comparative justice, we might discover a morally relevant reason for pulling over only speeders from this particular racial group. What would such reasons look like?

The officer's claim that she has a morally relevant reason for stopping only members of a particular race because there is a high probability that members of this group are drug offenders is false. This is not a good reason unless we add the further premises that (1) there is a high probability that stopping only speeders from this group would maximize arrests for drug offenses; (2) the benefit from maximizing such arrests would outweigh the disadvantage caused by the negative deterrent effect on speeders who are not members of this group; and (3) the specter of racism that this practice would raise in a society with a known history of racial discrimination would not cause the general level of racism in the society to increase. It is doubtful that all these premises are true and that such a rule would be the most rational alternative available to the officer. It is indeed questionable whether this is a rational alternative at all. So if likes should be treated alike, unless there is some morally relevant reason for treating them differently, then the alleged differences cited above do not seem to qualify as morally relevant differences.

In the examples above, we did not immediately reject our police officer's use of her discretion in a way that appeared to discriminate on the basis of race. A part of our willingness to allow the officer to single out members of one racial group is that they are wrongdoers. Members of this group cannot claim they did not do anything wrong, but only that they were being unfairly treated when compared to other wrongdoers. But in our assessment of their complaint on grounds of comparative justice, we found the officer's discretionary rule to be invalid when we put her rationale for discriminating against this group into a historical context and then accurately evaluated the utility and disutility of such a discriminatory rule.

Would it make a difference if the race of the police officer and of the group being singled out were identical? In practice it might, because in a society with our racial history it would be hard for many people to believe that the motives of the officer were pure if she was not from the same racial group as those who were singled out for ticketing. We should not ignore this reality because to do so would be to fail to appreciate the harmful negative consequences that can flow from people's perceptions. If we are to accurately calculate the efficacy of such a rule, then we cannot ignore people's perceptions about the fairness of the rule. In a society where there has been a long history of racial discrimination, it is difficult for many people to accept that a person is acting from nonracist motives when they engage in a controversial practice that primarily harms members of another racial group. These perceptions must be taken into account in deciding whether a particular discretionary rule is fair and wise.

Given our remarks about perceptions, the racial identity of the officer can have a bearing on the effectiveness of such a policy. In certain situations, we might be warranted in adjusting our discretionary practices according to the racial identity of the police officer. For example, in a racially explosive situation it might be better to have officers who are of the same racial group as the participants. They might be better able to bring calm to the situation. Nevertheless, although the race of the police officer could have some bearing in our revised case, I do not think that it is the decisive consideration. Even if the officer and those who felt that they were being unfairly singled out were of the same racial identity, the issue would not be resolved.

What if the group of speeders who are stopped are from different racial backgrounds, but the majority are members of one racial group? Should this alter our conclusion? I think it should. This modification would allow us to salvage some of the deterrent effect of stopping speeders in the first place; this would be so because all races would have reason to believe that if they speed they will be ticketed. But it would not completely resolve the deterrence issue because some speeders could still rationally infer that they had a lesser chance of being stopped for speeding simply by virtue of their racial identities. Therefore, all things considered, even in our modified case it would not be wise or fair for an officer to adopt such a discretionary rule.

But what about cases that do not involve race, in which the

officer uses her discretionary powers discriminatorily when it is unclear whether parties affected by her actions are guilty or negligent in some way? Consider the following case: A police officer decides to pull over mostly senior citizens at a vehicle inspection stop. Her reason for doing this is that the reaction time for seniors is greater than the reaction time for other drivers, and seniors would therefore be less likely to be able to respond effectively in the case of an emergency situation brought on by some mechanical failure. Is her reasoning sound? We can quibble about whether the typical senior citizen has a lower reaction time than younger drivers and about the connection between slow reaction time and accidents. But let us assume, for the sake of argument, that these claims are true. Would this justify the officer in pulling over senior citizens for inspection more frequently than younger drivers?

In this situation, the officer clearly could have noble motives for pulling over the elderly drivers. She may not wish to harm or disrespect older drivers. In fact, she may want only to protect the seniors and other drivers from possible harm. What should the officer do? Should she pull over only vehicles that have some obvious mechanical problems or should she use some random method for pulling over cars? Why can't she use her discretion and pull over elderly drivers if she thinks that accidents might be reduced by doing so? Do the elderly drivers really have good reasons for objecting to such a practice?

The answer to these questions is unclear. Perhaps we can gain some insight into this case by examining a similar case. During certain hours of the day, some store owners deny teenagers access to their stores. They do so because they believe that teenagers engage in a lot of shoplifting, considerably more than members of other age groups. In both of these cases, a generalization about members of a group is used to penalize particular members of that group, even those members who are completely innocent. Laurence Thomas has argued persuasively that the use of suspect characteristics like race and sex often involves a rush to judgment. He argues that there are usually much better social indicators than a person's race for picking out rule violators. For example, he claims that we would be better served by focusing on attire. According to Thomas, very few people are mugged by people in tweed sports coats and ties.[14] Thus it would not be rational to conclude that a person so attired, African-American or otherwise, would be a mugger. Using parity of reasoning, the same would hold for a person's age. Thomas's point is that our preoccupation with race and other suspect characteristics in American society inhibits our development of needed social monitoring skills. Our lack of interaction with people from various races ill equips us with the skills necessary to distinguish friend from foe. Thomas argues that we would be much better served by developing these social monitoring skills than by relying on statistical generalizations about race and other suspect characteristics to draw conclusions about what particular people will do.

David Wasserman, in his essay "Racial Generalizations and Police Discretion," generally supports Thomas's conclusions, but he warns us that we cannot totally do away with the need to depend on generalizations based upon suspect characteristics like race. He argues that a more diversified and experienced police force would make it less likely that a police officer would need to rely on racial sterotypes. He writes:

Years ago, riding around the Thirty-second Precinct with two dedicated white police officers with years of anticrime and narcotics experience between them, I was struck by how little of the boisterous, confrontational "street theater" we witnessed alarmed or even interested them. They had learned, or appeared to have learned, how to distinguish behavior intended to look threatening from behavior that really was threatening.[15]

Wasserman's conclusions are instructive, but I do not think they will completely succeed in changing actual police practice until evils like racism are greatly reduced in our society. Racism produces racial stereotypes. The stereotypes do not cause the racism. But given that the complete elimination of racism is not on the immediate horizon, what do we do for now? Clearly Wasserman's proposals are in the right direction, but alone they will be insufficient to help a responsible police officer who wants to use her discretionary authority in ways that do not discriminate unjustly against some citizens.

What are some of the things that individual police officers can do to reduce the likelihood that they will use their discretionary powers in unjust ways? Individual police officers in their day-to-day activities must strive to be more reflective in their decision making. They must calculate and anticipate the full range of consequences that might ensue from their decisions. I realize that this may be unrealistic in emergencies, or in life and death situations, but most police work does not consist of these types of situations. In most instances, police officers have time to evaluate the various alternatives open to them and to assess the possible consequences of those alternatives.

The claim that police officers never know what the next encounter will bring does not justify rash or uninformed judgments on their part. Erring on the side of caution does not entitle the officer to set aside deliberation in making discretionary decisions that could lead to unjust discrimination. We are not second-guessing police officers in asking them to make well informed discretionary judgments. Their deliberations should include an awareness of the negative impact on race and other relations caused by discretionary decisions that tend to intensify various divisions in society; a recognition that the discriminatory application of objective standards by the use of suspect characteristics may reduce the deterrent value of having the standards; and a realization that using suspect characteristics in discretionary decision making often means ignoring factors that may have greater reliability in identifying criminal conduct.

## The Contractarian Approach

A police officer who adopts a contractarian approach is concerned with rights and the integrity of the individual as well as the common good. The officer who follows this approach would be especially concerned to respect the presumption of innocence. If one takes this presumption of innocence seriously, one should have strong reservations about using racial generalizations as the primary reason for arresting or detaining a citizen. This is not to say that statistical inferences can never be used, but simply that the mere fact that a person is a member of a particular racial group is not good reason for the belief that a particular person has committed a crime. A contractarian, like Rawls, would be willing to sacrifice some expected utility in order to respect important individual rights. The assumption that a person is guilty cuts at that person's integrity. Such a presumption is especially harmful to persons who have a history of marginalization and unjust discrimination. Of course, a Bayesian might be sensitive to such rights, but only in a derivative way. Bayesians respect rights only if doing so promotes greater expected utility than not doing so.

A contractarian would argue that a rational and just police officer should use her discretionary powers in ways that would first respect fundamental rights and then promote social utility. So, for example, in the case of our elderly drivers who are pulled over more often than younger drivers for vehicle inspections, a just police officer would seek to ascertain whether such a practice would violate any fundamental rights. Should these inspections violate the rights of the elderly drivers, some alternative course of action ought to be pursued. For example, instead of stopping elderly drivers disproportionately, we might require that all drivers who have caused serious accidents submit their vehicles to inspection more often than persons who have not caused such accidents. By requiring this, we would judge drivers by their driving records and not by factors beyond their control (like their age). Such an alternative might better serve our desire to protect drivers from car accidents that can be attributed to vehicular failures and at the same time respect citizens' right to the presumption of innocence.

This appears to be a just and reasonable alternative to stopping all elderly drivers at random check points. But even if I am wrong about this particular alternative, it is likely that some modification of this proposal will suffice. I am less optimistic, however, about finding an alternative proposal for our speeding AfricanAmerican motorists case. Our elderly drivers case is easier to handle because the objects of our focus are unsafe vehicles. But in our speeding African-American motorists case, we are concerned with the behavior of the motorists. More specifically, we want to detect speeders who may be trafficking in illegal drugs.

Is there a more just and reasonable alternative for detecting such persons than one that relies on racial generalizations about drug traffickers? One might think so, though finding such a method is more easily said than done. Perhaps we could require all convicted drug traffickers to place an insignia on their vehicles that would identify them as convicted drug traffickers, but there is some question whether such a requirement would pass constitutional muster. Nevertheless, given the New Jersey Supreme Court's decision to uphold Megan's Law (a New Jersey statute that requires convicted child molesters to register with local authorities), there is some reason to believe that a law requiring convicted drug traffickers to place on their vehicles an insignia which identifies them as convicted drug traffickers may be judged constitutional by the present conservative US Supreme Court.

But even were such a requirement to be legal, it is extremely doubtful whether it would assist police officers in picking out speeders who are also drug traffickers. It is highly unlikely that drug traffickers would use their own vehicles. Perhaps we could deny driving privileges to convicted drug traffickers. However, it is very unlikely that this practice would deter police officers from using racial generalizations in a racist society if the majority of convicted drug traffickers were African-American. Unless we can reduce racism in our society, I doubt whether either the contractarian or Bayesian methods will help a well-intentioned police officer use her discretion in ways that do not discriminate unjustly against members of certain groups.

## What Can Police Administrators Do?

What can police administrators do to better enable individual police officers to avoid making discretionary decisions that discriminate unjustly against members of certain groups? In addition to the instructive proposals by Thomas and Wasserman, police departments should work to reduce the "hassle" contact that presently exists between police and particular racial and ethnic groups. A great deal of the discomfort experienced by many ethnic and racial minorities in their contacts with police has nothing to do with police arrests. Even members of these groups who have never been arrested do not have positive impressions of the police. Members of some racial groups believe that they are hassled rather than served by the police.

I think that these negative police perceptions regarding certain groups can be attributed in part to the way in which police view their role in the community. Do they see themselves more as an occupying army in a foreign land during wartime or as members of a community who are charged with the important responsibility of protecting and serving? Clearly, the way police view their role will have a tremendous bearing on how they do their jobs.

In Detroit, police officials have tried to combat the conception of police as an occupying army by allowing civilians to accompany them on patrol and to visit police precincts to view police in their day-to-day activities. These are useful programs because they foster a better understanding between civilians and the police. But it is also important to create programs that will allow police officers to get involved in the full life of the actual communities they serve.[16]

One way in which communities have attempted to get police more involved in the neighborhoods they serve is by placing a residency requirement on police officers. I do not think that this requirement has adequately addressed the problem, however. If you coerce the police into becoming members of a community, this will breed resentment rather than fraternity. Perhaps a better way to approach this problem would be to create incentives that will encourage police to get involved in community organizations and activities. Police Athletics Leagues, for example, have had a positive impact in this regard. But in times of budgetary crisis these programs are the first to go. Perhaps police, the community, and other public officials need to re-evaluate their priorities. Some things that may appear to be tangential to good police work may be more central than we realize. Unjust discrimination involves viewing people as the "other" or as "outsiders." Police officials must do all that they can to combat the alienation that exists between the police and the people they serve. These efforts will require full and open discussion of topics like racism and police involvement in the communities where they work.

## Notes

1   Ronald Dworkin, *Taking Rights Seriously* (Cambridge, MA: Harvard University Press, 1977), 31.

2   A. J. Reiss, Jr., "Discretionary Justice in the United States," *International Journal of Criminology and Penology*, 2, 2 (1974): 181.

3   Samuel Walker, *Taming the System: The Control of Discretion in Criminal Justice, 1950–1990* (New York: Oxford University Press, 1993), 23–5.

4   H. L. A. Hart, *Punishment and Responsibility* (New York: Oxford University Press, 1973), 8.

5   Ibid., 72–83.

6   Joel Feinberg, *Social Philosophy* (Englewood Cliffs, NJ: Prentice-Hall, 1973), 98–9.

7   Ibid., 102.

8   John Rawls, *A Theory of Justice* (Cambridge, MA: Harvard University Press, 1971), 179–83.

9   Thomas M. Scanlon, "Contractualism and Utilitarianism," in *Utilitarianism and Beyond*, ed. Amartya Sen and Bernard Williams (Cambridge: Cambridge University Press, 1982).

10  Michael Levin, "Responses to Race Differences in Crime," *Journal of Social Philosophy*, 23, 1 (Spring 1992): 5–29.

11  Jon Nordheimer, "N.J. Troopers Accused of Bias in Traffic Stops," Quincy (Massachusetts) *Patriot Ledger* (December 23, 1994): 1.

12  Jenifer McKim, "Arrest of Hispanic Drivers Challenged," *Boston Globe* (May 29, 1995): 15.

13  Laurence Thomas, "Statistical Badness," *Journal of Social Philosophy*, 23, 1 (Spring 1992): 31.

14  Ibid., 33.

15  David Wasserman, "Racial Generalizations and Police Discretion," in John Kleinig, ed., *Handled With Discretion* (New York: Rowman and Littlefield Publishers, 1996), 128.

16  Jack R. Greene and Stephen D. Mastrofski, eds, *Community Policing: Rhetoric or Reality* (New York: Praeger, 1988).

# 11

# DuBois, the New Conservatism, and the Critique of African-American Leadership

W. E. B. DuBois is clearly one of the important social theorists of the twentieth century. His views on education, leadership, race, and urban life continue to inform scholars working on these topics. In this chapter, I shall use some of DuBois's ideas on leadership to present and examine the so-called crisis of African-American leadership today. But before I do, I shall spend some time explaining DuBois's two accounts of leadership that I will draw on in my analysis of the present problem of African-American leadership.

## I

In 1910, DuBois argued that effective leadership is a necessary condition for uplifting African-Americans or any racial group who have experienced a prolonged history of racial discrimination. According to DuBois, African-Americans, as a group, will not be able to overcome the poverty, lack of education, and political powerlessness without effective leadership. DuBois certainly believed that some African-Americans could prosper without the assistance of effective leaders, but he clearly believed that the group as a whole could not.

According to DuBois, individual initiative and skills were not enough to uplift the African-American masses. In order for the group to prosper there must be a political component which sets the parameters for what should count as effective leadership.

Before 1940 this political component for DuBois was understood as cultural nationalism and after 1940 in terms of Marxism. But even when DuBois moved from cultural nationalism to Marxism, he continued to believe that race must be a crucial factor in any successful program for uplifting the African-American masses.[1] In this chapter, I will not directly examine DuBois's views on which is more fundamental, race or class, but I will comment briefly on this debate since my concern is with DuBois's ideas on the nature and role of leadership in uplifting African-Americans as a group.

In "The Talented Tenth" DuBois argued that in order to uplift the African-American masses ten percent of the best and brightest of the black race must be educated to provide leadership and service to the African-American community.[2] Remember, at the time of the publication of "The Talented Tenth," racial segregation was legal and the dominant moral and social norms supported racial segregation. So although DuBois supported racial assimilation as an end,[3] the social reality was a system of racial segregation. Given this reality, as a sociologist, DuBois dedicated his life to identifying the most effective means for achieving racial advancement for African-Americans as a group in a racially segregated society. DuBois was an idealist about achieving a racially assimilated society, but his idealism did not cloud his assessment of the existing legal, moral, and social realities.

In order to understand why DuBois supported the idea of educating ten percent of the African-American population to serve as leaders for their race, one must read his proposal in the light of several crucial ideas contained in one of his earliest works. In 1897 DuBois published a pamphlet entitled "The Conservation of Races."[4] In this pamphlet, he presented a definition of race and racism and a plea for the African-American community to reject racial hatred and to maintain a separate racial identity. In this paper, DuBois can be seen to be defending a kind of racial pluralism. The idea being that all races are valuable, but that no race is superior to any other race. According to DuBois, each race has its own special contribution to make towards social progress.

Of course, a number of critics have challenged DuBois's conception of race and his call for racial solidarity in "The Conservation of Races." These critics have argued that DuBois's argument for a social and historical definition of races is incoherent and thus his call for racial solidarity based upon this conception of race is also problematic. In particular, Anthony Appiah has argued that any attempt to develop a cogent social and historical definition of races will fail. Appiah believes that you cannot provide a coherent definition of races without appealing to genetic and biological definitions of races; something that leading figures in the scientific community reject.[5] I do not wish to join this debate, but I do wish to explain why DuBois thought that racial rather than cultural solidarity was necessary for racial uplift and how his account of racial solidarity related to his views on leadership developed in "The Talented Tenth."

The early DuBois believed that social progress occurs because of the behavior of racial groups rather than individuals and that there was historical evidence to support this contention. Given this belief, DuBois claimed that if African-Americans were to progress, it must be as a group. But before this progress can take place, African-Americans must close ranks as a group and make optimal use of the parts that make up the whole. What does DuBois mean by closing ranks? I believe that he had in mind here the idea of racial solidarity.[6] By racial solidarity, I mean when all or most members of a group share important interests, feel pride when one of the members does something noteworthy, feel shame when one of its members acts badly, and desire to act together to achieve common ends. But because racial solidarity exists, it would be wrong to assume that this was sufficient for racial progress.

DuBois was clearly cognizant of this fact. He thought that racial solidarity was necessary but not sufficient for racial uplift. The group also had to function as an effective unit which requires explicit chains of command, norms, and disciplinary codes. So, effective leadership was necessary to bring about racial solidarity and to create an effective mechanism for advancing group interests. DuBois's paper "The Conservation of Races" is intended to address the importance of group solidarity and "The Talented Tenth" was written to provide a mechanism for a group with solidarity to effectively promote its interests. So for the early DuBois, leaders had the responsibility to interpret common ends and steer the group towards these ends.

But even during DuBois's day, he was criticized for offering an account of leadership that was seen by some to be elitist and impractical.[7] It was judged to be elitist because in the minds of some only a narrowly defined subgroup was deemed to possess the qualities necessary for leadership. It was described as impractical because some felt that DuBois failed to appreciate the intragroup conflicts that exist, especially the ones that would result because of DuBois's concept of the talented tenth.

DuBois's response to the first criticism was that any group, if it is to prosper, needs good leaders and historically those groups who have been successful have chosen their leaders from the most talented among them. However, this response misses the force of the criticism. The critics were not denying that there should be some qualifications upon who should qualify as a leader, but rather that DuBois's qualifications were too narrow. In response to this complaint, DuBois argued against those who felt that leaders did not need a classical education.[8] He believed that leaders need to be able to conceptualize as well as strategize, and thus a classical education was necessary for doing the conceptual work that would be required in articulating the interests of the race.

His response to the second criticism was that African-Americans are not discriminated against because they are as individuals perceived to be uneducated and unworthy, but because they are perceived to be members of a group that lacks worth. The early DuBois saw race as a community where the fate of one member of the community is tied to the fate of others in the community. When one member is harmed because of his or her membership in the community, all others are harmed whether they realize it or not. The task of an effective leader is to reveal to the masses this inter-connectiveness of African-American interests.

But the early DuBois also thought that effective leaders must play a crucial role in defining the mission of the race. This, according to DuBois, would cause other races to see the worthiness of a group that had been placed so far down by slavery and a system of racial discrimination. But the talented tenth could not help the race to hone its racial mission if the group lacked racial solidarity.

Why did DuBois believe that members of the talented tenth would feel obligated to the other ninety percent of the population?

Was it because they had a more developed sense of moral obligation? I think not. According to DuBois, the basis for this sense of obligation was self-interest. Because of their training, they can see that their interests are intimately connected to the rest of the group. DuBois felt no special urgency to argue for this because the system of racial discrimination was so explicit at the turn of the twentieth century. He thought it was clear that all African-Americans had an interest in breaking down these barriers no matter their social and class position. The fact of legally enforced segregation also shaped DuBois's thinking. Even if the talented tenth wanted to use their talents to help other communities, they would not be able to do so because they would be barred from participating in institutions in the white community. If they wanted to practice their trade, it would have to be in African-American communities. So, for DuBois, one did not have to be a rocket scientist to see that it was in one's interest to unite with other African-Americans to gain the political and economic clout to combat an explicit system of racial discrimination.

## II

In the 1920s, DuBois began to have some misgivings with his early account of leadership. He began to see that his early account was imposed upon the African-American community instead of growing out of the lived experiences of the group. His attraction to Marxist thought made him more materialistic in his outlook.[9] Marx argued that workers would be moved to revolt by their material conditions and not because of moral or political ideals articulated by leaders in the working class. In a like manner, DuBois began to realize that the African-American masses would be motivated to unify to fight racial injustice because they perceived it to be in their self-interest to do so. They would not be moved to act by some idealistic proposal no matter how alluring it might sound. DuBois came to better appreciate that leaders must stay in touch with the African-American masses and that any educational process that prevented this would not produce effective leaders. It was for this reason, I think, that DuBois turned in his own life away from purely scholarly pursuits to an active public service. His work with the NAACP and his editorship of the *Crisis* magazine was indicative of this public turn.

It was at this stage in his life that DuBois realized, after years of struggling to inform people of the evils and pitfalls of racism, that racism was not simply the result of ignorance and different ideals of life, but that people knowingly acted in a racist fashion because it promoted their interests.[10] This new way of thinking about racism caused DuBois to concentrate on building racial unity to achieve a level of economic cooperation in the African-American community. DuBois felt that an effective leader must understand national and international economies and the role of black people in these economies. But an effective leader must also stay in touch with what is going on in the lives of ordinary black folks. DuBois began to stress the shared economic interests between African-Americans and African peoples throughout the world. He also questioned whether the African-American masses could be uplifted without overthrowing capitalism.

All of this led DuBois to conclude that effective leaders must move beyond building racial solidarity, to the unity of the working class. Was this truly the case? Some scholars have argued that DuBois never abandoned the idea of racial solidarity while others have claimed that he jettisoned the idea of racial unity in favor of class unity. In DuBois's important work *Black Reconstruction*, there is clear evidence that he had not totally abandoned the idea of racial solidarity. In this work, we find a mixture of Marxism and racial reasoning. By racial reasoning, I mean arguments that have premises which assert that a person's racial identity plays a crucial role in determining their life prospects. DuBois was unwilling to say that a person's race was less significant than their class position. In fact, he continued to believe that race was a significant factor until his death.

Those who claim that DuBois played down the significance of race in determining a person's fate dismiss DuBois's frequent criticisms of American Marxists.[11] They argue that Dubois was criticizing the tactics and strategies of the American communist party, but he was not criticizing the Marxist analysis of exploitation and oppression. While others argue that DuBois did continue to see race as significant, but he did so because he could not manage to escape the intense racial climate of his day.

I disagree with both positions. I do not think that DuBois was simply unable to escape the racism of his day nor was he guilty of racism in reverse by arguing for the necessity of strong African-American leadership. It is clear that DuBois was acutely sensitive to the principle that likes should be treated alike unless there was some morally relevant reason for treating them differently. However, DuBois firmly believed that African-Americans and whites were not equals. Whites enjoyed privileges and protections that African-Americans did not enjoy and these privileges and protections were based upon their race. DuBois believed that the pragmatics of race made race significant not some trans-historical ontological or moral view about races.

DuBois did not deny that there would come a time when race did not matter, but he did not think this time would come in the twentieth century. Recall his famous remark about the problem of the twentieth century being the color line. In the present debate over the significance of race and the permanence of racism, DuBois clearly sides with those who believe that race is significant, but that racism can be overcome. DuBois would reject Derrick Bell's view about the permanence of racism.[12] DuBois, like Cornel West,[13] believes that we must acknowledge race as a category in order to create a society where race is not used to unjustly discriminate against people.

But DuBois never abandoned the idea that African-American people needed to unify in order to defeat a worldwide system of racial and class exploitation. For Dubois this unity did not mean the exclusion of whites who also wished to work towards common goals. However, DuBois believed that African-Americans, even in the middle of the twentieth century, lived quite separate lives from whites and that this fact meant there were indeed separate communities with similar, but also different needs. These distinct needs could not be articulately and strongly addressed without a strong voice, clearly articulating these interests. Thus DuBois believed that there was still a need for African-American leaders and not just leaders who happened to be African-Americans.[14]

---
III
---

What can DuBois's views on leadership tell us about the current debate over African-American leadership? Cornel West, and other social critics, point to what they take to be a crisis of leadership in the African-American community. West writes: "There has not been a time in the history of African-American people in this country when the quantity of politicians and intellectuals was so great, yet the quality of both groups have been so low."[15] Is there a crisis of African-American leadership or is this simply a failure to see that leadership has changed with the times? I shall argue that it is a bit of both.

African-American intellectuals and politicians face a dilemma. On the one hand they are told by the popular press and the dominant political establishment that race does not matter, but on the other hand they see African-Americans in grossly disproportionate numbers failing to enter into the mainstream of American life.[16] If these leaders claim that race is significant, and attempt to organize to address concerns that specifically affect African-American people, they are accused of being racist or at best vulgarly nationalistic. If they play down the significance of race, they are accused by members of the African-American underclass of being sell-outs or worse. Is there no middle ground?

Cornel West attempts to take this middle ground,[17] but he is accused by those who claim that race is most of what matters, of ignoring or failing to appreciate the nature of modern racism and making too much of race by those who either believe that racism no longer exists or by those who think that racism exists but thatwe would be better served by exclusively focusing on class rather than race.

Are African-America leaders subject to intense criticism no matter which position they take? I think so. But the interesting question is why is this dilemma so acute at this historical juncture? Is it due to some failure on the part of the leaders? Are they less astute than their historical counterparts? West seems to suggest they are because they have not been able to convincingly assert that race does matter, but then go on to transcend race. According to West, "To be a serious black leader is to be a race-transcending prophet who critiques the powers that be (including the black component of the Establishment) and who puts forward a vision of moral regeneration and political insurgency for the purpose of fundamental social change for all who suffer from social induced misery."[18]

Perhaps DuBois's ideas on leadership might prove to be instructive in our examination of the crisis of African-American leadership. DuBois taught us that in American society racial political solidarity is built on clear opposition to clearly identifiable barriers to racial advancement. Frederick Douglass built his political program around clearly identifiable unjust laws, institutions, and practices. This was also true of all of the prominent black leaders in the nineteenth century and true of most, if not all, of the black leadership until the 1960s.

These leaders could point to clear and concrete unjust impediments to African-American advancement. They did not have to talk in terms of outcomes, their case was made in terms of the lack of opportunity. From Frederick Douglass to Martin L. King, Jr., African-American leaders could argue that all African-Americans had strong reasons to organize and work to abolish laws and practices that overtly discriminated against them. This was true for the poor southern share cropper as well as the affluent Northerner who was legally restricted from being a part of mainstream society.

However, today's leaders face a different set of circumstances. First, most, and some would say all, of the laws that explicitly discriminate against African-Americans have been removed from the books. So there is now a more intense debate in African-American communities about what is the cause of the lack of black advancement. As I have said, some argue that the external barriers no longer exist. Black neo-conservatives argue that many African-Americans fail to take advantage of existing opportunities because of a "victim's mentality."[19] This victim's mentality rather than racism is said to be the source of the lack of African-American advancement. Second, the above argument by black neo-conservatives is buttressed by highly visible examples of successful Black-Americans that we did not see before 1963. In fact, some African-Americans rank high on the list of Americans most respected by white Americans. Third, there have been structural changes in the economy which have had adverse impact on working people who are not highly skilled, particularly African-Americans. Fourth, the fact that survey after survey reveals that the majority of African-Americans from all walks of life still believe that American society is still racist.[20] Fifth, the rapid growth of a large urban underclass that is disproportionately African-American. So, on the one hand, real progress in race relations has been made. However, on the other hand, most African-Americans believe that there is still much work to be done.

These things are facts. Present African-American leadership cannot escape this reality. African-American conservatives tell us that effective African-Americans leaders must transcend race. But what do they mean by transcending race? What does it mean to rise above or go beyond race? West believes that we can take into account a person's racial identity as long as we do so in a way that does not violate his rights or rob him of his humanity. I am led to this interpretation because of West's strong advocacy of interracial coalitions. His idea of an interracial coalition is one where races come together with different ideas about what norms should govern society, and then they hammer out a political consensus about which norms will in fact prevail. With interracial coalitionary politics one does not reject claims of racial legitimacy in the process of consensus building.[21]

But the picture is more complex than West and the African-American conservatives realize. The crisis in African-American leadership is not because African-American leaders have been unwilling to go beyond race in their politics, I contend that today's leaders face a world that is far more ambiguous and subtle than their predecessors. Leaders in the past like Frederick Douglass and Martin L. King, Jr. believed that if we could wipe discriminatory laws from the books, this would go most of the way towards eliminating racism or greatly reducing its damaging effects. DuBois, for a large part of his life, shared this view. Given this belief, African-American leaders could speak with some authority about the prospects of moving to a time where race would truly not matter; to a time where people would have no need or desire to organize around race. DuBois clearly had these hopes, and over his long life, as he moved from a cultural analysis of race relations to an economic analysis, he never abandoned the view that African-Americans needed to unify and organize on the basis of race. Throughout his long life, DuBois continued to see race as significant because there were still clear legal barriers that stood in the way of African-American progress.

Present African-American leaders cannot speak with the same confidence because it is far less clear why African-Americans as a group are still out of the mainstream. For these leaders to speak of transcending race is seen by many of their fellow African-Americans, especially those who are down and out, as a denial of their predicament. West claims that courageous leaders can overcome these reservations by arguing for programs that will eliminate misery no matter what shade it comes in. But current efforts by African-American leaders to create social programs that help the needy are popularly criticized as hand-outs to undeserving African-Americans. For example, the African-American unemployment rate has been notoriously high in the African-American community for years, but the call by African-American leaders for extending unemployment benefits fell on deaf ears. However, when the unemployment rate began to rise slightly in the white population these benefits were extended. Of course, the supporters of extending unemployment benefits flatly deny that the race of the recipients played any role in their decision to extend benefits. They maintain that when the white unemployment rate began to rise the numbers became statistically significant. However, this explanation, even if true, does not set well with African-Americans who feel their interests are being devalued.

Another example involves Lani Guinier's proposals to rectify the unfairness that can result from tyranny of the minority by the majority in a democracy.[22] Her proposal of cumulative voting was offered as a progressive and race-neutral solution to tyrannical majorities. But instead of welcoming her proposal or seriously examining this proposal as a solution to an important political problem, her views were distorted, and she was ostracized even by many white liberals as being racist and undemocractic, when all she wanted to do was to give equal regard to the interests of African-American citizens. What was even more disturbing was when this same proposal was recommended in the South African context many of Guinier's critics hailed it as a brilliant solution to the problem.

These blatant inconsistencies cause many African-Americans, especially the poor, to doubt whether white America has any regard for African-Americans' interests. They also make it extremely difficult for African-American leaders to be race-transcending prophets. Given these two examples, and others like them, one can see the problems that African-American leaders face when they try to be race-transcending prophets. How can these leaders demonstrate to poor African-Americans they are genuinely sensitive to their concerns when any proposal to promote African-American interests, no matter how race-neutral, is rejected?

It is one thing to say that there should not be any racial barriers that prevent African-American advancement and quite another thing to say that African-American interests should be promoted. Today most African-American leaders are trying to find ways to promote legitimate African-American interests in a society that has demonstrated too little regard for these interests. This was not the problem confronting African-American leaders before 1963. Most white liberals and some white conservatives supported the efforts of early African-American leaders because these efforts were directed at clearly identifiable racist laws. But when African-American leaders begin to ask for an actual share of the pie, many liberals and progressives turned into former liberals and progressives.

One might object that I have failed to appreciate that before 1963 African-American leaders faced the same dilemma. Namely, even in the early part of the twentieth century some African-American leaders argued that African-American interests were not being served because of racism, while others argued that African-American interests could be promoted if African-Americans would only take full advantage of the opportunities that did exist.

But such an objection is misguided. For example, in the classic debates between DuBois and Booker T. Washington, their disagreement was not over whether there were explicit unjust racial barriers that blocked African-American advancement. Their disagreement was over what should be done given these barriers.

DuBois argued that African-Americans should vigorously protest these unjust restrictions. Washington, on the other hand, claimed that African-Americans should cast down their buckets where they were and forget protesting. Washington believed protest from a politically and economically powerless group was a mere appeal to pity; something he thought would harm the self-respect of African-Americans.[23]

For Washington, it was fruitless to conclude that white America would eliminate African-American suffering. Washington did not deny that there were racial barriers to African-American progress, but his pragmatism drove him to conclude that black self-help rather than political agitation would better serve the African-American masses.

Of course, Washington might have been wrong in reaching this conclusion. However, the truth of his position is not my concern here. My point is simply that the dispute between DuBois and Washington was not over whether serious racial barriers to African-American progress existed. Their disagreement was over what should be done given these barriers.

Today's black leaders, as I have said, do seriously debate whether such barriers continue to exist. Some, like Derrick Bell, have even argued that racial barriers are a permanent part of the fabric of American life.[24] However, whether they are permanent or impermanent does not mitigate the devastating impact on the psyche of African-Americans. If the barriers do not exist, then African-American leaders must find ways to uplift the African-American masses who may wrongly believe that their lack of progress is due to racial injustice. If the barriers do exist, but are not permanent, then leaders have the task of keeping their constituents motivated and engaged in order that they might tear down these barriers. And if the barriers are permanent as Bell suggests, then leaders must be able to sustain motivation and construct strategies without the hopeful premise that one day racism will be eliminated.

There are no universal necessary and sufficient conditions for effective leadership. These conditions are always tied to the specific economic, historical, and social conditions. We should realize that today's leaders may not be less astute or lacking in motivation, but they may simply face a very different set of political and social circumstances.

## Notes

1  My ideas have been shaped by the following texts: W. E. B. DuBois, *The Dusk of Dawn* (New Brunswick, NJ: Transaction Books, 1987); W. E. B. DuBois, *Black Reconstruction* (New York: Atheneum, 1970); W. E. B. DuBois, *The Souls of Black Folk* (New York: New American Library, 1969); W. E. B. DuBois, *Darkwater* (New York: Schocken Books, 1969); W. E. B. DuBois, *The Philadelphia Negro: A Social Study* (New York: Schocken Books, 1967); W. E. B. DuBois, "Socialism and the Negro Problem," *New Review*, February 1, 1913; W. E. B. DuBois, "Socialism and the Negro," *Crisis*, October 1921; W. E. B. DuBois, "Marxism and the Negro Problem," *Crisis*, May 1933; Herbert Aptheker, ed., *The Correspondence of W. E. B. DuBois*, vols 1 and 2 (Amherst: University of Massachusetts Press, 1976); Francis L. Broderick, *W. E. B. DuBois: Negro Leader in a Time of Crisis* (Stanford: Stanford University Press, 1959); Joseph P. DeMarco, *The Social Thought of W. E. B. DuBois* (New York: University Press of America, 1983); Shirley G. DuBois, *His Day is Marching On: A Memoir of W. E. B. DuBois* (New York: J. B. Lippincott Co., 1971); Julius Lester, *The Seventh Son: The Thought and the Writings of W. E. B. DuBois* (two volumes, New York: Random House, 1971); David L. Lewis, *W. E. B. DuBois: Biography of a Race 1868–1919* (New York: Henry Holt and Co., 1993); Arnold Rampersad, *The Art and Imagination of W. E. B. DuBois* (Cambridge: Harvard University Press, 1976); Elliot M. Rudwick, *W. E. B. DuBois: Propagandist of the Negro Protest* (New York: Atheneum, 1969).

2  W. E. B. DuBois, "The Talented Tenth," in Howard Brotz, ed. *Negro Social and Political Thought 1850-1920* (New York, Basic Books, 1966), 518–33.

3  W. E. B. DuBois, "Is Race Separation Practicable," *American Journal of Sociology*, 13 (May 1908): 834–8.

4  W. E. B. DuBois, "The Conservation of Races," in Brotz, 483–92.

5  Kwame Anthony Appiah, *In My Father's House* (Oxford: Oxford University Press, 1992), ch. 2.

6  See W. E. B. DuBois, "The Conservation of Races" and "The

Talented Tenth" in Howard Brotz, ed., *Negro Social and Political Thought 1850–1920* (New York: Basic Books, 1966).

7  See Marcus Garvey, "An Exposé of the Caste System Among Negroes," in Amy Jacques-Garvey, ed., *Philosophy and Opinions of Marcus Garvey* (New York: Atheneum, 1969), 55–61.

8  W. E. B. DuBois, "Negro Education," *Crisis* (February 1918); W. E. B. DuBois, "The Cultural Missions of Atlanta University," *Phylon*, III (1942).

9  W. E. B. DuBois, "Prospects of a World Without Race Conflict," *American Journal of Sociology*, 49 (March 1944); W. E. B. DuBois, *In Battle for Peace* (New York: Masses and Mainstream, 1952).

10  W. E. B. DuBois, *Dusk of Dawn*, 171.

11  For an example of this criticism by DuBois, see his "The Class Struggle," *Crisis*, August 1921.

12  Derrick Bell, *Faces at the Bottom of the Well: The Permanence of Racism* (New York: Basic Books, 1992).

13  Cornel West, *Race Matters* (Boston: Beacon Press, 1993).

14  Although DuBois continued to endorse the importance of African-American solidarity, in his later years he increasingly emphasized the international or Pan African character of this solidarity.

15  Cornel West, *Race Matters*, 35.

16  See William Julius Wilson, *The Truly Disadvantaged: The Inner City, the Underclass and Public Policy* (Chicago: University of Chicago Press, 1987), 134.

17  Cornel West, *Race Matters*, ch. 2.

18  Ibid., 46.

19  See Shelby Steele, *The Content of our Characters: A New Vision of Race in America* (New York: St. Martin's Press, 1990), chs 3 and 4; Thomas Sowell, *Ethnic America: A History* (New York: Basic Books, 1981), 203; and Walter Williams, *The State Against Blacks* (New York: McGraw-Hill, 1982).

20  See Jennifer L. Hochschild and Monica Herk, " 'Yes, But . . . ': Principles and Caveats in American Racial Attitudes," in John W. Chapman and Alan Wertheimer, eds, *Majorities and Minorities: Nomos XXXII* (New York: New York University Press, 1990).

21  Cornel West, *Race Matters*, ch. 2.

22  See Lani Guinier, *Tyranny of the Majority* (New York: Free Press, 1994).

23  Booker T. Washington, "The Intellectuals and the Boston Mob," in Brotz, *Negro Social and Political Thought,* 429.

24  Bell, *Faces at the Bottom of the Well*, esp. ch. 9.

# 12

# Racism, Social Justice, and Interracial Coalitions

Perhaps race should not matter, but it does. There are growing divisions between the races and the existence of a growing racialized underclass.[1] Cornel West has argued that race does matter, but he remains optimistic that we can transform the United States from a racist society to a non-racist one.[2] Derrick Bell, on the other hand, shares West's contention that race matters, but is less optimistic about the prospects for transforming the US into a non-racist society.[3] In this paper I wish to examine the connection between racial harmony and social justice and explore some of the proposals and difficulties that we encounter in our efforts to achieve racial harmony under conditions of justice in a pluralistic society having a long history of racial injustice. Special attention will be given to Cornel West's proposals for eliminating racism offered in his influential book *Race Matters*.[4]

In order to have racial harmony or peace, in a nation state that is pluralistic in terms of race, religion, and ethnicity, the basic institutions of the society must be arranged in a manner that all members of that society have good reasons for thinking these institutions are just and that they are legitimate members of the society. This does not mean that there will not be injustices, but the injustices will not be based upon institutional bias towards and exclusion of members of certain groups.

In our society many African-Americans and other people of color believe that institutions are not just and that this injustice can be traced to their skin color.[5] Even in the wake of the civil rights movement and the great society programs of the 60s and 70s, African-Americans from varied economic backgrounds still believe that the basic structure of society is unjust. In survey after survey this injustice is not just attributed to personal bias. There is the strong perception that there is systematic bias. Whether these perceptions are based upon fact or fiction, the evidence shows that these perceptions do exist.[6]

These perceptions produce frustration, especially in young African-Americans. Young African-Americans are told that racism is no longer prevalent in American society, but their lived experiences tell them otherwise. They still believe that they are excluded and the research of scholars like Andrew Hacker tends to provide support for their beliefs.[7] Of course, neo-conservatives, both black and white, deny that the inequalities experienced by African-Americans can be traced to racial bias. The joblessness, lack of education, and high crime rates amongst African-Americans are attributed to a failure by members of this group to shake the victim's mentality and to acquire the values and skills that are necessary for success in a market economy.[8]

The frustrations that African-Americans are said to experience have been described by writers like June Jordan as a kind of alienation.[9] According to Jordan, this form of alienation exists when the self is deeply divided because hostility by the dominant groups in society forces the self to see itself as loathsome, defective, or insignificant, and lacking the possibility of ever seeing itself in more positive terms. This type of alienation, according to Jordan, is not just estrangement from one's work or a particular plan of life, but an estrangement from ever becoming a self that is not defined in the hostile terms of the dominant groups.

The root idea here is not just that certain groups are forced to survive in an atmosphere in which they are not respected because of their group membership, but rather that they are required to survive in a society that is openly hostile to their very being. The hostility, according to this account of alienation, causes the victims to become hostile towards themselves. Those who are said to be alienated in this way are thought to be incapable of shaping their self-image in more positive terms because social forces impose upon them negative and hostile self-conceptions.

Liberal and progressive thinkers have recognized the ways that African-Americans are excluded from the mainstream of American life, but they have disagreed sharply over how to characterize and remedy this exclusion. Marxists and communitarians have criticized liberal accounts of justice and rights for failing to appreciate how we form a healthy self-concept in a community.[10] By this they mean African-Americans or any minority group that has been despised and subjugated will rightfully feel estranged from the dominant society if they are merely tolerated and not accepted as full-fledged members. But this theory, of course, assumes that we can identify some common values or ends that can serve as the foundation for our theory of community. This is something that liberals who give priority to the right over the good deny.

As I have said, it seems to be clear that significant numbers of African-Americans still feel alienated and excluded. Recent surveys confirm these feelings.[11] Is this a problem? Should a society that is concerned with social justice worry about these feelings? Clearly they should if these feelings are based upon the existence of racial injustice or bias, but what if they are based upon false beliefs?

According to John Rawls, it is not enough that the basic structure of society be just, it must be perceived as such by members of the society. So even if African-Americans are wrong about their perceptions, a society that values justice has an obligation to show them why they are wrong.[12]

According to Rawls, the belief that social institutions are just provides us with good reasons for embracing these institutions and for doing our part in maintaining them. We also tend to feel guilty when we fail to honor our duties as defined by just institutions even though we don't feel any special relationship like friendship to all of those who are affected by these institutions. A common allegiance to justice also provides a unified perspective from which people can adjudicate their differences. And finally a conviction that institutions are just creates reasons to work for (or at least not to oppose) these institutions. Thus the belief of many African-Americans that the basic institutions of their society are unjust tends to undermine the positive features of human cooperation that occur when people share a common sense of justice.[13]

Several proposals have been offered to remedy the growing disparities between African-Americans and whites and to address the perceptions of injustice by African-Americans. According to the first proposal, the basic institutions are not unjust; the fault lies not with the society, but with African-Americans. African-Americans have not acquired the appropriate values and skills that will allow them to be competitive and secure in a market economy. At one time the deplorable condition of African-Americans could be traced to injustice, but this is thought to no longer be the case. African-American perceptions about institutional injustice are dismissed as an inability to shed the victim's mentality. However, the proponents of this proposal rarely spend the time or resources to explain how people can rid themselves of these false perceptions and become happy and productive members of society. Most of the time is spent blaming those who see themselves as the victims of injustice.

The second proposal admits that present institutions and attitudes need to be changed, but it stops short of saying that the present institutional design is unjust. According to this proposal, the institutions ought to be redesigned because they are not as efficient as they could be, but they are not unjust. This proposal focuses on the waste in human capital when a society does not tap all of its resources.

A third proposal says that there is institutional injustice, but we must adopt an impartial perspective in deciding what should be the just design of social institutions. According to this proposal, people are asked to blind themselves to things like race and sex in our efforts to define norms and principles.

The fourth proposal, like the third proposal, says that present institutions are unjust but that we cannot decide how to make these institutions just by appealing to some impartial decision procedure. According to this proposal, we must get our hands dirty in the give and take of political dialogue in order to gain consensus about the just design of institutions. On this view, we do not discover the correct principles of justice, we agree upon them. This proposal prides itself on including the voices of all, particularly those who have been historically excluded from the discourse.

The final proposal says that there is a problem with the present design of social and economic institutions, but that we cannot resolve the problem without eliminating capitalism. The advocates of this position are of two minds. One group thinks that the elimination of capitalism is sufficient for achieving a society that treats all of its members with dignity and respect. The other believes that the elimination of capitalism is necessary, but clearly not sufficient. On this account, African-Americans are estranged from themselves and others because of their laboring activity or lack of it. They view themselves in hostile terms because they are defined by a mode of production that stultifies their truly human capacities and reduces them to human tools to be used by those who have power and influence. However, critics of this proposal have been skeptical because they believe that the conditions of African-American and white workers are not identical and that this difference is not merely a difference in terms of things like income, or political and social status. For these critics the injustice and alienation that African-Americans experience occurs apart from the labor process and cuts much deeper.[14]

Can any of these proposals truly address the perceptions by African-Americans that their society does not treat them justly? Perhaps they can, but to date they have not, but not because those who advocate these solutions have all been ingenious or because their theories are clearly wanting. Rather, it is because there has not been a clear understanding of the problem. The perceptions of injustice that African-Americans experience cannot simply be attributed to poverty or a lack of education. These are consequences of racism and they can be devastating to the well-being of persons. But these are only symptoms of a more basic problem. The problem is the alienation that results from the exclusion of African-Americans. Exclusion often generates poverty and a lack of education, but it does not entail them.

As I said in chapter 1, this alienation and exclusion has been felt by African-Americans from all walks of life. By highly visible celebrities like Bill Cosby and the late Arthur Ashe to ordinary citizens. Just before he died, Arthur Ashe said that one of the toughest aspects of his life was his struggle against the alienation and feelings of exclusion caused by racism. This exclusion or marginalization has also been acutely felt by African-American intellectuals.

All five of the proposals described above fail to fully appreciate the power of this alienation and exclusion and thus they fail to adequately address it. The first proposal either flatly denies this exclusion or marginalization or claims that if it exists, it can be traced to things like a victim's mentality. (Something that is self-imposed rather than caused by an unjust racist society.) This proposal tends to ignore, rather than engage, African-Americans in good faith dialogue about their feelings and perceptions. The second proposal says that we have to eliminate black poverty, inferior education, and marginalization not because it is unjust, but because it makes the society less productive. This proposal focuses on aggregate good rather than individual or group rights and therefore it tends to underestimate or ignore the damaging psychological consequences of ignoring a minority group's perceptions of injustice. Justice takes a back seat to things like social utility.

Proposal three makes a good faith effort to be sensitive to the experiences of African-Americans, but I don't think it succeeds because it fails to hear or fully acknowledge the authority of African-Americans to describe reality as they perceive it because of an allegiance to the idea of a universal impartial perspective that does not need to be modified, particularized, or supplemented by any particular cultural perspective. According to this view, we have to blind ourselves to things like race if we are to be impartial. However, efforts at producing this impartial perspective have always depended upon some actual particular perspective. Most often the perspective of those who have power and influence.

Proposals four and five attempt to develop a sense of community by recognizing there are different perspectives because of things like peoples' race, sex or class position, but they face the practical problem of developing strategies and mechanisms for including these voices in the public and political discourses. In a society that has a firm allegiance to individual rights, how do you find the common ground and public space when you are dealing with individuals who believe that their rights entitle them to act in ways that even they would consider contrary to the good of the community?

None of the five proposals above have been shown to be logically inconsistent or theoretically incapable of adequately addressing the perception by African-Americans that US society is unjust. However, proposals four and five come closer to correctly characterizing the problem because of their emphasis on inclusion and dialogue.

If the first step to a resolution is a clear understanding of African-American perceptions of alienation and exclusion, and if we cannot understand these perceptions without having a genuine dialogue, then we need an atmosphere where these things can be examined in the spirit of free and open inquiry. The academy is not perfect, but it is still one of the best places to begin such an inquiry.

African-American scholars have begun to address this exclusion and marginalization by working to bring the experiences of African-Americans into sharper focus and to the attention of the wider community. But in order for this effort to truly bear fruit, African-American intellectuals must overcome the distrust and suspicion that exists between African-American intellectuals and the wider African-American community.

West, in his "Dilemma of the Black Intellectual," attributes this distrust and suspicion to the refusal by many African-American intellectuals to remain, in some visible way, linked with African-American cultural life.[16] This detachment makes it difficult for African-American intellectuals to articulate the concerns and values in African-American culture. The other reason he cites is the fact that American scholarship has placed African-American scholars on the defensive. By this he means that African-American scholars spend an inordinate amount of time and energy responding to the attack on the humanity of African-Americans rather than in developing creative ways to bridge the gap between African-American intellectuals and the wider community. According to West, white intellectuals also have a role to play in combating the marginalization of African-American scholars and African-Americans in general. They must address the failure by mainstream scholarship to make the concerns of African-Americans visible in intellectual discourses, especially in the pages of leading journals that have as their charter the discussion of cultural, political, and moral issues. Unfortunately, there are fewer discussions of issues that directly relate to the lived experience of African-Americans in scholarly journals today than there were thirty or forty years ago. Such a climate breeds separation and exclusion, and works against the kind of free and open dialogue that allows people from different experiences to identify common concerns and values.

But it is clearly not enough for whites or African-Americans to be inclusive when it comes to the intellectual contributions that flow from various cultures. Intellectuals must join with the wider community and resist the temptation to acquiesce in wrongdoing on the ground that they did not cause it. Decent people do not cause or support known injustice, so they often take comfort in viewing themselves as innocent bystanders. Although they condemn the wrongdoing they did not cause, they feel no sense of responsibility when it comes to ending or reducing its damaging effects. As I have argued in chapter 5, to adopt such a posture is to shirk one's role as a morally responsible person. Not all of us have the courage and wherewithal to fight injustice, but we can disassociate ourselves from injustice when there are reasonable avenues available for doing so. Our disassociation shows that we do not condone the injustice, and signals to the perpetrators of injustice that we are not among their ranks. [17]

Good faith efforts to disassociate from unjust practices that we did not cause are important first steps in building the bonds of trust that make coalitions possible. Any realistic proposal for ending the injustices or perceptions of injustice caused by racism must be based upon creating trust and bonds of commitment across races. The creation of mechanisms that will allow for racial diversity is something that must be forged through human interaction and struggle and not discovered by appeal to impartial procedures. Without a shared sense of community there can be no justice. And without justice there can be no peace.

But how do we build the bonds of commitment and trust between races that see themselves as different? Some philosophers and social critics have argued that we must eliminate the idea of racial difference. According to this view, acknowledging or institutionalizing racial differences serves to weaken or destroy bonds of commitment and trust. For them the goal of the good or just society is racial assimilation. By this they mean a society where a person's race is morally, legally, and socially irrelevant. On their view, if we eliminate racial differences, then there will not be a basis for racial discrimination.[18]

On the other hand, there are those who oppose racial assimilation and argue we should recognize differences between races because failing to do so devalues those who will be forced to embrace the culture and identity of the dominant and powerful group through the process of racial assimilation. This position is popularly known as cultural or racial pluralism. The cultural or racial pluralist recognizes and acknowledges differences, but insists that no culture or race is superior to any other, and that all cultures and races have the right to exist in accordance with the constraints of justice.[19]

Who is correct? The assimilationists or the pluralists? Each approach has its positive and negative aspects. However, with either approach, we are still left with the problem of how to create the bonds of commitment or trust that are necessary to eliminate racism. How do we build commitment and trust between racial groups in a society with a long history of racial injustice?

How should we conceptualize our task? Should we see ourselves as attempting to identify and agree on impartial norms to protect non-cooperative racial groups against each other? Or should we admit that there is a level of cooperation between racial groups and see our task as building upon this cooperation in order to shape negotiated norms that will allow us to tolerate each other as we pursue common and different ends?

West has embraced the second option. His notion of coalitions takes the form of consensus-building. As I have said, his account of coalitions is real rather than hypothetical. His goal is to build actual consensus in real political contexts. He is not interested in developing a theory about what hypothetical reasoners would agree to under certain imaginary conditions.

Clearly, West does not believe that present political arrangements are sufficient for achieving justice. Although he clearly endorses strong voter participation in a free and open democracy, he does not believe that racist institutions and practices can be overcome without groups of individuals from varied backgrounds coming together to achieve social justice. Voting and consensus-building are not identical. Consensus-building is a process of synthesizing many diverse elements together. Voting assumes that people have competing preferences and that agreement can be reached only by compromise. Consensus assumes that people are willing to agree with each other and that conflict can lead to creative, intelligent, and mutually beneficial decisions. A very crucial aspect of consensus building is that the process requires everyone's participation. Each person should speak and listen, and each member's contribution is valued as a part of the collective solution. It is, of course, possible for one person or a minority to sway the entire group, but participation should always remain equal. Consensus requires that all people be able to express themselves in their own words. Genuine consensus must assure that everyone has the right to speak and be heard, though it is extremely difficult in practice to achieve these things.

West argues that interracial coalitions are crucial if we are to achieve racial harmony and social justice.[20] But will interracial coalitions allow us to build the bonds of commitment that are necessary to achieve racial harmony and social justice? According to West, interracial coalitions are necessary, but not sufficient. We also need a redistribution of wealth, large-scale governmental intervention to assure access to basic social goods, and courageous leadership. All of the ingredients of West's proposed solution are sensible, but I am not sure how realistic they are in today's climate. If what I argued above was sound, it is not sufficient to create a society that is in fact just if we want racial harmony or peace; we must create a society that is perceived as such by its members, especially by racial minorities who are especially sensitive to injustice.

Even though West favors interracial coalitionary politics as opposed to any form of racial separatism, he is well aware that these coalitions are difficult to maintain and they require constant maintenance for their continued existence. West clearly recognizes that good will is not enough. But what is enough? Why will these coalitions survive?

Will they survive because different racial groups depend upon each other to solve clearly identifiable common problems that could not be solved without assistance from other groups? What West has in mind here is coalitions like the coalition of different racial groups in New Brunswick, New Jersey, to fight for affordable housing for poor people. But if this is so, will these coalitions evaporate when the clearly identifiable problem has been solved? Will we be able to use these coalitions to tackle more long-range and intractable problems?

West argues that even after we have solved a clearly identifiable short-term problem, a level of commitment between members of the coalition will exist. This commitment, I suppose, will result from the positive interactions that occur from the struggle to solve a common problem.

Is West correct or is he overly optimistic? Some say that it is the latter because West's optimism is based more on his Christian beliefs in hope and human redemption rather than in the logic of coalitions. Coalitions are built upon perceived self-interest and I imagine they break down because members of the coalition do not see it to be in their best interests to continue. This can occur because it is not in their interest to remain a part of the coalition, or it may occur because of some misunderstanding between members of the coalition. Let us examine each of these reasons in turn.

When we talk about the interests of members of interracial coalitions, we should note that there are long-term and short-term interests. Very often it is extremely hard for people to look at their long-term interests, especially when they seem to conflict with their short-term interests. West might point out, however, that courageous leaders can play an important role in getting people to focus on short-term as well as long-term interests.[21] They can educate people to see that it is not always in their interests to adopt a narrow short-term interpretation of their best interest. I suspect he would say that when this is done, people from different races will come to see that they have a great deal in common.

West is right that racial groups do have a great deal in common, but I am not so sure that we can educate people in a racist, competitive society to look to their long-term interests. Maybe if people did not have to worry about their basic needs, then this would seem more likely. But in order to develop a society that adopts more egalitarian principles of distribution, we must first greatly minimize racism. But in the United States, programs that are designed to address basic needs are unfortunately most often perceived by the white majority as handouts to undeserving racial minorities. This perception continues to exist even when it is clear that larger numbers of whites benefit from such programs.

What about a lack of understanding between groups? Is this the chief reason for the failure of interracial coalitions? West tends to think that it is not so much that interests conflict, but rather that there is a lot of misunderstanding. He believes that the proper social interaction between groups can lead to better understanding. A common complaint is that members of the coalition have very different views about the nature of racial oppression. In fact, racial minorities often complain that members of the dominant group minimize or fail to appreciate the nature of racial injustice. They contend that members of the dominant group fail to see the subtle forms of racism, and that they are unable to recognize the mani-festations of subtle forms of racism in varied contexts. Uma Narayan has argued that people of color and women have what she calls "epistemic privilege" when it comes to understanding the evil of racial and sexual oppression.[22] If this is true, or if people of color believe that it is true, then this will work against building trust between different racial groups because of a lack of understanding.

In a similar vein, a frequent complaint by whites in interracial coalitions is that people of color expect them to go too far in prov-ing their commitment and good will. Racial minorities are said to expect more from whites than they do from other racial groups. Given the history of the interaction between whites and racial minorities, it would not be surprising to find that this is true. African-Americans and whites may have very different ideas about what counts as a sign of commitment and good will. Often the members of the white majority believe that the expectations of African-Americans are too high and that whites are expected to go too far to reasonably demonstrate their commitment and good will. Should members of both groups be more understanding? Perhaps they should, but in reality this is very often not the case. These difficulties have led some people to believe that these misunderstandings are so deep and widespread that whites and African-Americans will not be able to have the frank and pro-longed dialogues that are necessary to work across their differences.

In order to answer this question, we need to take a closer look at the logic of interracial coalitions. What are the aims of the participants in the coalition approach? Is it to achieve the common good? I think not. Each participant is not attempting to achieve the common good, they are attempting to maximize the interests of the members of their group. A by-product of their efforts may be the promotion of common interests, but this is not the aim of the participants. In this regard, the coalition approach is quite similar to the social contractarian approach in political philosophy. In the social contractarian approach, members of the state of nature or in the original position in the case of early Rawls are rational egoists who are attempting to agree on principles that will maximize their own interests. However, by securing their own interests through the use of a fair or impartial decision procedure they will protect the rights and interests of all.

The coalition approach is not an impartial decision procedure, but it does involve the idea that the coalition is a dialogical process that must meet certain requirements of fairness, e.g., all parties to the coalition must be free to interpret and express their perceived interests. But unlike the dialogue procedures offered by liberal writers like Bruce Ackerman, there is no requirement that the dialogical process must conform to some neutrality constraint.[23] A neutrality constraint places conditions on what can qualify as a good reason in the dialogue or conversation between those who hold conflicting views. According to Ackerman, a reason advanced in support of one's claim to legitimacy is a good reason only if it assumes that all conceptions of the good embraced by parties to the dialogue have equal value or that no party to the dialogue has a conception of the good which makes her superior to any one else in the conversation.[24] West would reject Ackerman's approach because it is just another attempt to reduce the plurality of moral subjects and situations to a false unity by demanding that these judgments be detached, dispassionate, and neutral.

West does not adopt the view that parties to the coalition must embrace an impartial perspective in their discussions, but clearly he believes there are rules that govern their conversations. Unfortunately, West does not tell us what these rules are. Are they epistemological rules, moral rules, political rules or religious rules? An answer to this question is extremely important. Does West believe that the parties in the dialogical process share the same

basic moral principles? If so, is this a fair assumption? Are the conflicts between African-Americans and whites based upon disagree-
ments about what are the correct moral, political or religious
principles? Or is it the case that African-Americans and whites
share the same principles, but disagree about the applications of
these principles?

Given some of the other things that West is committed to, like
cultural pluralism, there are good reasons for thinking that he may
question whether the conflicts that exist between African-
Americans occur only in application rather than on the level of
principle. Also, as a pragmatist, West is weary of the idea that there
are true and universal moral principles that can be known through
some process of impartial reasoning. West sides with those who do
not see morality or politics as a process of discovering the true
moral and political principles. He sees the search for principles as
a process of agreement rather than discovery. This is consistent
with his belief that there are no privileged persons or perspectives
in the process.

If what I have said above is true, does West's coalition approach
begin to look like Rawls' recent strategy for arriving at principles
of justice through a process of overlapping consensus? Rawls dis-
tinguishes political philosophy from moral philosophy and politics.[25] According to Rawls, political philosophy in our times should
be free of moral assumptions that are in question and should not
rest upon any metaphysical foundations. The political philosopher
is searching for a shared stock of ideas that are dormant in the culture and acceptable to all in the culture no matter what their metaphysical or moral views might be. Rawls is describing political
reasoning in our times. By this he means political reasoning in the
latter part of the twentieth century in modern western democratic
societies. These societies are characterized by certain conditions
which are said to make Rawls' version of political reasoning possible. These conditions are moderate scarcity of primary goods,
permanent pluralism that can only be overcome through repressive
measures, and the fact the people in the society realize that there
are important things to be gained through a scheme of social
cooperation. According to Rawls, our times dictate this methodology. Rawls' account of justice, and the liberalism that it reveals,

does not rest on a comprehensive conception of human good.[26]

Although West never says it, I think that his argument might take a form quite similar to the one endorsed by the later Rawls. This may be why West goes to some lengths to describe what he takes to be the sociological and spiritual state of modern racist capitalistic consumer societies before he proposes his strategy for transforming these societies into non-racist societies. Like Rawls, West does not want to get bogged-down in endless disputes over metaphysical and moral issues of a foundationalist sort. It appears that he believes these issues can be taken off the agenda until we have agreed upon certain basic principles of what constitutes the right or just.

By suggesting that West might be adopting a strategy that is similar to Rawls' strategy for arriving at shared principles of social justice, I am not claiming that West embraces Rawls' liberalism. West's commitment to democratic socialism ties him to a level of egalitarianism that goes beyond Rawls' commitment to equality. Recall that Rawls' difference principle maintains that inequalities are justified only if they work to the advantage of the least-advantaged members of society.[27] So, for Rawls, we could still have large disparities in terms of income and wealth, provided this worked to the advantage of the least well-off members of society. West's commitment to socialism would not allow him to describe such inequality as just. He would insist that a just society should embrace a more radical form of egalitarianism than the one endorsed by Rawls.

Even though Rawls and West may have very different visions of the just society, they may embrace similar methodologies. Both the later Rawls and West reject basing their conceptions of justice on transcendental metaphysical and moral truths. Rawls rejects any form of moral intuitionism or moral constructivism in favor of what he describes as "political constructivism." Political constructivism is a method for arriving at shared principles to govern the terms of cooperation in modern democratic societies between free and equal citizens that are characterized by reasonable pluralism.[28] West roots his conception of justice in his own version of pragmatism.[29]

Although I believe that the later Rawls and West may share

some things in common, they do not share the same method. Rawls' method for achieving a consensus between people who believe that they have a right to hold and act on different conceptions of the good, rests on the distinction that Rawls draws between the rational and the reasonable.[30] For Rawls, the reasonable allows for public criteria for adjudicating differences while the rational does not. So, for Rawls, certain positions that are rational can be rejected because they do not pass his criteria for public reasonableness. The later Rawls still wants to exalt the role of reason, though now it has a more public face.

West, on the other hand, would approach Rawls' idea of public reasonableness with some caution. Even though Rawls has now backed away from Kantian rationalism, he may still be too metaphysical and moralistic for West. To truly reach a consensus between people with varied conceptions of the good might require a greater turn to the give and take of politics than Rawls is willing to accept.

If West does take this approach, are there any questions or issues that should be removed from the discourse? And if there are such questions and issues, what grounds should we use in removing them? Rawls' answer is that they are moral or metaphysical in their nature. But why should this matter? His response is that they are hopelessly controversial, and they are hopelessly controversial because of the natural result of the unrestricted use of human powers in a context of freedom. Rawls thinks that our society allows for conceptions of the good that are not merely incompatible with each other, he also thinks there is no overarching standard that can be used to arbitrate these different conceptions.

But if this is West's position, then his theory is wanting because it puts to the side questions that many would take to be crucial if we are to achieve a non-racist society. If West adopts Rawls' strategy, would this mean that we should not try to convince racists in the dialogue to change their racist beliefs? Is the belief that some races are naturally inferior to others a metaphysical or moral belief that can be put to one side? Perhaps we do not have to worry about changing racists' beliefs and attitudes if we can change the unjust behavior of racists. Social psychologist like D. J. Bem states that we can change behavior without changing attitudes.[31] If this is so, as long as we have principles of justice that forbid unjust discrimination on the basis of race, it should not matter whether people harbor racist beliefs and attitudes.

But racism can take subtle, but harmful forms. Will we be able to construct principles that are sensitive to the subtle forms that racism can take without addressing the issue of the natural inferiority of races in a direct way? I think not. But if we address the issue in a direct way, will this not create endless controversy and confrontations? I think so. Can fragile coalitions between racial groups survive these confrontations? It is doubtful, but not impossible. But an even greater worry might be that these confrontations will require that we challenge people's conception of the good, something liberal society says that we have no right to challenge.

So if what I have said about using a Rawlsian-like strategy to address racism is true then the task of eliminating racism by attempting to achieve an overlapping consensus, without basing this consensus on some overarching standard of the good, faces some serious difficulties. It is hard to imagine consensus being achieved between the races if they don't respect each other's basic humanity. But perhaps in the end West does not have to appeal to such a strategy. Maybe he can argue that (1) our natures are good and that we only have to work to remove those obstacles that prevent our good natures from manifesting themselves or that (2) our natures are not naturally good, but that we can identify some common conception of the good that will allow us to see ourselves as moral equals or (3) that the society will eventually become so violent and harsh that fear will compel us to work across our racial difference in order to achieve protection and peace. There is some evidence that suggests that West could have something like (3) in mind. However, this is a discussion for another occasion.

Despite these problems, I would like to think racial coalitions can be used to create a racially harmonious and just society. But we must realize that in a society where there has been and continues to be widespread racism, any small disagreement between members of different racial groups can serve to undermine any common ground that has been established through coalitionary politics. Of course, I have not exhausted all of the possible methods for building trust and commitment to common institutions in a racially diverse society. I only hope my remarks will stimulate others to join this discussion.

## Notes

1  Bill E. Lawson, *The Underclass Question* (Philadelphia: Temple University Press, 1992).
2  Cornel West, *Race Matters* (New York: Beacon Press, 1992).
3  Derrick Bell, *Faces at the Bottom of the Well* (New York: Basic Books, 1992).
4  John Rawls, *Political Liberalism* (New York: Columbia University Press, 1993).
5  Monica Herk and Jennifer Hochschild, " 'Yes, But ... ': Principles and Caveats in American Racial Attitudes," in John W. Chapman and Alan Wertheimer, eds, *Majorities and Minorities: Nomos XXXII* (New York: New York University Press, 1990).
6  Herk and Hochschild, " 'Yes, But . . . ': Principles and Caveats in American Racial Attitudes," 316–20.
7  Andrew Hacker, *Two Nations: Black and White, Separate, Hostile, Unequal* (New York: Scribner's, 1992).
8  See Thomas Sowell, *Race and Economics* (New York: David McKay, 1975); and Shelby Steele, *The Content of Our Characters* (New York: St. Martin's Press, 1990).
9  See June Jordan, *On Call* (Boston: South End Press, 1985); and Howard McGary, "Alienation and the African American Experience," *The Philosophical Forum*, 24, 1–3 (1992).
10  See Will Kymlicka, *Liberalism, Community, and Culture* (Oxford: Oxford University Press, 1991), 47–58 and 100–27.
11  Herk and Hochschild, "'Yes, But . . . ': Principles and Caveats in American Racial Attitudes," 317, 330.
12  John Rawls, *A Theory of Justice* (Cambridge, MA: Harvard University Press, 1971).
13  Rawls, *A Theory of Justice*, 474.
14  Bernard Boxill, *Blacks and Social Justice* (Lanham, MD: Rowman & Littlefield Publishers, 1992), ch. 3, and Howard McGary, "The Nature of Race and Class Exploitation," in Zegeye, Harris and Maxted, eds, *Exploitation and Exclusion: Race and Class in Contemporary US Society* (London: Hans Zell Publishers, 1991), 14–27.

15  Jordan, *On Call*, 123.
16  Cornel West, "The Dilemma of the Black Intellectual," *Cultural Critique*, 1, 1 (1985).
17  Howard McGary, "Morality and Collective Liability," in Larry May and Stacey Hoffman, eds, *Collective Responsibility* (Lanham, MD: Rowman & Littlefield Publishers, 1991), 77–87.
18  Richard Wasserstrom, "Racism and Sexism," in his *Philosophy and Social Issue* (West Lafayette, IN: University of Notre Dame Press, 1980).
19  Iris Young, *Justice and the Politics of Difference* (Princeton: Princeton University Press, 1990), chs 6 and 8.
20  West, *Race Matters*, 28.
21  Ibid., ch. 3.
22  Uma Narayan, "Working Across Differences," *Hypatia*, 3, 1 (1988): 34–41.
23  Bruce Ackerman, *Social Justice in the Liberal State* (New Haven, CT: Yale University Press, 1980), 10–12.
24  Ibid., 11.
25  John Rawls, "The Idea of an Overlapping Consensus," *The Oxford Journal of Legal Studies*, 7, 1 (1987): 24–5.
26  Ibid., xvi–xxiv, 59, 177.
27  Rawls, *A Theory of Justice*.
28  Rawls, *Political Liberalism*, 89–130.
29  Cornel West, *The American Evasion of Philosophy* (Madison, WI: University of Wisconsin Press, 1989).
30  Rawls, *Political Liberalism*, 50.
31  D. J. Bem, *Beliefs, Attitudes, and Human Affairs* (Belmont, CA: Wadsworth, 1970).

# Bibliography

## Black Studies

Alkalimat, Abdul, et al. *Introduction to Afro-American Studies: A People's College Primer*, 6th edn (Chicago: Twenty-first Century Books and Publications, 1986). An introduction to the black American experience in Africa, during the slave trade, civil rights movement, and the black nationalist and Marxist movements.

Asante, Molefi. *The Afrocentric Idea* (Philadelphia: Temple University Press, 1987). An attempt to provide a definition of "Afrocentricity."

ben-Jochanan, Yosef. *Cultural Genocide in the Black and African Studies Curriculum* (New York: Alkebu-Lan Books, 1972). An Afrocentric critique of black and African studies programs.

Clark, Cedrick. "Black Studies or the Study of Black People," *Black Psychology*, ed. Reginald L. Jones (New York: Harper and Row, 1972). A thoughtful critique of the philosophy and psychology of black studies.

DuBois, W. E. B. "The Field and Function of the Negro College," in *W. E. B. DuBois: The Education of the Negro People – Ten Critiques, 1900–1960*, ed. Herbert Aptheker (Amherst: University of Massachusetts Press, 1973). An examination of black colleges.

Frye, Charles. *Towards a Philosophy of Black Studies* (San Francisco: R. & E. Research Associates, 1978). An early attempt by a professional philosopher to provide an Afrocentric account of black studies.

Huggins, Nathan. *Afro-American Studies* (New York: Ford Foundation, 1985). A report to the Ford Foundation that highlights successes and failures of black studies at American universities.

Karenga, Maulana. *Introduction to Black Studies* (Inglewood, CA: Kawaida Publications, 1982). A text book that covers the standard topics taken up in a course in the Introduction to Black Studies.

Kilson, Martin. "Reflections on Structure and Content in Black Studies," *Journal of Black Studies*, 3: 3 (1973): 297–314. A rigorous critique of black studies programs and their content.

Robinson, Armstead L., Foster, Craig C., and Ogilvie, Donald, eds. *Black Studies in the University: A Symposium* (New Haven: Yale University Press, 1969). A collection of papers from an early conference on black studies.

Turner, James E., ed. *The Next Decade: Theoretical and Research Issues in Africana Studies* (Ithaca, NY: Cornel University Africana Studies and Research Center, 1984). A collection of essays on the history, the status, and the theory and practice of Africana Studies.

## African-American / Black Philosophy
### Books and Special Issues of Philosophical Journals

Allen, Anita. *Uneasy Access: Privacy for Women in a Free Society* (Savage, MD: Rowman and Littlefield, 1988). An examination of the right to privacy in the context of women's issues.

Appiah, Anthony. *In My Father's House* (Oxford: Oxford University Press, 1992). An excellent collection of essays on identity, race, and ethnophilosophy.

Boxill, Bernard R. *Blacks and Social Justice* (Totowa, NJ: Rowman and Allenheld, 1984). An excellent discussion of some of the major issues in the black experience, e.g., affirmative action, civil disobedience, forced busing to achieve school integration, and the racial integrationist and separatist debate.

Davis, Angela. *Women, Culture and Politics* (New York: Random House, 1989). An analysis of the relationship of culture and politics from the perspective of women.

——. *Women, Race, and Class* (New York: Vintage Books, 1983). An excellent examination of the interplay between gender, race, and class.

Gordon, Lewis R. *Existence in Black* (New York: Routledge, 1997).

——. *Bad Faith and Antiblack Racism* (New York: Humanities Press, 1995).

Harris, Leonard, ed. *Philosophy Born of Struggle* (Dubuque, IA: Kendall/Hunt, 1983). A good collection of papers by African-American philosophers and African-American scholars with philosophical interests.

——, ed. *The Philosophy of Alain Locke* (Philadelphia: Temple University Press, 1989). An excellent collection and discussion of Locke's philosophical writings.

Hodge, J., Struckmann, D., and Trost, L. *Cultural Bases of Racism and Group Oppression* (Berkeley: Two Riders Press, 1975). A philosophical examination of racism and group oppression with an extensive focus on culture.

King, Martin Luther, Jr. *Why We Can't Wait* (New York: Harper and Row, 1963). A good discussion of civil disobedience.

Lawson, Bill, ed. *Meditations on Integration: Philosophy and the Urban Underclass* (Philadelphia: Temple University Press, 1992). A collection of papers by African-American philosophers on the problems of the urban underclass.

McDade, Jesse, and Lesnor, Carl, eds. *The Philosophical Forum*, 9 (1978). A special issue of this journal devoted to Philosophy and the Black Experience. A good source for courses in African-American philosophy.

McGary, Howard, ed. *The Journal*, 1 (1984). A collection of papers by African-American philosophers on topics ranging from the nature of Africana philosophy to issues of racism and sexism.

McGary, H., and Lawson, B. *Between Slavery and Freedom: Philosophy and American Slavery* (Bloomington, IN: University of Indiana Press, 1992). A philosophical discussion of some of the moral and social issues raised by slavery.

Mills, Charles W. *Blackness Visible: Essays on Philosophy and Race* (Ithaca: Cornell University Press, 1998).

_____. *The Racial Contract* (Ithaca: Cornell University Press, 1997). A discussion of race and the social contract tradition in Political Philosophy.

Outlaw, Lucius. *On Race and Philosophy* (New York: Routledge, 1996). A discussion of the interplay between race, racism, and the practice of philosophy.

Thomas, Laurence. *Living Morally: A Psychology of Moral Character* (Philadelphia: Temple University Press, 1989). Subtle uses of the black experience in the development of a theory of moral character.

_____. *Vessels of Evil: American Slavery and the Holocaust* (Philadelphia: Temple University Press, 1993). A critical examination of the concept of evil through the use of American slavery and the holocaust.

Washington, Johnny. *Alain Locke and Philosophy: A Quest for Cultural Pluralism* (Westport, Conn.: Greenwood Press, 1986). A fair discussion of Locke's philosophical ideas.

West, Cornel. *Prophesy Deliverance: An Afro-American Revolutionary Christianity* (Philadelphia: The Westminster Press, 1982). A very good philosophical discussion of the conflicts and problems of African-Americans and their responses to them.

_____. *The American Evasion of Philosophy: A Genealogy of Pragmatism* (Madison, Wisc.: University of Wisconsin Press, 1989). In chapter four, West attempts to situate W. E. B. DuBois within the American pragmatist tradition.

_____. *Race Matters* (Boston: Beacon Press, 1993). A lively discussion of some of the key issues in the debate over ways to overcome racism.

Zack, Naomi. *Race and Mixed Race* (Philadelphia: Temple University Press, 1993).

## Articles

Allen, Anita L. "The Role Model Argument and Faculty Diversity," *Philosophical Forum*, 24, 1–3 (1992–3).

Appiah, Anthony. "The Uncompleted Argument: DuBois and the Illusion of Race," in H. L. Gates, ed., *Race, Writing, and Difference* (Chicago: University of Chicago Press, 1986). A first-rate analysis of DuBois's argument in "The Conservation of Races."

_____. "Racisms," in Goldberg, D. T., ed., *Anatomy of Racism* (Minneapolis: University of Minnesota Press, 1990). A carefully argued paper about race theorizing.

_____. "Racism and Moral Pollution," *The Philosophical Forum*, 18 (1987). A special issue of the journal on Racism in South Africa. A critique of the argument that moral taint or pollution is a good moral reason for divesting.

Boxill, Bernard. "The Race and Class Question," in L. Harris, *Philosophy Born of Struggle* (Iowa: Iowa University Press, 1983), 107–16.

_____. "The Morality of Preferential Hiring," *Philosophy and Public Affairs*, 7, 3 (1978).

_____. "Self-Respect and Protest," *Philosophy and Public Affairs*, 6 (1976). An excellent examination of the arguments in the debate between Booker T. Washington and W. E. B. DuBois over the necessity of protest.

_____. "The Morality of Reparations," *Social Theory and Practice*, 2 (1972): 113–22.

DeMarco, Joseph P. *The Social Thought of W. E. B. DuBois* (New York: University Press of America, 1983).

DuBois, W. E. B. "The Class Struggle," *Crisis*, August 1921.

_____. "Negro Education," *Crisis*, February 1918.

_____. "The Cultural Missions of Atlanta University," *Phylon*, Vol. III (1942).

_____. "Prospects of a World Without Race Conflict," *American Journal of Sociology*, Vol. 49 (March 1944).

_____. *In Battle for Peace* (New York: Masses and Mainstream, 1952).

_____. "Is Race Separation Practicable?" *American Journal of Sociology*, Vol. 13 (May 1908): 834–8.

Garcia, Jorge L. A. "The Heart of Racism," *Journal of Social Philosophy*, 27, 1 (1996). An excellent analysis of the concept of racism.

Lawson, Bill. "Locke and the Legal Obligations of Black Americans," *Public Affairs Quarterly*, 3 (1989). An examination of the virtues and limitations of Locke's account of political obligation by focusing on the black experience in America.

Loury, Glenn. "The Moral Quandary of the Black Community," *Public Interest*, 79 (Spring 1985): 9–22.

McGary, Howard. "Alienation and the African American Experience," *The Philosophical Forum*, 24 (1992).

_____. "Morality and Collective Liability," in Larry May and Stacey Hoffman, eds, *Collective Responsibility* (Lanham, MD: Rowman & Littlefield Publishers, 1991), 77–87.

_____. "The Nature of Race and Class Exploitation," in A. Zegeye, L. Harris, and J. Maxted, eds, *Exploitation and Exclusion: Race and Class in Contemporary US Society* (London: Hans Zell Publishers, 1991), 14–27.

_____. "Reparations, Self-Respect, and Public Policy," in D. T. Goldberg, ed., *Ethical Theory and Social Issues* (New York: Holt, Rinehart and Winston, Inc., 1989).

_____. "Teaching Black Philosophy," *Teaching Philosophy*, 7 (1984). A description of an introductory course in African-American philosophy.

_____. "Morality and Collective Liability, *The Journal of Value Inquiry*, 20 (1986). An argument for collective moral liability for gross wrongs committed against groups by groups.

_____. "South Africa: The Morality of Divestment," *The Philosophical Forum*, 18 (1987). An examination of some of the moral and political arguments offered against divestment.

_____. "Justice and Reparations," *The Philosophical Forum*, 2–3 (1977–8): 250–63.

_____. "Reparations and Inverse Discrimination," *Dialogue*, 17, 1 (1974).

Menkiti, I. A. "The Resentment of Injustice: Some Consequences of Institutional Racism," *Philosophical Forum*, 9 (1977–8): 227–49.

Mills, Charles. "Sums: Philosophy and the African-American Experience," *Teaching Philosophy*, 17 (1994). A good description of a first course in African-American Philosophy.

_____ "Alternative Epistemologies," *Social Theory and Practice*, 14 (1988). An examination of the challenge by black and feminist writers to a neutral and universalist theory of cognitive norms.

Narayan, Uma. "Working Across Differences," *Hypatia*, 3, 1 (1988): 34–41.

Piper, Adrian. "Higher Order Discrimination," in O. Flanagan, and A. Rorty, eds, *Identity, Character, and Morality* (Cambridge, MA: MIT Press, 1990). A careful analysis of subtle forms of discrimination.

Thomas, Laurence. "Statistical Badness," *Journal of Social Philosophy*, 23, 1 (Spring 1992): 31.

_____. "Jews, Blacks, and Group Autonomy," *Social Theory and Practice*, 14 (1988). An examination of group autonomy by focusing on the experiences of blacks and Jews.

_____. "Sexism and Racism: Some Conceptual Differences," *Ethics*, 90 (1980). An analysis of the differences between racism and sexism.

_____. "Morality and Our Self-Concept," *The Journal of Value Inquiry*, 12 (1978): 258–68.

## Classic and Primary Texts in African-American Thought

Aptheker, Herbert, ed. *The Correspondence of W. E. B. DuBois*, vols 1 and 2 (Amherst: University of Massachusetts Press, 1976).

_____, ed. *A Documentary History of the Negro People of the United States* (Secaucus, NJ: Citadel Press, 1974).

Baldwin, James. "Everybody's Protest Novel," *Notes of a Native Son* (Boston: Beacon Press, 1955).

_____. *The Fire Next Time* (New York: Dell, 1963).

_____. *Go Tell It On The Mountain* (New York: Grosset's Universal Library, 1961).

Bambara, Toni Cade. *The Black Woman: An Anthology* (New York: New American Library, 1970).

Barbour, Floyd B., ed. *The Black Power Revolt* (Boston: Extending Horizons Books, 1968).

Bell, Derrick. *Faces at the Bottom of the Well: The Permanence of Racism* (New York: Basic Books, 1992).

Bennett, Lerone, Jr. *Before the Mayflower: A History of the Negro in America 1619–1962* (Chicago: Johnson Publishing Co., 1962).

Bernal, Martin. *Black Athena: The Afroasiatic Roots of Classical Civilization* (New Brunswick, NJ: Rutgers University Press, 1987).

Blassingame, John. *The Slave Community* (New York: Oxford University Press, 1972).

____. *Slave Testimonies* (Baton Rouge: Louisiana State University Press, 1977).

Bracey, John H., Meir, August, and Rudwick, Elliott M., eds. *Black Nationalism in America* (Indianapolis: Bobbs-Merrill, 1970).

Broderick, Francis L. *W. E. B. DuBois: Negro Leader in a Time of Crisis* (Stanford: Stanford University Press, 1959).

Brotz, Howard, ed. *Negro Social and Political Thought, 1850–1920* (New York: Basic Books, 1966).

Chestnut, Charles W. *The Conjure Woman and Other Tales* (Darby, PA: Arden Library, 1978).

Cruse, Harold. *The Crisis of the Negro Intellectual* (London: W. H. Allen, 1969).

Delgado, Richard, ed. *Critical Race Theory: The Cutting Edge* (Philadelphia: Temple University, 1995).

Diop, Chekh Anta. *The African Origin of Civilization: Myth or Reality* (Westport, Conn.: Lawrence Hill & Co., 1974).

Douglass, Frederick. *Life and Times of Frederick Douglass* (London: Collier Books, 1962).

Drake, St Clair, and Clayton, Horace R. *Black Metropolis* (New York: Harcourt, Brace, 1945).

DuBois, Shirley G. *His Day is Marching On: A Memoir of W. E. B. DuBois* (New York: J. B. Lippincott Co., 1971).

DuBois, W. E. B. *Black Reconstruction* (New York: Atheneum, 1970).

____. *The Souls of Black Folk* (New York: New American Library, 1969).

____. *Darkwater* (New York: Schocken Books, 1969).

____. *The Philadelphia Negro: A Social Study* (New York: Schocken Books, 1967).

____. "Socialism and the Negro Problem," *New Review*, February 1, 1913.

____. "Socialism and the Negro," *Crisis* (October 1921).

____. "Marxism and the Negro Problem," *Crisis* (May 1933).

____. *The Dusk of Dawn* (New Brunswick, NJ: Transaction Books, 1987).

____. *Darkwater: Voices from Within the Veil* (New York: Schocken Books, 1920).

____. *Dusk of Dawn: An Essay Toward an Autobiography of a Race Concept* (New York: Harcourt Brace, 1940).

____. *The Souls of Black Folks* (New York: New American Library/Signet Classics, 1969).

Ellison, Ralph. *The Invisible Man* (New York: Vintage, 1995).

_____. *Shadow and Act* (New York: Random House, 1964).

Essien-Udom, E. U. *Black Nationalism: A Search for Identity in America* (Chicago: University of Chicago Press, 1962).

Garvey, Marcus. *Philosophy and Opinions of Marcus Garvey*, ed. Amy Jacques Garvey, two volumes (New York: Atheneum, 1969).

Gates, Henry Louis, Jr., ed. *The Classic Slave Narratives* (New York: American Library, 1987).

_____, ed. *"Race", Writing, and Difference* (Chicago: University of Chicago Press, 1986).

Genovese, Eugene. *Roll, Jordan, Roll: The World the Slaves Made* (New York: Pantheon, 1974).

Guinier, Lani. *Tyranny of the Majority* (New York: Free Press, 1994).

hooks, bell. *Ain't I a Woman* (Boston: South End, 1981).

Hughes, Langston, and Bontemps, Arna, eds. *The Book of Negro Folklore* (New York: Dodd, Mead and Co., 1958).

Hull, Gloria, et al., eds. *All the Women are White, All the Blacks are Men but Some of us are Brave: Black Women's Studies* (New York: Feminist Press, 1981).

Hurston, Zora Neale. *Mules and Men* (New York: Harper & Row, 1935).

James, C. L. R. *A History of Negro Revolt* (London: Race Today, 1985).

_____. *The Black Jacobins* (New York: Allison, 1938).

Johnson, James Weldon. *The Autobiography of An Ex-Colored Man* (New York: Hill and Wang, 1960 reprint).

Jones, Leroi. *Blues People* (New York: William Morrow & Co., 1963).

King, Martin Luther, Jr. *Why We Can't Wait* (New York: Harper & Row, 1963).

Lerner, Gerder, ed. *Black Women in White America: A Documentary History* (New York: Pantheon Books, 1972).

Lester, Julius. *The Seventh Son: The Thought and the Writings of W. E. B. DuBois*, two volumes (New York: Random House, 1971).

Lewis, David L. *W. E. B. DuBois: Biography of a Race 1868–1919* (New York: Henry Holt and Company, 1993).

Malcolm X. *The Autobiography of Malcolm X*, with the assistance of Alex Haley (New York: Ballantine, 1977).

Marable, Manny. *Race, Reform, and Rebellion: The Second Reconstruction in Black America, 1945–1982* (New York: Macmillan, 1984).

Morrison, Toni. *Beloved: A Novel* (New York: Alfred Knopf, 1987).

Osofsky, Gilbert, ed. *Puttin' On Ole Massa* (New York: Harper & Row, 1969).

Rampersad, Arnold. *The Art and Imagination of W. E. B. DuBois* (Cambridge: Harvard University Press, 1976).

Robinson, Cedric J. *Black Marxism: The Making of the Black Radical Tradition* (London: Zed, 1983).

Rudwick, Elliot M. *W. E. B. DuBois: Propagandist of the Negro Protest* (New York: Atheneum, 1969).

Simonson, Rick, and Walker, Scott, eds. *The Graywolf Annual Five: Multicultural Literacy* (Saint Paul: Graywolf Press, 1988).

Sowell, Thomas. *Race and Economics* (New York: David McKay Company, Inc., 1975).

Toomer, Jean. *Cane* (New York: Liveright Publishing Corp., 1975).

Truth, Sojourner. *Narrative of Sojourner Truth: With a History of Her Labors and Correspondence Drawn from her "Book of Life,"* ed. Olive Gilbert (New York: Arno, 1968).

Walker, David. *David Walker's Appeal* (1829), ed. Charles M. Wiltse (New York: Hill and Wang, 1965).

Washington, Booker T. *Up From Slavery: An Autobiography* (New York: Airmont Publishing Co., 1975).

———. "Atlanta Exposition Address," and "The Intellectuals and the Boston Mob," both in *Negro Social and Political Thought, 1850–1920*, ed. Howard Brotz (New York: Basic Books, 1966).

Wilson, William J. *The Truly Disadvantaged: The Inner City, the Underclass, and Public Policy* (Chicago: University of Chicago Press, 1987).

———. *The Declining Significance of Race: Blacks and Changing American Institutions* (Chicago: University of Chicago Press, 1980).

## General Articles and Texts

Ackerman, Bruce A. *Social Justice and the Liberal State* (New Haven, Conn.: Yale University Press, 1980).

Aristotle. *Nicomachean Ethics,* translated by Martin Ostwaid (New York: Bobbs-Merrill Company, Inc., 1962).

Barber, Benjamin. *Strong Democracy* (Berkeley: University of California Press, 1994).

Barker, L. J., and McCorry, J. J., Jr. *Black Americans in the Political System* (Cambridge: Winthrop Publishers, Inc., 1976).

Barry, Brian. "The Public Interest," *Proceedings of the Aristotelian Society*, supp. vol. 38 (1964): 1–18.

Bem, D. J. *Beliefs, Attitudes, and Human Affairs* (Belmont, CA: Wadsworth, 1970).

Berlin, Isaiah. *Two Concepts of Liberty* (Oxford: Clarendon Press, 1961).

Bittker, Boris. *The Case for Black Reparations* (New York: Random House, 1973).

Blassingame, John. *The Slave Community: Plantation Life in the Antebellum South* (New York: Oxford University Press, 1972).

Block, N. J., and Dworkin, Gerald. "I.Q., Heritability, and Equality," in *The I.Q. Controversy*, ed. Block and Dworkin (New York: Random House, 1976), 410–540.

Blyden, Edward W. "The African Problem and the Method of its Solution," in *Negro Social and Political Thought 1850–1920,* ed. Howard Brotz (New York: Basic Books, Inc., 1966).

Brodbeck, May. "Methodological Individualism: Definition and Reduction," in May Brodbeck, *Readings in the Philosophy of the Social Sciences* (New York: Macmillan, 1968).

Buchanan, Allen E. *Marx and Justice: The Radical Critique of Liberalism* (New York: Rowman and Littlefield, 1982).

Cahn, Steven M., ed. *Affirmative Action and the University: A Philosophical Inquiry* (Philadelphia: Temple University Press, 1993).

Chomsky, Noam. *For Reasons of State* (New York: Random House, 1973).

Cowan, J. L. "Inverse Discrimination and Morally Relevant Characteristics," *Analysis*, 33, 1 (1972).

Cross, Theodore L. "On Scapegoating Blacks for Grade Inflation," *The Journal of Blacks in Higher Education*, 1, 1 (1993).

Delany, Martin R. "The Condition, Elevation, Emigration, and Destiny of the Colored People of the United States" (abridged), in *Negro Social and Political Thought 1850–1920*, ed. Howard Brotz (New York: Basic Books, Inc., 1966).

Dickens, Charles. *A Tale of Two Cities* (New York: Random House, 1990).

DuBois, W. E. B. *Dusk of Dawn* (New Brunswick, NJ: Transaction Books, 1987).

_____. *The Souls of Black Folk* (New York: New American Library, 1969).

Dworkin, Ronald. *Taking Rights Seriously* (Cambridge, MA: Harvard University Press, 1977).

Elkins, Stanley. *Slavery: A Problem in American Institutional and Intellectual Life* (Chicago: University of Chicago Press, 1976).

Ellison, Ralph. *The Invisible Man* (New York: New American Library, 1953).

Elster, John, ed. *Karl Marx: A Reader* (Cambridge: Cambridge University Press, 1986).

Eze, Emmanuel C., ed. *Race and the Enlightenment: A Reader* (Cambridge, MA: Blackwell, 1997).

Ezorsky, Gertrude. *Racism and Justice: The Case for Affirmative Action* (Ithaca: Cornell University Press, 1991).

Feinberg, Joel. *Social Philosophy* (Englewood Cliffs, NJ: Prentice-Hall, Inc., 1973).

_____. "Collective Responsibility," and "Problematic Responsibility in Law and Morals," both in *Doing and Deserving* (Princeton: Princeton University Press, 1970).

Frankena, William K. *Ethics* (New Jersey: Prentice-Hall, 1973).

French, Peter A. *Individual and Collective Responsibility: The Massacre at My Lai* (Cambridge: Schenkman, 1972).

Fullinwider, Robert. *The Reverse Discrimination Controversy: A Moral and Legal Analysis* (Totowa: Rowman and Littlefield, 1980).

Garvey, Marcus. *Philosophy and Opinions of Marcus Garvey on Africa for the Africans* (London: Frank Cass and Co., Ltd., 1923).

Goldberg, David Theo. *The Anatomy of Racism* (Minneapolis: University of Minnesota Press, 1990).

_____. *Racist Culture: Philosophy and the Politics of Meaning* (Oxford: Blackwell, 1993).

Goldman, Alan. *Justice and Reverse Discrimination* (Princeton: Princeton University Press, 1979).

Goldman, Alvin I. *A Theory of Human Action* (Englewood Cliffs, NJ: Prentice-Hall, 1970).

Gomperz, H. "Individual, Collective and Social Responsibility," *Ethics*, 49 (1939): 329–42.

Gottfredson, Linda S. "Societal Consequences of the g Factor in Employment," *Journal of Vocational Behavior*, 29, 3 (1986): 379–410.

Greene, Jack R., and Mastrofski, Stephen D., eds. *Community Policing: Rhetoric or Reality* (New York: Praeger, 1988).

Hacker, Andrew. *Two Nations: Black and White, Separate, Hostile, Unequal* (New York: Scribner's, 1992).

Hart, H. L. A. *Punishment and Responsibility* (New York: Oxford University Press, 1973).

Hart and Honore. *Causation in the Law*, 2nd edn (Oxford: Oxford University Press, 1985).

Held, Virginia. "Reasonable Progress and Self-Respect," *The Monist*, 57, 1 (1973).

Herk, Monica, and Hochschild, Jennifer. "'Yes, But . . . .': Principles and Caveats in American Racial Attitudes," in John W. Chapman and Alan Wertheimer, eds, *Majorities and Minorities: Nomos XXXII* (New York: New York University Press, 1990).

Herrnstein, Richard J., and Murray, Charles. *The Bell Curve: Intelligence and Class Structure in American Life* (New York: Free Press, 1994).

Hill, Thomas E., Jr. "The Message of Affirmative Action," in *Autonomy and Self-Respect* (Cambridge: Cambridge University Press, 1991).

_____. "Symbolic Protest and Calculated Silence," *Philosophy and Public Affairs*, 9 (1979): 83–102.

_____. "Servility and Self-Respect," *The Monist*, 57 (1973): 87–104.

Hobhouse, L. T. *Morals in Evolution* (London: Chapman and Hill, 1951).

Hook, Sidney. "Discrimination Against the Qualified," *New York Times*, Opposite editorial page, November 5, 1971.

Hughes, Graham. "Reparations for Blacks," *The New York University Law Review*, 43 (1968): 1063–74.

Hunter, J. E. "Cognitive Ability, Cognitive Attitudes, Job Knowledge, and Job Performance," *Journal of Vocational Behavior*, 29, 3 (1986): 340–62.

Iltis, Hugo. *Life of Mendel*, trans. Eden and Cedar Paul (New York: W. W. Norton and Co., 1932).

James, William. *Psychology: The Brief Course*, ed. Gordon Allport (New York: Harper and Row, 1961).

Jensen, A. R. "g: Artifact or Reality?" *Journal of Vocational Behavior*, 29 (1986): 301–31.

_____. *Genetics and Education* (New York: Harper & Row, 1972), 69–204; and "How Much Can We Boost IQ and Scholastic Achievement?" *Atlantic Monthly* (September 1971): 43-64.

Jones, Leroi. "The Need for a Cultural Base to Civil Rites and B power Moments," in *The Black Power Revolt*, ed. Floyd B. Barbour (New York: Collier Books, 1968): 136–44.

Kamin, Leon J. "Heredity, Intelligence, Politics, and Psychology: II," in N. J. Block and Gerald Dworkin, eds, *The I. Q. Controversy* (New York: Random House, 1976), 376–81.

Karenga, Maulana Ron. "From the Quotable Karenga," in *The Black Power Revolt*, ed. Floyd B. Barbour (New York: Collier Books, 1968).

Kennedy, Randall. *Race, Crime and the Law* (New York: Pantheon Books, 1997).

King, Martin Luther, Jr. "I Have a Dream," *Negro History Bulletin* (1968).

Kinsley, Michael. "Equal Lack of Opportunity," *Harper's* (1983): 8.

Kuhn, Thomas. "The Structure of Scientific Revolutions," *Foundations of the Unity of Science*, 2, 2 (1970).

Kymlicka, Will. *Liberalism, Community, and Culture* (Oxford: Oxford University Press, 1991).

Lecky, Robert S., and Wright, H. E. *Black Manifesto: Religion, Racism and Reparations* (New York: Sheed and Ward, 1969).

Levin, Michael. "Responses to Race Differences in Crime," *Journal of Social Philosophy*, 23, 1 (Spring 1992): 5–29.

Lewis, William A. *Race Conflict and Economic Development* (Cambridge, MA: Harvard University Press, 1985).

Locke, John. *Two Treatises of Government*, edited by Peter Laslett, 2nd edn (Cambridge: Cambridge University Press, 1967).

MacIntyre, Alasdair. *After Virtue* (Notre Dame, Ind.: University of Notre Dame Press, 1981).

Malcolm X. *Malcolm X Speaks*, ed. G. Breitman (New York: Grove Press, 1966).

Malcolm X (with assistance of Alex Haley). *The Autobiography of Malcolm X* (New York: Grove Press, 1965).

Martin, Tony. *Race First* (Westport, Conn.: Greenwood Press, 1976).

Marx, Karl. "On the Jewish Question," in L. Easton and K. Guddhat, eds, *Writings of the Young Marx on Philosophy* (New York: Doubleday Publishers, 1976).

May, Larry, and Hoffman, Stacey, eds. *Collective Responsibility: Five Decades of Debate in Theoretical and Applied Ethics* (Savage: Rowman and Littlefild, 1991).

McGary, Howard, Jr. "The Nature of Race and Class Exploitation," in A. Zegeye, L. Harris, and J. Maxted, eds, *Exploitation and Exclusion: Race and Class in Contemporary US Society* (London: Hans Zell Publishers, 1991).

_____. "The Black Underclass and the Question of Values," in William Lawson, ed., *The Underclass Question* (Philadelphia: Temple University Press, 1992): 57–70.

McKim, Jenifer. "Arrest of Hispanic Drivers Challenged," *Boston Globe*, 29 (May 1995): 15.

Miles, Robert. *Racism* (London: Routledge, 1989).

Mill, John Stuart. *Utilitarianism*, ed. Oskar Piest (Indianapolis: Bobbs-Merrill Company, Inc.)

Montagu, Ashley. *Man's Most Dangerous Myth: The Fallacy of Race* (New York: Oxford University Press, 1974).

_____. *The Concept of Race* (London: Collier-Macmillan, 1969).

_____. *Race, Science, and Humanity* (New York: Van Nostrand Reinhold, 1963).

Muhammad, Elijah. *Message to the Black Man in America* (Chicago: Muhammad Mosque of Islam No. 2, 1965).

Myrdal, Gunnor. *An American Dilemma: The Negro Problem and Modern Democracy* (New York: Harper and Row, 1969).

Nagel, Thomas. "Equal Treatment and Compensatory Discrimination," *Philosophy and Public Affairs*, 2 (1973): 348–63.

Newton, Lisa H. "Reverse Discrimination as Unjustified," *Ethics*, 83, 4 (1973).

Nickel, J. W. "Classifications by Race in Compensatory Programs," *Ethics*, 84 (1974).

———. "Discrimination and Morally Relevant Characteristics," *Analysis*, 32, 4 (1972).

———. "Should Reparations be to Groups or Individuals," *Analysis*, 34, 5 (1973).

Nordheimer, Jon. "N.J. Troopers Accused of Bias in Traffic Stops," *Quincy (Massachusetts) Patriot Ledger*, December 23, 1994: 1.

Nozick, Robert. *Anarchy, State and Utopia* (New York: Basic Books, 1975).

Nunn, William A. "Reverse Discrimination," *Analysis*, 34, 5 (1974).

Ollman, Bertrell. *Alienation* (Cambridge: Cambridge University Press, 1976).

Omi, Michael, and Winant, Howard. *Racial Formation in the United States: From the 1960s to the 1980s* (New York: Routledge and Kegan Paul, 1986).

Patterson, Orlando. *Slavery and Social Death* (Cambridge, MA.: Harvard University Press, 1982).

———. *Ethnic Chauvinism: The Reactionary Impulse* (New York: Stein and Day, 1977), 102.

———. "Towards a Future that Has No Past: Reflections on the Fate of Blacks in America," *The Public Interest*, 27 (1972).

Popkin, Richard. "Hume's Racism Reconsidered," *The Journal*, 1 (1984): 61–71.

———. "Hume's Racism," *The Philosophical Forum*, 9 (1977–8): 211–26.

Pritchard, Michael S. "Human Dignity and Justice," *Ethics*, 82 (1971–2): 299–313.

Rawls, John. "The Idea of an Overlapping Consensus," *The Oxford Journal of Legal Studies*, 7, 1 (1987).

———. *A Theory of Justice* (Cambridge, MA: Harvard University Press, 1971).

Reiss, A. J., Jr. "Discretionary Justice in the United States," *International Journal of Criminology and Penology*, 2, 2 (1974).

Rothenberg, Paula. *Racism and Sexism: An Integrated Study* (New York: St. Martin's Press, 1988).

Sandel, Michael. *Liberalism and the Limits of Justice* (Cambridge: Cambridge University Press, 1982).

Scanlon, Thomas M. "Contractualism and Utilitarianism," in *Utilitarianism and Beyond*, ed. Amartya Sen and Bernard Williams (Cambridge: Cambridge University Press, 1982).

———. "Rights, Goals and Fairness," Stuart Hampshire, ed., *Public and Private Morality* (Cambridge: Cambridge University Press, 1978).

Schmitt, Richard. "A New Hypothesis about the Relations of Class, Race and Gender: Capitalism as a Dependent System," *Social Theory and Practice*, 14, 3 (1988): 345-65.

Shockley, William. "Dysgenics, Geneticity, Raceology: A Challenge to the Intellectual Responsibility of Educators," *Phi Delta Kappan* (January 1972): 297–307.

Sowell, Thomas. *The Economics and Politics of Race* (New York: Morrow, 1983).

_____. *Race and Economics* (New York: David McKay, 1975).

Steele, Shelby. *The Content of Our Characters: A New Vision of Race in America* (New York: St. Martin's Press, 1990).

Thalberg, Irving. "Reverse Discrimination and the Future," in *Women and Philosophy*, ed. Carol Gould and Marx Wartofsky (New York: G. P. Putnam's Sons, 1976).

_____. "Reverse Discrimination and the Future," *Philosophical Forum*, 5, 1–2 (1973–4).

Thomas, Laurence. In *The New York Times*, August 13, 1990.

Thomson, Judith Jarvis. "Preferential Hiring," *Philosophy and Public Affairs*, 2, 4 (1971).

Thorndike, R. L. "The Role of General Ability in Prediction," *The Journal of Vocational Behavior*, 29, 3 (1986): 332–9.

Tucker, Robert C., ed. *The Marx-Engels Reader* (New York: W. W. Norton & Co., 1978).

_____. *The Marxian Revolutionary Idea* (New York: Norton Publishing Company, 1969).

Vlastos, Gregory. "Justice and Equality," in A. I. Meldin, ed., *Human Rights* (Belmont: Wadsworth Publishing, 1970).

Waldron, Jeremy. "A Right to Do Wrong," *Ethics*, 92, 1 (1981): 21–39.

Walker, Samuel. *Taming the System: The Control of Discretion in Criminal Justice, 1950–1990* (New York: Oxford University Press, 1993).

Warren, Mary Ann. "On the Moral and Legal Status of Abortion," in R. Wasserstrom, ed., *Today's Moral Problems* (New York: Macmillan, 1985).

Wasserman, David. "Racial Generalizations and Police Discretion," in John Kleinig, ed., *Handled With Discretion* (New York: Rowman and Littlefield Publishers, 1996).

Wasserstrom, Richard. "Rights, Human Rights, and Racial Discrimination," in A. I. Meldin, ed., *Human Rights* (Belmont: Wadsworth Publishing, 1970).

_____. "On Racism and Sexism," and "Preferential Treatment," both in R. Wasserstrom, ed., *Philosophy and Social Issues* (Notre Dame: Notre Dame University Press, 1980).

_____. "Racism, Sexism and Preferential Treatment: An Approach to the Topics," *UCLA Law Review*, 24 (1977): 581.

Williams, Bernard. "The Idea of Equality," in P. Laslett and W. G. Runciman, eds, *Philosophy, Politics and Society*, 2 (Oxford: Blackwell, 1962).

Williams, Walter. *The State Against Blacks* (New York: McGraw-Hill, 1982).

Wilson, William Julius. "Studying Inner-City Social Dislocations: The Challenge of Public Agenda Research," *American Sociological Review*, 56, 1 (1991): 1–14.

_____. *The Truly Disadvantaged* (Chicago: University of Chicago Press, 1987).

Wood, Allen. "The Marxian Critique of Justice," *Philosophy and Public Affairs*, 1 (1972).

Young, Iris. *Justice and the Politics of Difference* (Princeton: Princeton University Press, 1990).

# Index

self-evaluation, 67–8
self-identification, 11, 28
self-interest, 56, 185
self-reliance, 76–7
self-respect, 14, 20, 21
  affirmative action, 137–40
  racial separatism, 49–50
  Rawls on, 13, 100
  reparations, 112, 121
  requirements for, 100
  slavery, 121
  social institutions, 13, 111, 113,
    114, 122–3n
separatism *see* cultural separatism;
  racial separatism
sex, as morally relevant characteristic,
  131–2, 133
sexism, 12, 70–1
sexual exploitation, 27, 34
Shockley, W., 150
Shoshone people, 106–7
sickness, 13
Simpson, O. J., vii
single-family households, 69
slavery
  alienation, 20, 21
  disassociation from, 90
  effect on underclass, 21
  importance of supportive
    communities, 22
  loss of African heritage, 51
  moral status, 116
  non-personhood, 39
  reparations, 96–7
  self-concept, 20
  self-respect, 121
  values, 71
social indicators, 174–5
social institutions
  belief in justness of, 198–200
  influence on the way people think,
    63
  racism, 112–14, 196–7, 198
  Rawls on, 13, 65, 123n, 198

self-respect, 13, 111, 113, 114,
  122–3n
solidarity, 27
  *see also* group solidarity;
    racial solidarity
*The Souls of Black Folk*, 11
South Africa, 191
Southern Christian Leadership
  Conference, 52
Sowell, Thomas, 74
state authority, 64
state coercion, 36
state intervention, 62, 67, 148
Steele, Shelby, 23–4, 74
stereotypes,
  African-Americans, 10, 15, 111,
    113, 118, 175
  women, 12
supportive communities, 20–3, 24
*Sweatt v. Painter*, 102, 103–4

"The Talented Tenth," 182, 183
Texas Law School, 102
Thomas, Laurence, vii, 16, 171,
  174–5, 178
Thomson, Judith Jarvis, vi, 130, 135
Till, Emmett, 56
*Time* magazine, 155
traditions, 51
traits
  inheritance of, 27–8
  required for personhood, 39
tribalism, 81
*The Truly Disadvantaged*, 22, 62
truth, as a value, 149

underclass, 3, 22, 24, 62–78
  characteristics of, 62, 66
  conservatives on, 62–4, 74–5
  effect of slavery on, 21
  laziness, 66–73, 74, 75
  liberals on, 62–4, 67
  rapid growth of, 190, 196
unemployment, 191